THE CAR CULTURE

W9-ACJ-267

THE CAR CULTURE

James J. Flink

The MIT Press
Cambridge, Massachusetts, and London, England

Copyright © 1975 by
The Massachusetts Institute of Technology

This book was set in CRT Baskerville,
printed on R&E Book,
and bound in Columbia Millbank Vellum MBV-4934
by The Colonial Press Inc.
in the United States of America.

First MIT Press paperback edition, 1976

Second printing, September 1976

Library of Congress Cataloging in Publication Data

Flink, James J
  The car culture.

  Includes bibliographical references and index.
  1. Automobiles—History. 2. Automobile industry and trade—United States—History. 3. Automobiles—Social aspects—United States. I. Title.
TL23.F572   301.24′3   74-31191
ISBN 0-262-06059-0 (hardcover)
ISBN 0-262-56015-1 (paperback)

To the memory of my niece,
Tiffany Ann Rudd.
Born December 11, 1969.
Killed while at play by
an automobile on
May 1, 1971, my thirty-ninth
birthday.

CONTENTS

PREFACE

This book is dedicated to Tiffany. It is her book. I hope most of all that the younger generation will like it. My life was greatly changed by her death, which caused me to reexamine my basic values and my views about the car culture.

Much of the material in the opening chapters is abstracted from my first book, *America Adopts the Automobile, 1895–1910*. However, the perspective here is very different because I have tried to write primarily for people under thirty, in whom I have great confidence. Increasingly I prefer their values over those of my generation.

I have intended that Tiffany's book, like most young people I know, be concerned about social justice, outspoken, iconoclastic, critical of the status quo, and optimistic about the future. The young dislike long-windedness. So I have tried to be concise. Since the reference notes are at the back of the book, where they will not intrude on an impatient reader's attention, I have omitted a bibliography.

Tiffany and I are indebted to many people. Her aunt, Iona Rogers Flink, contributed much to shaping my point of view, was an empathic critic of the text, and did all the typing. Dialogue with my students and colleagues helped clarify and sharpen my ideas. We are particularly indebted to those who commented on the manuscript: Dave Bruce, Pete Clecak, Raul Fernandez, Gil Gonzalez, and Dick Tashjian. Thomas C. Cochran, my mentor, urged me to write it. Bruce Kuklick suggested countless improvements in my prose that add up to an immeasurably more readable text.

Because scholarship is a cumulative process, our greatest debt is to my fellow automotive historians. A revisionist synthesis of the car culture would have been unthinkable were it not for John B. Rae's pioneering books and articles. John has always been exemplary in his ability to comment objectively on scholarship that proceeds from premises different from his own, and I appreciate more than I can say both his support for my work over the years and his generous criticism. He also corrected several important factual errors. I have learned much, too, from those who challenged key contentions of my first book. Blaine A. Brownell, especially, has influenced my maturing conception of the car culture, and his perceptive reading of the manuscript enhances my confidence in it. Without the collaboration of Glenn A. Niemeyer, the Durant chapter could never have been written.

The help of all these good people was invaluable, and they should share credit for any merits the reader finds in the text. I tried to write a perfect tribute to the memory of a perfect child. But I know that every book has faults for which its author is solely responsible. That is why there is no end to the making of books and why this one attempts to be provocative rather than safe in its generalizations. I think that Tiffany, who never played it safe, would have wanted her book this way.

James J. Flink
Irvine, California
September 28, 1974

THE CAR CULTURE

INTRODUCTION

At the 1893 annual meeting of the American Historical Association in Chicago, Frederick Jackson Turner presented his bold paper, "The Significance of the Frontier in American History." As George Rogers Taylor says, the Turner thesis, "which has become the most widely known essay in American history, revolutionized historical thought in the United States." A generation of historians accepted as an article of faith Turner's contention that "the existence of an area of free land, its continuous recession, and the advance of American settlement westward, explain American development." [1] The frontier hypothesis was to come under scathing attack and, ultimately, revision as a special case of more general theories of abundance, migration, and institution building by a later generation of historians.[2] Yet among scholars as well as the general public the idea remains pervasive that a significant turning point in American historical development was reached with the closing of the frontier announced by Turner in 1893.

The frontier, as defined by Turner, offered Americans a unique form of geographic and social mobility that centrally influenced the development of nineteenth-century American institutions and values. But in 1893 neither Turner nor anyone else foresaw that a new form of mobility was to become even more significant in shaping the lifeways of twentieth-century Americans. Six motor vehicles were displayed at the 1893 Columbian Exposition in Chicago. That same year two bicycle mechanics, Charles E. and J. Frank Duryea, built the first successful American gasoline automobile in Springfield, Massachusetts. Few Americans knew about either event. From these inauspicious beginnings, however, automobility* was rapidly to

---

* For the term "automobility" I am indebted to John C. Burnham. The term conveniently sums up the combined impact of the motor vehicle, the automobile

develop into a force with a deeper and broader influence than Turner's frontier. As a presidential commission surveying contemporary changes in American life concluded about the automobile in 1933, "It is probable that no invention of such far reaching importance was ever diffused with such rapidity or so quickly exerted influences that ramified through the national culture, transforming even habits of thought and language." [3] Father R. L. Bruckberger, a French observer of American civilization, goes so far as to state that Henry Ford's innovation of the five-dollar, eight-hour day, along with the moving-belt assembly line, alone has had more important consequences in the twentieth century than Lenin's socialist revolution.[4] While this is clearly a debatable and premature assessment, few would disagree that these innovations at Ford, the Model T, and the Fordson tractor more profoundly influenced twentieth-century American historical development than the collectivity of reforms emerging from the so-called Progressive Era and the New Deal combined.

As long ago as 1948 Thomas C. Cochran made clear the untenability of the prevailing national political periodization for synthesizing American history in his seminal essay, "The 'Presidential Synthesis' in American History." [5] Yet neither the social science movement in historiography nor the New Left revisionists have come to grips with the main thrust of Professor Cochran's argument by developing an alternative technoeconomic synthesis. A first step in this formidable task of constructing a more meaningful and socially relevant synthesis for the recent American past is obviously consideration of the impact of automobility.

Professional historians have devoted relatively little attention to the American automobile revolution. Except for the publication of two revised doctoral dissertations on the automobile industry in

industry, and the highway plus the emotional connotations of this impact for Americans. See Burnham's "The Gasoline Tax and the Automobile Revolution," *Mississippi Valley Historical Review*, 48:435–459 (December 1961).

1928,[6] which have become classics for serious students of automotive history, scholarly interest in the automobile revolution remained dormant until the 1950s. The publication of the monumental study of the Ford Motor Company undertaken by Allan Nevins in collaboration with Frank E. Hill marked an impressive awakening of interest.[7] But it remains the only multivolume history of any aspect of the American automobile revolution. And John B. Rae is the only historian of note whose career has been primarily identified with automotive history. The publisher of Professor Rae's excellent but brief volume, *The American Automobile*, could claim as late as 1965 on its dust jacket that the book was "the first complete, authoritative treatment of the whole span of the automobile industry, which has given American society its pace and direction and stimulated an amazing number of related industrial and social changes." [8]

This lack of scholarly interest has meant that most automotive history has been written by and for the automobile buff. We are indebted to him for much of what we know about the history of automobile racing and the mechanical evolution of the modern motorcar. But for the general reader as well as the scholar, the automobile buff's approach to automotive history leaves much to be desired. Invariably beginning with a statement about the author's long and passionate love affair with the car, such books are often uncritical, esoteric, and antiquarian. Many are simply high-priced picture books, soon to be remaindered at bargain prices, and designed primarily to be attractive ornaments for the coffee table.

The history of American automobility has also suffered from the misplaced emphases of the available literature. Until very recently, its primary focus has been on the internal dynamics of the automobile industry and its prominent personalities. The treatment of these topics has been more often appreciative and apologetic than critical and analytic. In particular, the popular cult of Henry Ford and the Model T has been unduly emphasized. The understandable result is that most historians, who ought to know better, as well as the general public, still tacitly accept a misleading heroic interpretation of the diffusion of the automobile in the United States, one that glorifies the contributions of Ford at the expense of misinterpreting the basic processes of social change in modern American civilization.

On December 29, 1971, at its eighty-sixth annual meeting in New York City, the American Historical Association gave formal recognition to a growing interest in automotive history by holding its first session on the impact of the automobile. The session emanated from and reflected a shift in automotive historiography away from narrow, uncritical concentration on the automobile industry. An emphasis upon automobility as a force influencing American life was common to new books on diverse aspects of the automobile revolution. They include, in addition to my earlier volume, works by John B. Rae, Lawrence J. White, and Reynold M. Wik.[9] Those of us who participated in the session were keenly aware that these developments in scholarly interest and awareness had in turn been conditioned by the new, critical attitudes toward automobility that had emerged in the United States during the 1960s.[10] Just as the centrality of Turner's frontier could be perceived only after the frontier had closed, so the overwhelming impact of automobility had to wait for formal recognition by the historical profession until the automobile and the automobile industry no longer called the tune and set the tempo of American life.

My paper, "Three Stages of American Automobile Consciousness," [11] presented a long overdue programmatic synthesis of the American automobile revolution. This book is an expansion and amplification of that paper. It was conceived as an opening argument in what promises to become an important historical debate over the significance of automobility for synthesizing American history. The reader who is seeking a definitive, "objective" study of the automobile and the automobile industry had therefore best look elsewhere. My intention here is to be suggestive, partisan, and controversial.

1 PROLOGUE: THE AUTOMOTIVE IDEA, ANTIQUITY TO 1900

Automotive historians have long held that "the automobile is European by birth, American by adoption." [1] The evidence is unequivocal that Europeans were a decade ahead of Americans in the development of the gasoline-powered car. But evidence of parallel development of the automotive idea in America during the nineteenth century is equally clear. As L. Scott Bailey says, "So often the view is taken that the automobile was virtually non-existent in America until it was introduced to these shores from Europe; America did not develop the automotive idea, she merely borrowed it. This simply is not true." [2]

The idea of the self-propelled road vehicle dates from at least as early as the speculations made by Roger Bacon and Leonardo da Vinci in the thirteenth and fourteenth centuries. Its development during the nineteenth century was multinational and involved the independent discovery or invention of the basic elements of automotive technology and their synthesis by many individuals. To put much emphasis on "firsts" or to search for tenuous "influences" is unrealistic. Cultural differences reflected by national political boundaries were far less significant than the fact that a modern urban-industrial social order was evolving both in Western Europe and in the United States. This involved a widely disseminated, shared state of scientific and technological knowledge. It was thus inevitable that a number of people on both sides of the Atlantic would independently perceive the possibility and social utility of the automotive idea—the combination of a light, sprung, wheeled vehicle; a compact, efficient power unit; and hard-surface roads.

The earliest experiments with cumbersome steam-powered vehicles failed to get very far. Between 1765 and 1770 Nicholas Joseph

Cugnot, a Swiss engineer, was subsidized by the French government to experiment with steam trucks for carrying cannons. Cugnot's 1769 vehicle was less efficient than horses, and further development was halted when a change in government policy cut off his funds. Richard Trevithick, a Cornish engineer who pioneered the development of the high-pressure steam engine in England, built steam carriages in 1801 and 1803. Although his vehicle ran reliably at speeds up to 12 mph, Trevithick was unable to obtain financial backing. Oliver Evans, an American inventor, obtained a patent from the Maryland legislature in 1787 giving him exclusive rights to operate steam-powered vehicles on public roads. In 1792 the newly formed United States Patent Office granted Evans a patent on his high-pressure steam engine. In 1805 a steam dredge that he built for the city of Philadelphia, the "Orukter Amphibolos" or "Amphibious Digger," moved under its own power through the streets of Philadelphia at about 4 mph. Onlookers thought the vehicle would be too slow for turnpike travel, and Evans was unable to raise the $3,000 he needed to launch an experimental company to build steam-powered wagons.

These initial, abortive experiments were a prelude to many other demonstrations of self-propelled road vehicles during the first half of the nineteenth century. In both England and the United States, attempts were made to establish stage lines utilizing steam-powered road vehicles for the long-distance transportation of freight and passengers. The main reason these attempts failed was that the railroad was a far superior technological alternative, given the bulk and weight of the steam engines and the incredibly poor roads of the day. Competition from cheaper, as well as more reliable and comfortable, water transportation was also a major factor in the United States. In England, under the influence of vested horse-drawn interests, the turnpike trusts that administered the highways levied discriminatory tolls against mechanical road vehicles. Then in 1865 Parliament passed on behalf of the railroad monopolists the notorious Locomotives on Highways Act, which further stultified development of the automotive idea in Great Britain until its repeal in 1896. This so-called Red Flag Act limited the speed of "road locomotives" to 2 mph in towns and 4 mph on the open highway and required that an attendant walk sixty yards ahead carrying a red flag by day and a red lantern by night. [Although such absurd discriminatory legislation was absent in the United States, the rapid development of the railroad network, heavily subsidized by government here, reduced the stage lines to the role of short-haul feeders and discouraged the building of improved roads.]

The automotive idea had the best chance for early implementation in France. Even before the French Revolution, the French government had perceived the need for good roads upon which to move the heavy wheeled traffic of its armies and had given special attention to building a national highway network since the founding of the École des Ponts et Chaussées in 1747. Cugnot's experiments are only one indication that the French were also the first to recognize the military potential of the self-propelled vehicle.

The implementation of the automotive idea throughout Western Europe and the United States by the 1890s depended upon a reawakening of interest in highway transportation. Early in the nineteenth century John L. McAdam (1756–1836) and Thomas Telford (1757–1834) in Great Britain developed new techniques of highway design and construction that made possible much smoother, tougher road surfaces and easier grades. This "highway renaissance" soon collapsed under competition from the steam locomotive running on fixed rails. Interest in improved roads was revived in Great Britain and the United States by the bicycle craze of the 1880s and 1890s. With the introduction of the geared, low-wheeled "safety bicycle" by James Kemp Starley of Coventry, England, in 1885 and after quantity production reduced the price of a bicycle to about $30, use of the bicycle became widespread. Since the bicycle required much better roads than the horse, bicycle organizations both here and abroad energetically began to agitate for improved roads. Their early efforts gained a broader base of support as the popularity of the bicycle increased in the 1890s. The bicycle also made contributions to automotive technology, such as the development of the pneumatic bicycle tire by John B. Dunlop in Ireland in 1888. But probably the greatest contribution of the bicycle to the implementation of the automotive idea was that it made the average person aware of the possibilities of individualized, long-distance highway transportation. It created a demand that neither the horse nor the railroad could satisfy.[3]

The crest of the bicycle movement in the United States coincided with the climax of several decades of agrarian discontent. The Farmers Alliances and the Populist movement had made the abuse of monopoly power by the railroads a prime target. Farmers were beginning to perceive highway transportation as an alternative and to complain about the lack of good farm-to-market roads. Good roads thus became a popular political issue during the 1890s, and strong good-roads planks were incorporated into the state platforms of the two major political parties. At the national level, a petition to Congress drafted by the League of American Wheelmen, headed by Colonel Albert A. Pope, the nation's leading bicycle manufacturer, resulted in the creation of the Office of Road Inquiry in the Department of Agriculture in 1893. The National League for Good Roads, with branches in most states, was founded by General Roy Stone at the 1893 Columbian Exposition, and later that year a Good Roads Convention was held in Washington, D.C.[4]

This new interest in highway transportation provided a fertile climate for the commercial exploitation of the advances in automotive technology of the preceding decades. Considerable progress had been made since the mid-nineteenth century in developing more compact and efficient power units. During the 1860–1890 period light-weight, high-pressure, self-condensing steam engines with automatic controls were developed; the introduction of the flash boiler, an instantaneous steam generator, in the late 1880s meant that it was no longer necessary to wait to get up steam before a vehicle could be operated. The electric motor had similarly progressed to the point that an electric car built in 1890 by William Morrison of Des Moines, Iowa, could operate for thirteen consecutive hours at 14 mph. But from the perspective of even the short-range implementation of the automotive idea, the most significant progress was in the development of the internal-combustion engine.

The internal-combustion engine had no single inventor. Two-cycle internal-combustion engines were patented by Stuart Perry, a New York inventor, in the United States in 1844 and 1846 and by Etienne Lenoir, a Belgian mechanic, in France in 1860. Their work was paralleled by Dr. Alfred Drake, a Philadelphian who began work on an engine similar to Lenoir's in 1835, and by a Captain Brown, who as early as 1824 demonstrated a carriage propelled by a "gas vacuum" engine in London. Undoubtedly there were others. Credit for being "first" is generally given to Lenoir because his engine was commercially successful.

The demand for a cheap and simple source of power from farmers and small industrial plants stimulated the development of more advanced internal-combustion engines. The two-cycle engine patented by George B. Brayton of Boston, Massachusetts, in 1872 deserves mention here because it played an important role in the Selden patent controversy, the legal battle over threatened monopolization of the early American automobile industry. But from the standpoint of automotive technology the most important advance was a four-cycle engine introduced by Nicholas Otto, a German manufacturer, in 1876. The original Otto engine, conceived as a stationary source of power, was too cumbersome and slow to be efficient in a self-propelled vehicle. However, by 1885 Gottlieb Daimler, who had been one of Otto's engineers, and his assistant, William Maybach, had developed a 1.5-horsepower, 110-pound,

600-rpm, vertical "high-speed" engine that proved to be the prototype of the modern motorcar's power plant. To demonstrate the capability of their engine, Daimler and Maybach built four experimental motor vehicles between 1885 and 1889.

The idea of substituting a motor for the horse occurred to so many inventors during the 1860–1890 period that a full recounting of credits becomes merely a catalog of names and dates. In the United States alone, at least a dozen inventors built operable steam cars. The most important was Sylvester H. Roper of Roxbury, Massachusetts, who began his experiments in 1859 and built ten or more steam-powered road vehicles in the next two decades. Undoubtedly, the antiquarians will in time add even more names to a pre-Benz, pre-Duryea list that is already more than long enough to prove its main point: no one could claim to have invented the automobile. Yet this audacious claim was made by George B. Selden, a Rochester, New York, patent attorney and neophyte inventor, who was granted United States patent no. 549,160 on November 5, 1895, for an "improved road engine" powered by "a liquid-hydrocarbon engine of the compression type." [5]

The Selden patent covered the basic elements necessary for constructing a gasoline-powered automobile. Selden got his idea for the vehicle after seeing a two-cycle Brayton engine at the Philadelphia Centennial Exposition. His original patent application was filed in 1879. He then used evasive legal tactics to delay the patent's acceptance until conditions seemed favorable for commercial exploitation, which enabled him to maintain adequate security for his claims while he deferred the start of the seventeen-year period of exclusive rights to his invention provided by law. Meanwhile, Selden assiduously kept track of developments in the automotive field. His hand was forced in 1895—in part because the Patent Office was tightening its rules on delayed applications but more because events indicated that the time was now ripe for implementing the automotive idea. Selden had not yet built an operational model of his design when the patent was issued, and the state of the prior technological art at that time in no sense supported his allegation of priority.

The decade 1885–1895 saw a flurry of automotive activity both in Western Europe and in the United States. We have already noted the experiments of Daimler and Maybach. Even more significant were the contributions of Karl Benz and Emile Constant Levassor. Benz, a German manufacturer of stationary gas engines, pioneered the automobile to the stage of commercial feasibility. He built his first car, a tricycle powered by a one-cylinder engine, in 1886. His third vehicle was exhibited at the Paris Exposition in 1887 and was sold shortly afterward to a Frenchman named Emile Roger, who became Benz's agent in France. Motor vehicles were now for the first time offered for sale to the public. The 1891 Benz was a vastly improved four-wheel car with a redesigned engine capable of 700 rpm. Given the limited market and low performance expectations of the day, the 1891 Benz sold well and was fairly reliable. It was widely imitated. Benz retained the same basic design for ten years and was soon surpassed technologically by other manufacturers.

Benz's most important competitor was Emile Constant Levassor, who innovated the basic mechanical arrangement of the modern motorcar. Having acquired the French manufacturing rights for the Daimler motor in 1890, the newly founded engineering firm of Panhard and Levassor radically altered motor vehicle design in its 1891 model. The engine was placed vertically in front of the chassis instead of under the seats or in the back, which put the crankshaft parallel with the longitudinal line of the car instead of parallel with the axles. This mechanical arrangement marked the abandonment of the carriage silhouette in automotive design. Its great importance was that it made possible the accommodation of larger, more powerful engines in motor vehicles. Then in 1895 Panhard and Levassor began to use the new two-cylinder, 750-rpm Daimler "Phoenix" engine. Levassor drove one of these cars over the 727-mile course of the 1895 Paris-Bordeaux-Paris race at the then incredible average speed of 15 mph, with the longest stop for servicing being only twenty-two minutes.

That race, which began on June 11, 1895, underlined French superiority in automotive technology. By 1895 several French firms were issuing regular catalogs and producing motor vehicles in quantity for sale. The automobile was already a common sight on the streets of Paris. In 1894 *Le Petit Journal*, aware of public enthusiasm, had sponsored a 78-mile reliability run from Paris to Rouen, in which all thirteen entries powered by internal-combustion engines and four of the eight steam-driven entries managed to finish. The Automobile Club of France was founded soon afterward, in early 1895, to encourage the development of the motor vehicle and to regulate future automotive sporting events. The 1895 Paris-Bordeaux-Paris race was the new club's initial endeavor. Nine of the twenty-two vehicles that started ultimately completed the then formidable distance, and the best driving time was Levassor's impressive forty-eight hours. Although he was ostensibly the winner, Levassor was disqualified on a technicality, and first place was given to a Peugeot that finished eleven hours behind him. Eight of the nine successful entries were powered by internal-combustion engines.

The extensive, favorable coverage given to the French contest by newspapers and magazines had an immediate impact in the United States. The event demonstrated to Americans that the eventual displacement of the horse by the motorcar was more than an idle dream and suggested the possibility of a golden age of highway transportation. The results of the race also demonstrated the superiority of the gasoline-powered car over self-propelled steam and electric vehicles. European automobiles were soon being imported for sale by three New York City department stores; two specialized American automobile periodicals were inaugurated—*Motocycle* in October and *Horseless Age* in November 1895; and by September

1895 over 500 applications for patents relating to motor vehicles were on file in the United States Patent Office. On the first page of its first issue, *Horseless Age* nicely summed up current opinion: "Those who have taken the pains to search below the surface for the great tendencies of the age, know what a giant industry is struggling into being there. All signs point to the motor vehicle as the necessary sequence of methods of locomotion already established and approved. The growing needs of our civilization demand it; the public believe in it, and await with lively interest its practical application to the daily business of the world." [6]

Horseless Age was well aware that the French lead in automotive technology did not imply any lack of interest in the automotive idea in America: "All over the country mechanics and inventors are wrestling with the problems of trackless traction. Much of their work is in an unfinished state; many of their theories lack demonstration; but enough has already been achieved to prove absolutely the practicality of the motor vehicle." [7] The periodical reported that in late 1895 more than three hundred companies or individuals in the United States were or had been engaged in building experimental automobiles. American accomplishments since the late 1880s had been most notable in the areas of steam and electricity, which were rapidly to become the backwaters of automotive technology after the turn of the century. But several American inventors had managed to build experimental gasoline-powered cars by 1895. Compared with the 1895 French models, these cars were crude, motorized horse buggies, and they were not produced in quantity for sale. Nonetheless, they represent independent native attempts to build automobiles.

Credit for building the first successful American car powered by an internal-combustion engine is generally given to two Springfield, Massachusetts, bicycle mechanics, Charles E. and J. Frank Duryea, who were motivated to design their own automobile after reading a description of the Benz car in *Scientific American* in 1889. The Duryeas completed their first car in 1893. Their feat was duplicated in 1894 by Elwood P. Haynes, superintendent of the Indiana Gas and Oil Company, who built his vehicle with the help of two Kokomo, Indiana, machinists, Edgar and Elmer Apperson, and their assistant, Jonathan D. Maxwell. A number of other American automotive pioneers also began to build experimental gasoline automobiles about this time. Significant among those who had succeeded by 1896 were Hiram Percy Maxim, Charles B. King, Ransom E. Olds, Alexander Winton, and Henry Ford. We now know that American gasoline cars were built before the Duryeas': by Henry Nadig (1891), John W. Lambert (1891), Gottfried Schlomer and Frank Toepfer (1892), W. T. Harris and William Hollingsworth (1892), and Charles H. Black (1893). There were probably others.[8] However, these individuals made no lasting contribution to the implementation of the automative idea in America. The Duryeas, in contrast, went on to win the 1895 *Times-Herald* race, gained national publicity for their accomplishment, and initiated the manufacture of motor vehicles for a commercial market in the United States in 1896.

The *Chicago Times-Herald* sponsored the first American automobile race, held on Thanksgiving Day, November 28, 1895. Just five of the eleven entrants started, and only two vehicles were able to complete the 55-mile distance: the Duryea car that won and a Benz driven by Charles B. King. J. Frank Duryea's winning average speed was less than 8 mph. Nevertheless, the *Times-Herald* report the following day stressed that the race had been run in thirty-degree temperatures "through deep snow, and along ruts that would have tried horses to their utmost." Eastern newspapers viewed the contest as a convincing demonstration that the Duryea and Benz cars could perform tolerably under the worst possible conditions and prophesied the demise of the horse. Herman H. Kohlsaat, the publisher of the *Times-Herald*, received an open congratulatory letter from P. H. Studebaker, whose family firm was then the world's leading producer of carriages and wagons. And Thomas A. Edison told a reporter from the *New York World* that "the horseless vehicle is the coming wonder. . . . It is only a question of time when the carriages and trucks in every large city will be run with motors." It was generally believed that the *Times-Herald* race had advanced by at least five years the formation of the American automobile industry.[9]

Capitalizing on their success in the *Times-Herald* contest, the Duryeas made the first sale of an American gasoline car in February 1896 and produced twelve more vehicles of the same design that year. In 1897 their firm became the Duryea Manufacturing Company of Peoria, Illinois. No heed was paid to the Selden patent by the Duryeas or by several other manufacturers of gasoline-powered cars that soon entered the competition. Elwood P. Haynes and the Apperson brothers also took advantage of their early start and in 1898 began to build cars in Kokomo, Indiana, in quantity for sale. Alexander Winton, a Cleveland, Ohio, bicycle manufacturer, formed the Winton Motor Carriage Company. In the summer of 1897 he gained national recognition by driving one of his cars 800 miles from Cleveland to New York City in less than seventy-nine hours' driving time. Winton sold his first automobile in March 1898 and by December had delivered twenty-two vehicles.

There were even more advocates of steam and electricity who started to manufacture motor vehicles for a commercial market in the late 1890s. The quantity production of steam cars was initiated in the Boston area in 1898 by George E. Whitney and by Francis E. and Freelan O. Stanley. In 1899 two companies that made identical steam cars—the Locomobile Company of America at Bridgeport, Connecticut, and the Mobile Company of America at Tarrytown, New York—were established by Amzi Lorenzo Barber, an asphalt magnate, and by John Brisbane Walker, the owner of *Cosmopolitan Magazine*, respectively. The Electric Carriage and Wagon Company, formed by Henry G. Morris and Pedro G. Salom, began operating twelve of its electric cars as a fleet of public cabs on the streets of

New York City in January 1897. The company later moved to Hartford, Connecticut, and was absorbed by the Electric Vehicle Company, a New Jersey holding company. The most important early producer not only of electrics but of all motor vehicles in the United States was the nation's leading bicycle manufacturer, the Pope Manufacturing Company of Hartford, Connecticut. Its motor vehicle division, started by Hayden Eames in 1895, began to make electric cars in 1897 and had produced some 500 electric and 40 gasoline automobiles by the end of 1898. In 1899 it was consolidated with the Electric Vehicle Company.

Allowing for changes of name and early failures, thirty American automobile manufacturers produced an estimated 2,500 motor vehicles in 1899, the first year for which separate figures were compiled for the automobile industry in the *United States Census of Manufactures.* Ten New England firms that concentrated on producing electric and steam cars were responsible for the most significant part of that output. The remaining firms were equally dispersed between the Middle Atlantic states and the Middle West, which even then was the center for the manufacture of gasoline automobiles.[10] *Motor Age*, one of several recently launched automobile trade journals, reported in 1899 that, in addition to these manufacturers, experimental automobile work was "being carried on on such a scale that if the conditions in New England were approached in other parts of the country. . . . it may perhaps be estimated that one thousand such shops exist in the United States today, and probably one hundred of them have been in operation for two years or longer without yet having advanced to the stage of manufacture, except in a very few instances."[11]

The formation of an embryonic American automobile industry in the years 1895–1899 and the feverish automotive activity by scores of backyard inventors augured well for implementing the automotive idea in America on the eve of the turn of the century. Within a decade it would become obvious to the general public that the keynote of twentieth-century American life was automobility. The early speculations of Roger Bacon and Leonardo da Vinci would turn out to be as American as apple pie, the Declaration of Independence, and the stars and stripes.

2 EARLY IMPLEMENTATION IN AMERICA

During the first decade of the twentieth century, automobility became an integral part of American life. Contrary to popular myth, the introduction of the motorcar was greeted with enthusiasm by Americans. Shortly after the turn of the century, predictions began to become commonplace that a cheap, reliable car for the masses would soon be built and that within the foreseeable future a utopian horseless age would dawn. By 1905 the annual New York Automobile Show was the nation's leading industrial exhibit. By 1907 the automobile was commonly referred to as a necessity. Despite the drawbacks that cars were then sold on a cash-on-delivery basis without warranty and left much to be desired in performance, the demand for motorcars far exceeded the supply. The new firms operated in an unprecedented seller's market for an expensive item. By 1910 automobile manufacturing leaped from 150th to 21st in value of product among American industries and had become more important to the national economy on all measurable criteria than the wagon and carriage industry. Some 458,500 motor vehicles were registered in the United States in 1910, making America the world's foremost automobile culture.[1]

A mass market for automobiles existed in popular sentiment long before volume production of the Ford Model T made it a reality. The early automobile industry faced formidable technological and organizational problems. But from the introduction of the motor vehicle, public opinion about the potential of the innovation was always in advance of the industry's progress in producing reliable, moderately priced cars in quantity. A result of automotive historians' too narrow emphasis on the internal dynamics of the industry and its prominent personalities has been a production-oriented automotive history that tends to cast the industry in the heroic role of having created our automobile culture against overwhelming odds, including an apathetic or adverse populace. Their writings accord well with the flattering image that early automotive pioneers later were to develop about themselves. The fault is that automotive historians have not given adequate attention to the sociocultural milieu within which the early automobile industry developed.

[By the time the Ford Motor Company was organized in 1903, the belief that the automobile would soon supersede the horse was commonplace] Henry Ford could have derived his conception of a universal car for the masses from any of a large number of newspaper and magazine articles. In a statement released in late 1900 through the Boston News Bureau, a financial information agency, Colonel Albert A. Pope, then the nation's leading bicycle and automobile manufacturer, said: "The automobile will in time be the universal means of transportation, and the future of the American Bicycle Co. rests on the adoption and development of the automobile. . . . I predict that inside of ten years there will be more automobiles in use in the large cities of the United States than there are now horses in these cities." He further declared that 15,000 of his bicycle agents throughout the country were "fairly howling" for automobiles to meet an "enormous demand." [2] Other contemporary observers agreed with Pope. As the principal examiner at the United States Patent Office stated in early 1901, "To say that the future of the automobile is assured is merely to voice an impression which is as common as it is usually vague." [3] John W. Anderson, one of the original investors in the Ford Motor Company, expressed the early popular enthusiasm for the automobile in a letter from Detroit to his father just before the Ford incorporation in 1903: "Now the demand for automobiles is a perfect craze. Every factory here . . . has its entire output sold and cannot begin to fill orders. Mr. Malcomson has already begun to be deluged with orders, although not a machine has been put on the market and will not be until July 1.

. . . And it is all spot cash on delivery, and no guarantee or string attached of any kind." [4]

Newspapers and magazines in the United States, knowing that automobile news fascinated readers from all walks of life, gave the motorcar generous and extensive coverage. Even as early as the turn of the century, *Automobile* felt that "the unprecedented and well nigh incredible rapidity with which the automobile industry has developed . . . is largely due to the fact that every detail of the subject has been popularized by the technical and daily press." [5] In 1902 another journal reported that "a dozen publications thrive in the interests of the industry, while every newspaper of repute has its automobile department, hundreds of special articles are to be found in periodicals of general circulation, the advertisements of makers and dealers find places in almost every high-class publication, and numerous books have come from the publishers." [6] *Horseless Age* in 1903 commented that "fanatical opposition to the automobile is on the whole very rare in this country. The metropolitan dailies occasionally print strong editorials denouncing speed excesses and careless driving, but the whole press is practically unanimous in recognizing the automobile as a legitimate pleasure vehicle and as destined to a great future in the commercial world." [7]

Close cooperation between the press and the automobile industry was established early. On May 13, 1897, Colonel Albert A. Pope initiated the custom of the press interview as an established part of introducing new automobile models to the public. He invited reporters to a private showing of his first electric cars, allowed them to operate the vehicles, and supplied pictures for publication. The press interview was soon institutionalized and became more elaborate. Manufacturers commonly brought reporters long distances at company expense to be entertained and given a preview of new models in the hope that "free" publicity would follow. Automobile clubs, too, undertook "a campaign of education among the newspaper men," which consisted of demonstration rides and furnishing free news copy on the motorcar. *Automobile* found "nothing ulterior in the motives of a club that undertakes a campaign along the lines suggested—it is merely placing the moulders of public opinion in a position to weigh the subject with unbiased minds." [8]

No automobile manufacturer exploited the press more consciously or to better advantage than Alexander Winton, whose high regard for the power of the printed word can be traced to his 1897 drive from Cleveland to New York. The trip resulted in so much favorable publicity that he decided to repeat it in 1899 with Charles B. Shanks, a newspaper reporter. The articles written by Shanks to publicize the journey attracted much attention and drew interested crowds all along their route. James R. Doolittle, writing the first comprehensive history of the industry in 1916, called Shanks's articles "the first real effort at intelligent publicity with which the new industry had been favored." He estimated that "when Winton reached New York a million people saw his car and part of the credit for that crowd must be given to Shanks." The fact that Winton's 1899 Cleveland–New York run had taken less than forty-eight hours' driving time, combined with Shanks's effective publicity, appears to have stimulated popular demand for automobiles. Other manufacturers gave Winton credit for a general increase in sales. Winton's own records show that before the trip his "sales were made almost exclusively to engineers who desired to buy and experiment with an automobile that would really run, but after the trip, the sales were made to the public at large." [9]

Winton's practical demonstration of the motorcar was emulated many times during the next few years. Automobiles became drawing cards at county fairs around the turn of the century; and the annual automobile show, after its inauguration in five American cities in 1900, became a popular institution. But it was the long-distance reliability run that most excited the average person's imagination about the romance of motoring. In contrast, track and road races, which placed primary emphasis upon speed, were more important for their contributions to automotive technology as tests for weaknesses in design than as publicity for the motorcar. Track races were viewed by the public as little more than exciting spectacles, involving as they did specialized monstrosities designed for maximum speed rather than practical road vehicles. Road races were considered to be dangerous exhibitions, unwarranted because their relation to the development of a reliable family car seemed remote. The man in the street was more impressed by the imminent personal automobility promised by the long-distance reliability run.

In the fall of 1901 Ransom E. Olds decided to have Roy D. Chapin, then a tester at the Olds factory, drive a new curved-dash Oldsmobile (1901–1906) from Detroit to the New York automobile show. The curved-dash Olds was the zenith of surrey-influenced automotive design. It sold for a moderate $650, making ownership of a fairly reliable car for its time possible for middle-class Americans. The Olds Motor Works was by 1901 committed to the volume production of the curved-dash, having been the first company to mass-produce gasoline automobiles by manufacturing some 425 cars that year. A New York City to Buffalo endurance run sponsored by the newly formed Automobile Club of America (ACA) in 1901 indicated the possibility of long-distance touring by private owners, and Olds hoped to capture the market in the heavily populated eastern cities by providing convincing evidence that his moderately priced light car was as reliable for touring as more expensive heavy vehicles. Chapin left Detroit on October 27. Despite the handicap of extremely muddy roads, he arrived in New York City on November 5, with an average speed of 14 mph for the 820-mile distance. Olds sold a record 750 cars in New York City alone the following year.

Chapin's feat was a prelude to three successful crossings of the American continent by automobile in 1903. The first was made by Dr. H. Nelson Jackson, a physician from Burlington, Vermont, and his chauffeur, Sewall K. Crocker. They traveled from San Francisco to New York City in a new Winton in sixty-three days. Transcontinental tours by a Packard and a curved-dash Olds under the auspices of their manufacturers followed. For Ransom E. Olds this important achievement helped him to lead the industry with nationwide sales of 4,000 in 1903. More important, the reliability of the moderately priced light car was now established in the mind of the public. An estimated several thousand Americans were encouraged to take cross-country automobile vacations in 1904, marking the inauguration of long-distance automobile touring by the average automobilist.

Charles J. Glidden, a millionaire automobile enthusiast who wished to encourage touring by private owners, sponsored the famous Glidden reliability tours. They were run between 1905 and 1913 for handsome trophies. To keep the events from becoming simply publicity stunts for automobile manufacturers, Glidden stipulated that each car entered must be driven by its owner. But since any executive of the automobile industry could comply with the rule by driving one of his firm's most recent models himself, most contestants were representatives of the automobile industry. The first Glidden tour was held from July 11 to July 22, 1905, over an 870-mile route from New York City through New England and return. Twenty-seven of the thirty-four entries finished, the first being a heavy Pierce touring car carrying five passengers. A participant summed up the results: "The tour has proved that the automobile is now almost foolproof. It has proved that American cars are durable and efficient. It has shown the few who took part how delightful their short vacation may be, and it has strengthened our belief in the permanence of the motorcar." [10]

That tour obviated the need to prove further that the motorcar was reliable for long-distance transportation. The point was unequivocally underlined for the public by the performance of the automobile during the 1906 San Francisco earthquake. Walter C. White organized a caravan of motortrucks to bring supplies to the disaster area, and some 200 privately owned local automobiles were immediately impressed for emergency service by the authorities. The gasoline automobiles used an estimated 15,000 gallons of fuel donated by the Standard Oil Company. After tires exploded from the heat of the pavement, cars were run for days on their wheel rims at as fast a speed as possible over obstacle-laden streets. Passenger cars were called upon to tow several moving vans after the horses pulling them had expired from the heat and strain. Mechanical failures under these extremely severe conditions turned out to be surprisingly infrequent. Little need remained to demonstrate the reliability of the motor vehicle. By 1907, gasoline economy runs had replaced reliability runs as the focus of public interest.

Motor vehicle sales increased substantially in 1907 despite the general business recession and an apparent saturation of the upper-class market. No one doubted that a broad middle-class market for cars was becoming a reality. The number of starting cars in the annual Glidden tours dwindled from forty-nine in 1907 to thirteen in 1909. One of the 1909 Glidden officials explained that the decline occurred because automobile manufacturers "were enjoying too much prosperity. They said, 'Why should we enter this contest when we are unable to supply the demand now? The advertising will do us no good.' " [11] *Automobile* observed: "The riding and driving clubs all over the country are losing membership, and even closing their clubhouse doors, and livery stables are losing money or being transformed into garages. The remaining stronghold of the horse is guarded solely by low prices." [12]

After 1905, recognizing that the early upper-class market was nearing saturation and aware of a great demand for outmoded buggy-type cars and secondhand conventional automobiles, the more enterprising manufacturers turned to the developing middle-class market. The most successful was Henry Ford, who led the industry in developing the reliable, moderately priced, four-cylinder, conventional runabout with his $600 Model N (1906–1907). Its successor, Ford's legendary Model T (1908–1927), became the universal car that had been anticipated by many Americans since the turn of the century. John B. Rae has aptly stated: "By the end of the first decade of the twentieth century the automobile could no longer be regarded either as a novelty or as a rich man's plaything; it was already potentially what it would become in fact—an item of incredible mass consumption." [13]

While the automobile remained an adjunct of social status in Europe, automobility quickly became a mass movement in the United States. The only people deeply prejudiced against the automobile were horse breeders and livery stable owners, whose vested economic interests were threatened by the motorcar. Carriage manufacturers and blacksmiths, on the other hand, accommodated to the motorcar because they were able to profit from the ensuing new demands for their products and services. Even antispeed organizations maintained that they were proautomobile and only against its abuse. The legal counsel for the Long Island Protective Society, one of the most virulent antispeed organizations, said typically upon its incorporation in September 1902: "Our purpose is to enforce the speed law against the reckless drivers of automobiles and also those of fast horses. . . . It is not a society antagonistic to automobiles. We recognize that the automobile is the twentieth-century vehicle, and that it is with us to stay. Many of our members own and operate automobiles, but we are for a free highway and a safe highway and intend to harmonize the interests of the automobilists, the horse drivers, and the pedestrians." [14]

Early attempts to regulate the motor vehicle pitted the auto enthusiast against the general public, who, appalled by speeding and reports of accidents in the daily press, demanded that government take action. But the legislation passed was overly lenient and not motivated by prejudice against the motorcar. After the turn of the century it became increasingly obvious even to auto enthusiasts that special motor vehicle legislation was needed to supplement the few laws regulating horse-drawn traffic. Motorcars had much higher average and top speeds than horse-drawn vehicles, and melding motor vehicles into the normal flow of horse-drawn traffic was a problem.

Local automobile ordinances were soon superseded by state laws. These local and state laws usually reflected the thinking of the automobile clubs, who lobbied energetically to forestall prejudicial legislation. The American Automobile Association (AAA) and the National Association of Automobile Manufacturers (NAAM) went so far as to campaign for a national motor vehicle law. Beginning in 1905 in the Fifty-ninth Congress, they introduced several federal automobile bills, which died in committee because legislators doubted that federal regulation of the motorcar was either necessary or constitutional.

In 1901 New York was the first state to require registration; by 1910 motor vehicle registration was compulsory in thirty-six states. Motorists at first resented registration, which had as its main purpose the identification of speeders and reckless drivers. However, because the general practice in most states was to use funds from registration fees for road improvement, motorists after 1905 came to favor higher and annual registration fees as one means of securing better roads.

About 1905, motorists also began to agitate for the licensing of all motor vehicle operators. They felt that safety demanded that the operators be not only licensed but also required to pass an examination to determine their competence. The certification of operators was common in Europe, but state governments here were reluctant to assume the responsibility. As late as 1909, only twelve states and the District of Columbia required all automobile drivers to obtain licenses, and in seven other states only professional chauffeurs had to obtain licenses. The application forms for an operator's license in these nineteen states as a rule asked for little more information than the applicant's name, address, age, and the type of car he claimed to be competent to drive. The form might have to be notarized, but in the vast majority of these states a license to drive an automobile could still be obtained by mail.

As of 1902, only four states had passed any special regulations governing use of the automobile. The lowest speed limit on the open highway in any of these states was 15 mph, and the municipal ordinances then in effect almost never restricted the motorcar to lower speeds than the top speeds of horse-drawn vehicles—that is, 6 to 8 mph in business sections and 10 to 12 mph in other parts of cities. By 1906 most states had adopted motor vehicle legislation that provided for maximum speed limits of 20 to 25 mph on the open highway. The narrow, winding, dirt roads of the day, combined with the predominance of horse-drawn traffic on them, meant that these speed limits represented the very limit of safety. The 1905–1906 period marked the high point of restrictive speed laws. Before this few speed laws had been enacted; later, with the rapid diffusion of the motorcar, speed laws became progressively more lenient.

The sentiment against speeding and reckless driving was especially strong in rural areas, where the ire of farmers was aroused with the advent of informal automobile touring. Their hostility was misconstrued by many early auto enthusiasts to be directed against the automobile itself rather than the automobilist. Inconsiderate automobile tourists constituted a danger both to stock and to horse-drawn traffic, and automobiles raised clouds of dust that damaged crops and settled on farmhouses and barns. In addition, most automobile manufacturers made no attempt to design cars suited to the farmers' needs until forced to do so by the saturation of the urban luxury market after 1905. Although feelings against the city automobilist were extreme in some localities, the important point is that antiautomobile sentiment among farmers remained localized, was directed against speeding and reckless driving, and was pretty much confined to the years 1904 through 1906. William Jennings Bryan, the leading national spokesman for rural America, used motor vehicles in the campaigns of 1896 and 1900. By 1904, politicians were finding the motorcar useful for stumping tours of rural districts, where its novelty was considered "an effective aid to the oratorical talents of the spellbinder in drawing a crowd." [15] At the high point of the farmers' reaction to the motorcar, in November 1905 at the thirty-ninth annual session of the National Grange, Patrons of Husbandry, a resolution was passed by the delegates that the automobile was "an innovation in modes of travel which must be accepted." [16]

The increasing prosperity of farmers, combined with the appearance of rugged, moderately priced cars such as the Ford Model N and Model T, led to the rapid development of a rural market for automobiles after 1906. Industry spokesmen such as Alfred E. Reeves of the American Motor Car Manufacturers' Association (AMCMA) were impressed by 1909 that "manufacturers are relying on two great new purchasing factors—the farmer and the man with the middle-class income." [17]

The middle-class base of the American market for automobiles was evident well before Henry Ford came out with his Model T. The expense of automobile ownership meant, of course, that cars were initially bought by persons with much higher than average incomes. Ralph C. Epstein gathered data showing that the first purchasers of several makes of cars were mainly moneyed businessmen, ranging from self-designated "capitalists" to dry-goods merchants, but physicians and engineers were also well represented. Merchants and physicians predominated among the early purchasers of the curved-dash Oldsmobile.[18] The local doctors were invariably among the first persons to purchase cars in any community, and physicians emerged as the most innovative group in the United States in adopting the automobile. Thus from its inception the automobile movement in the United States was neither exclusively nor primarily the "fad of the idle rich" that horse breeders and livery stable owners tried to label it.

What is striking in retrospect is how rapidly automobile ownership became general in the United States, not its initial, false association with the exceptionally affluent. As early as 1903 George A. Banker, one of the largest eastern automobile dealers, reported: "Of course the wealthy classes are still our chief customers. . . . But they are no longer the exclusive buyers, even of moderately expensive cars, as was the case a year ago. The bank clerk and similar young men with plenty of time and earning good salaries are now found among our customers." [19] Data presented in the Lynds' classic study of Muncie, Indiana, illustrate how rapidly automobile ownership became more widespread than the ownership of horses and buggies: "A local carriage manufacturer of the early days estimates that about 125 families owned a horse and buggy in 1890, practically all of them business folk. . . . The first real automobile appeared in Middletown in 1900. About 1906 it was estimated that 'there are probably 200 in the city and county.' " [20] By 1907, conservative bankers were beginning to worry that too many people were mortgaging their homes to finance automobile purchases.

Automobility remained a mass movement mainly in sentiment until after 1910 only because cars were expensive. Until well after 1910 the initial price of an automobile involved a staggering expenditure for the family of average means. And there is good evidence that prices were not lowered as rapidly as possible. The average selling price of cars produced by the Association of Licensed Automobile Manufacturers (ALAM) went from $1,170 in 1903 to an exorbitant $1,784 in 1905. As long as the early luxury market lasted, most automobile manufacturers, who were able to sell all the high-priced cars they could produce, spurned the idea of making lower-priced cars at lower unit profits. *Outlook* explained as late as 1907, for example: "One firm . . . whose first reputation was made on a low-priced car of unusual excellence, now makes that style only on order and does not exhibit or generally advertise it. It is now turning out higher-priced cars, of which, as a representative said, 'we can sell all that we make.' " [21] Installment sales were not looked upon favorably by the automobile industry until the market for new cars began to approach saturation in the early 1920s. Industry opinion about time sales before 1910 was summed up well by *Motor World* at the end of 1904: "There is no excess of cars, and customers are to be found for all of reputable make that are produced. To deviate from the cash system now in universal use is to invite disaster without any corresponding gain in the unlikely event of success. No sane businessman will bring himself to do this." [22]

Early upper-class owners were equally shortsighted about the implications of the developing mass market. Taking the aristocratic national automobile clubs of France and Great Britain as a model, a self-appointed New York City automobile elite founded the Automobile Club of America (ACA) on June 7, 1899, with a view toward being the national voice and conscience of American motorists. The ACA was quickly recognized as "an ultra-fashionable coterie of millionaires who have taken up the new and expensive fad of auto-locomotion and banded themselves together for its pursuit and the incidental notoriety attributed to all the functions of upper swelldom." [23] Competing automobile clubs, also drawing their membership almost exclusively from the affluent and socially prominent, were soon founded in other large cities. Elegant clubhouses that included elaborate garage facilities were built; memberships were restricted to a few hundred individuals; and social functions were almost as important as agitation for improved roads and reasonable motor vehicle laws, sponsoring tours and automobile shows, and providing essential services for the motorist.

The hegemony of the early aristocratic big-city clubs in the automobile movement was undercut as local clubs mushroomed in medium-sized cities and small towns and as middle-class motorists in large cities formed competing associations that combined limited services with open membership policies. Automobile clubs outside the large cities attracted members from all walks of life and needed "some different sort of local association, better suited to the semirural environment and less expensive to a small [and less affluent] membership." [24] As the public garage became an established institution and as motoring came to be considered utilitarian rather than a "sport," in large cities as well the future belonged to clubs such as the Chicago Motor Club. It was organized in August 1906 with no clubhouse, no social features, and the goal of attracting as many members as possible at nominal fees.

The American Automobile Association (AAA) was formed in March 1902 as a loose federation of local clubs under the auspices of the elite big-city clubs, who expected to dominate it. But the AAA quickly came to reflect the interests of the middle-class motorist as memberships skyrocketed in the more democratic local clubs with their more limited goals. Piqued by its loss of control over the affairs of the AAA, the Automobile Club of America withdrew from the AAA on March 12, 1908. William H. Hotchkiss, the president of the AAA, responded: "I do not regret the resignation, but welcome it. It is high time that motorists understand whether a mere name adopted in the infancy of the motor vehicle in this country, and which has since become a misnomer, entitles any local club in any city, no matter how great, to lord it over hundreds of other clubs in other parts of the country. . . . whether the American Automobile Association represents those motorists or whether they are to be represented by a small clique of gentlemen who manage a local social club. I, therefore, hail the issue and have no doubt of the results." [25]

Thus the ACA failed in its attempt to transplant the European pattern of highly centralized control over a national automobile movement by an elite group of automobilists. To exercise effective national influence in the United States, any automobile association had to reckon with the predominant democratic ethos of American culture, the widespread ownership of automobiles, and the decentralized governmental powers of our federal political system. As *Motor World* had prophesied in 1901, "Aristocracy never has survived a transplanting to American soil, and this automobile club idea will not be an exception to the rule of failure. No club, no matter how rich or exclusive its membership may be, can arrogate to itself the right to pose in any way as supreme ruler of the present or future of the motor vehicle." [26]

There are many reasons why, in contrast with Europe, an automobile culture developed so rapidly in the United States. To begin with, the volume production of standardized commodities became well established early in our industrial history. Our abundance of natural resources, combined with a chronic shortage of labor, resulted in low costs for raw materials and the mechanization of industrial processes, which necessitated the standardization of products. In addition, the absence of tariff barriers between the states encouraged sales over a wide geographic area. Most important were our higher per capita income and more equal income distribution relative to those in European countries.[27] It is significant, for example, that Morris Motors, the most important British automobile manufacturer, did not install a moving assembly line until 1934—two decades after it had been innovated at Ford. The income distribution in Great Britain fixed the demand for cars there at too low a level to justify the investment.[28] Because of these differences between Europe and the United States, the European pattern of small-scale, individualized production of motor vehicles stood no chance of becoming characteristic of the American automobile industry.

The lack of early governmental subsidization of the motorcar in the United States turned out to be a blessing in disguise. Our War Department showed little interest in the motorcar until about 1909. The automobile trade journals complained as late as 1909 that "the Washington government has not given to the motorcar that support which a new method of transportation deserves, or has that government given even a semblance of support compared with the financial and legislative aid that have been rendered by many of the governments of Europe to their motoring interests." [29] The governments of France, Germany, and England had realized the military potential of the motor vehicle by the mid-1890s. They conducted extensive military experiments with motor vehicles and offered substantial subsidies to encourage the development of motor vehicles suitable for military purposes. The early governmental subsidization in Europe delayed the manufacture of light cars for the family driver by emphasizing the development of heavy touring cars and trucks that were better suited for officers' staff cars, weapons carriers, and transporting troops and supplies.

Lacking our decentralized federal political system and tradition of minimal government, European countries early adopted national legislation regulating the construction and operation of motor vehicles. In contrast, the American policy of laissez faire and caveat emptor meant that many American cars did not meet even the extremely low minimal safety requirements of the period. The national automobile laws common in Europe had the advantage of imposing uniform, reasonable standards upon all of a nation's motorists and ensured the basic competence of everyone who drove an automobile on the public roads. European practice was clearly superior from the standpoint of automotive safety. But the minimally restrictive attitude of government in the United States ensured that the American consumer could purchase cars that were cheap, if unsafe, by European standards and encouraged the average person to believe that everyone was competent to drive.

Perhaps it was inevitable that our democratic production and consumption ethics would be applied to motorcars, given only that the automobile from its introduction seemed, on utilitarian grounds, to be superior to other forms of transportation. The motorcar combined the flexibility of the horse with the speed of the locomotive or electric trolley, without the costly liability of a system of fixed rails and overhead wires. The general adoption of the automobile promised to relieve taxpayers of the high cost of removing tons of excreta daily from city streets and to eliminate huge expenditures for endless miles of railroad track, overhead wires, and networks of tunnels, and with this the graft and corruption that too often seemed to be associated with building urban mass-transit systems.

In New York City alone at the turn of the century, horses deposited an estimated 2.5 million pounds of manure and 60,000 gallons of urine on the streets every day. Traffic was often clogged by the carcasses of overworked dray horses who dropped in their tracks during summer heat waves or were destroyed after stumbling on slippery pavements and breaking their legs. On the average, New York City removed about 15,000 dead horses from its streets each year. A 1908 estimate that tried to take all factors into account concluded that the cost of not banning the horse from New York City was approximately $100 million a year. Urban sanitation departments were not only expensive but typically inefficient and graft- and corruption-ridden. As prize political plums for the ward bosses, sanitation departments were staffed by "old and indigent men," "prisoners who don't like to work," and "persons on relief." Arguing for the displacement of the horse by the electric trolley, United States Commissioner of Labor Carroll D. Wright pointed out in 1892 that, in addition to the expense of horses, "the vitiation of the air by the presence of so many animals is alone a sufficient reason for their removal, while the clogged condition of the streets impedes business, and involves the safety of life and limb." [30]

After its introduction in the late 1880s, the electric trolley rapidly displaced horses on streetcar lines. It was sanitary, not subject to organic malfunctions, and faster than the horse. But an urban transportation system based on the electric trolley involved huge expenditures for rails, overhead wires, and tunnels or elevated platforms. Freight still had to be moved by horse-drawn trucks, and passengers had to get from the trolley stop to their ultimate destinations by horse, bicycle, or foot. The electric trolley was less flexible than the horse, and if a single trolley got stalled on the tracks, the normal flow of traffic was halted. The expense of an urban rail transportation system meant that it was practical only in areas of high-density population, thus stifling suburban development because it was not feasible to extend facilities out to the sparsely settled outskirts of the city. As construction costs mounted during the 1890s, it began to become apparent even in large cities that building adequate mass-transit rail systems was an insurmountable task.

The motor vehicle offered an attractive alternative. It was facilely assumed that the cost of improving city streets for antiseptic automobile traffic would be negligible. Further, it was anticipated that urban traffic congestion and parking problems would disappear because automobiles were more flexible than streetcars running on fixed rails, and they took up only half the space of horse-drawn vehicles. According to an 1896 article in *Scientific American*, for example, "the existence of a double line of cars moving on a fixed track and claiming the right of way over other vehicles is a hindrance to traffic and is itself delayed." If these rails were removed, the street asphalted from curb to curb, and the streetcars replaced by motor vehicles that could pass one another at will, "the whole volume of traffic would move with less interruption than at present, and . . . the cars themselves would make faster time." [31] The idea of asphalt pavement, too slippery for horses, was obviously predicated on a horseless city, with streets free from accumulated excreta and the carcasses of dead animals. From the perspective of American values there was the bonus that dependence upon private passenger cars for mass transit promised to place the burden of the costs of an urban transportation system squarely on the shoulders of the individual.

The motorcar was considered cleaner, safer, more reliable, and more economical than the horse. The car promised to be vastly improved and lowered in price in the near future, while the expense and liabilities of the horse seemed insurmountable. As *Harper's Weekly* said in 1899, "a good many folks to whom every horse is a wild beast feel much safer on a machine than behind a quadruped, who has a mind of his own, and emotions which may not always be forestalled or controlled." [32] Lacking the physical strength needed to control a spirited, skittish team, women in particular were impressed with the advantages of the motorcar, especially with the noiseless, odorless electric car that did not involve the problem of learning to shift gears. Even the crude brakes on early motorcars were vastly superior to those on horse-drawn vehicles, and it was widely believed that an automobile going twenty miles an hour could be stopped in less space than a horse-drawn rig being driven at a moderate trot. The motor vehicle was also much more maneuverable than the horse-drawn vehicle, requiring considerably less space for turning around because of its shorter length. In addition, it was impervious to weather conditions and to fatigue. Countless tests demonstrated to the public that the motor vehicle was cheaper than the horse. It depreciated less rapidly and did about three times the work for the same amount in operating expenses. Medical doctors, who drove their horses hard on calls, invariably reported that the motorcar was more economical as well as more reliable. The average automobile owner, however, did not use his car enough to realize these economies. Nonetheless, everyone agreed: "So far as we can at present see, the displacement of the horse will cheapen living and travel, certainly not increase them." [33]

From its introduction, the automobile was thus compared quite favorably with the horse-drawn rig. But the motorcar was always judged on tougher criteria. People anticipated that the automobile, unlike the horse, would be substantially improved and available at a much lower price in the near future. *Motor Age* explained in 1903: "In one way the automobile is its own enemy. It has accomplished so much and has become able to do so much, that the public has reached a point of unlimited expectation. For instance take the man who asks for automobiles at about $400 or less. What does he want for the price of a good horse and buggy outfit? A car equal in capabilities to the horse and buggy? Not by any means. He wants a car which will go from four to six times as fast, and travel twice or three times as far at the same expense. . . . [The public] puts the automobile in a class by itself out of comparison with other means of travel—and then kicks because the first cost is greater than that of a side bar runabout and a spavined gray mare." [34]

The long-range liabilities of the mass adoption of the automobile were not foreseen at the time. No one envisioned that the mass ownership of motorcars would ultimately entail a total per capita expenditure for cars, fuel, repairs, road building and maintenance, insurance, and loss of life and income through accidents considerably in excess of the cost of any conceivable mass-transit trolley and railroad system. Nor was it evident that the best case for the relative efficiency and economy of the motor vehicle from the perspective of either the transportation system as a whole or the individual could be made for the limited use of motor-driven trucks and buses along with rail transportation, not the widespread adoption of private passenger cars. That automobile exhaust would become a more dangerous and expensive pollutant than horse excreta was not foreseen. It was also overlooked that the average family did not use a horse and buggy enough, or spend enough on trolley and railroad fares, to realize a saving from switching to the automobile, the relative economy of which became apparent only when a substantial amount of driving was done.

Even had the experts recognized some of the long-range liabilities of the mass use of private passenger cars, the automobile was developed as a consumer-goods item and was diffused in response to the demands of a capitalist market economy. Americans have historically had unbounded faith in technological progress. They have accepted as an essential aspect of American democracy that the marketplace and the profit motive should determine the fate of technological innovations defined as consumer-goods items. And they have assumed that any adverse unanticipated consequences would be corrected in time either by the market or by other technological innovations. In the early 1900s both the experts and the public concluded that the automobile promised to raise significantly the quality of life and to restructure American society through technology along lines dictated by traditional cultural values. These considerations were undoubtedly as important as the utilitarian ones in the rapid development of our automobile culture.

Individualism—defined in terms of privatism, freedom of choice, and the opportunity to extend one's control over his physical and social environment—was one of the important American core values that automobility promised to preserve and enhance in a changing urban-industrial society. Mobility was another. The automobile tremendously increased the individual's geographic mobility, which was closely associated with social mobility in the United States. It was certain to be prized by Americans. In our traditionally mobile society the motorcar was an ideal status symbol.[35]

In a culture that has invariably preferred technological to political solutions to its problems, automobility appeared to the expert and to the man in the street as a panacea for many of the social ills of the day. Most people believed that the general adoption of the automobile would significantly raise the quality of life in cities. Better public health conditions were the main benefits anticipated. Medical authorities pointed out that tetanus was introduced into cities in horse fodder and that dysentery and diarrhea, serious health problems among city children at the time, were caused by "street dust," which in the main consisted of germ-laden dried horse dung. The excreta that littered city streets irritated nasal passages and lungs in the form of "street dust" during dry weather, making it unpleasant to open windows for ventilation, then became a syrupy mass to wade through and track into the home whenever it rained. Insurance actuaries established that infectious diseases, including typhoid fever, were much more frequently contracted by livery stable keepers and their employees than by other population groups. It was well known that the flies that bred on the ever-present manure heaps carried over thirty communicable diseases, and public health officials were convinced by the turn of the century that the first step in eradicating the housefly was to eliminate the horse from cities. The unsightliness and stench of the stable meant that most urban owners of horses "boarded and baited" them at public facilities an inconvenient distance from their residences. The stress and strain associated with urban living were also widely attributed to the iron wheels of countless horse-drawn vehicles clattering on the cobblestone pavement that horses required for a foothold. As pointed out in *Scientific American* in 1899, "The improvement in city conditions by the general adoption of the motorcar can hardly be overestimated. Streets clean, dustless and odorless, with light rubber tired vehicles moving swiftly and noiselessly over their smooth expanse, would eliminate a greater part of the nervousness, distraction, and strain of modern metropolitan life." [36]

To a population that had deeply internalized what Richard Hofstadter called the "agrarian myth," [37] however, the chief value of automobility was that it permitted escape from the supposedly debilitating environment of the city without cutting oneself off from the advantages only the metropolis offered. Henry Ford once phrased nicely the motorist's paradigm for urban reform: "We shall solve the city problem by leaving the city." [38] The ultimate answer to the tenement house slum was that everyone should buy a motorcar and commute to suburbia, and a projected suburban real estate boom soon became another anticipated benefit of automobility. The utopian effects of a mass movement to suburbia seemed obvious: "Imagine a healthier race of workingmen, toiling in cheerful and sanitary factories, with mechanical skill and trade-craft developed to the highest, as the machinery grows more delicate and perfect, who, in the late afternoon, glide away in their own comfortable vehicles to their little farms or houses in the country or by the sea twenty or thirty miles distant! They will be healthier, happier, more intelligent and self-respecting citizens because of the chance to live among the meadows and flowers of the country instead of in crowded city streets." [39]

Automobility also seemed an ideal solution to the farm problem. A predominant fear during the 1900–1910 decade was that the siphoning off of the rural population into cities would soon deplete the number of farmers to the point that a critical food shortage would result. Rising prices for farm products disturbed city consumers, who were confronted with higher prices for food, yet the financial rewards of farming were still not sufficient to keep talented and ambitious rural youth tied to a life of isolated drudgery. The general adoption of the automobile by farmers promised to break down the isolation of rural life, lighten farm labor, and reduce significantly the cost of transporting farm products to market, thus raising the farmers' profits while lowering the food prices paid by city consumers. *Outing Magazine* predicted in 1902, for example, that with the adoption of the automobile "the millions of our rural population will be brought into closer relations with the towns and with neighbors, and the loneliness of farm life, which drives so many to the cities, with detriment to all, will no longer retard our agricultural growth, nor prevent a proper distribution of population for the national welfare." [40] By 1907 it seemed obvious that the automobile would "remove the last serious obstacle to the farmer's success. It will market his surplus product, restore the value of his lands, and greatly extend the scope and pleasure of all phases of country life." [41]

Viewed as a solution to these major social problems, the general adoption of the automobile was the most important reform of the pre–World War I era, an especially attractive reform to Americans because it did not involve collective political action. It is no wonder that automobility, for two generations after Henry Ford initiated the volume production of the Model T at his Highland Park plant in

1910, became the most important force for change in American civilization. In retrospect, we can see that many of the changes wrought by automobility were antithetical to the expectations of our forebears and that many consequences of the automobile revolution have proved either illusory or deleterious. But we need to recognize also that the American automobile movement was democratic in its inception and that our automobile culture was a vast improvement over the horse and rail culture that it superseded. For these considerations mean that automobility was until recently a progressive force as well as the predominant one in American historical development.

3 THE RISE OF THE GIANTS

Some 515 separate companies had entered automobile manufacturing by 1908, the year in which Henry Ford introduced his Model T and General Motors was founded by William C. Durant. No industry in American history required less capital to enter or promised greater profits. *Horseless Age* was concerned by 1902 that "the attitude of the public has, in fact, been so favorable to the new vehicle that promoters and manufacturers have in many cases taken advantage of it to impose upon the public worthless stocks and imperfect vehicles . . . [to] the detriment of the industry as a whole." [1] *Motor World*, appalled that the well-watered combined capitalization of automobile companies organized during 1900 came to $329.5 million, prophesied: "Not one-tenth of these concerns will ever get any nearer turning out a motor vehicle than the permission to do so, which appears in their incorporation papers. But what a sad commentary the whole thing is upon the credulity of humanity and the never deviating certainty that fools can always be counted upon to rush in where angels, celestial, not financial ones, would hesitate to tread or even fly." [2]

The managerial and technical expertise needed to enter automobile manufacturing presented little problem. It was most commonly diverted from other closely related business activities. John B. Rae has pointed out that most of the successful early automotive entrepreneurs "were less likely to be individual inventors starting a completely new business than men who added the production of automobiles to an existing operation. Most frequently, they were bicycle or carriage and wagon manufacturers, or operators of machine shops, but there were a variety of odds and ends." Rae has also established that, although the great majority of the more important figures in the early automobile industry had received only practical training as machinists or mechanics, "the number of college-trained engineers in this first generation of automotive entrepreneurs is surprisingly large, considering that engineering degrees were something of a rarity in the United States until the twentieth century." [3]

The requirements for fixed and working capital were met mainly by shifting the burden to parts makers, distributors, and dealers. The automobile was a unique combination of components already standardized and being produced for other uses—for example, stationary and marine gasoline engines, carriage bodies, and wheels. The manufacture of components was jobbed out to scores of independent suppliers, minimizing the capital requirements for wages, materials, expensive machinery, and a large factory. So once the basic design of his car was established, the early automobile manufacturer became merely an assembler of major components and a supplier of finished cars to his distributors and dealers. The modest assembly plant needed could be rented as easily as purchased, and the process of assembling was shorter than the thirty- to ninety-day credit period the parts makers allowed. Operating on this basis, the Ford Motor Company was able to start in business in 1903 with paid-in capital of only $28,000, a dozen workmen, and an assembly plant just 250 feet by 50 feet.

The demand for automobiles was so high that manufacturers were able to extract exorbitant concessions from distributors and dealers in exchange for exclusive territorial rights. Advance cash deposits of 20 percent were required on all orders, with full payment demanded immediately upon delivery through a sight draft attached to the bill of lading. And cars had to be accepted according to a prearranged schedule, regardless of current retail sales, thereby allowing the manufacturer to gear shipments to production. Roy D. Chapin, organizer of the Hudson Motor Car Company, stated that as late as 1909, when Hudson was beginning in the industry, "dealers' deposits often paid half the sum necessary to bring out a full year's production; and if the assembling were efficiently directed, drafts against the finished cars could be cashed as rapidly as the bills from parts makers came in." [4]

Closure of entry into automobile manufacturing did not occur until the market for new cars reached saturation in the late 1920s. But by 1910 it was evident to perceptive entrepreneurs that the era of freewheeling competition was about over and that the industry was tending toward oligopoly. Considerably heavier outlays of capital were becoming necessary to ensure success. With a view toward reducing unit costs of production, improving the quality of the product, and ensuring the supply of components, the better-managed firms early turned toward a policy of reinvesting their high profits in the expansion of plant facilities, both to increase the output of completed cars and to undertake the manufacture of many components formerly jobbed out. The results of this trend were pointed out well by Walter E. Flanders, the Ford production manager from August 1906 until he left in April 1908 to go into business for himself with the EMF car. Flanders knew that "to equal in quality cars now selling at $700 to $900, it is not only necessary to build them in tremendous quantities, but to build and equip factories for the economical manufacture of every part." The formation of General Motors and the opening of Ford's elaborately equipped Highland Park plant gave substance to Flanders's assertion that "henceforth the history of this industry will be the story of a conflict between giants." [5]

The mortality rate among early automobile companies was extremely high, and prominence in the early industry was most often fleeting. With Darwinian ruthlessness, the competition weeded out firms that exhibited organizational weaknesses, made technological blunders, or failed to adjust to changes in demand. These factors were most often interrelated and were the rule rather than the exception among early manufacturers. Many were fly-by-night operations or stock-jobbing ventures. Most enjoyed brief careers before failing.

One major source of failure was the poor choice to back either the electric car or the steamer. The electric car was far more expensive than the gasoline automobile to manufacture and about three times more expensive to operate. Its range was only twenty to fifty miles before the batteries had to be recharged; charging facilities were scarce outside cities; the storage batteries of the day deteriorated rapidly; and its hill climbing ability was poor because of the excessive weight of the batteries for the horsepower generated. In addition to the water it consumed, the steamer used as much petroleum fuel as the gasoline-powered car. And by 1901 the development of the steamer had reached a technological stalemate that was in sharp contrast with the rapid improvement of the gasoline automobile. Once the internal-combustion engine had been made more powerful for its weight and more flexible through better basic design and closer precision in the machining of parts, the steamer could not compete in horsepower generated for weight of engine and fuel supply carried. At the turn of the century there was general agreement that the gasoline automobile "developed more all around good qualities than any other carriage." [6] It rapidly became obvious that the gasoline-powered car was much more susceptible to short-range technological improvement than the electric or the steamer.

As experience proved the superiority of the gasoline automobile, the geographic center of automobile manufacturing shifted from New England, the home of the electric and the steamer, to the Middle West. The early, overwhelming choice of the internal-combustion engine by middle western manufacturers was influenced by the region's poor roads, which were nearly impossible for electrics to negotiate, and by the universal availability of gasoline for fuel in sparsely settled rural areas lacking electricity. As the demand for electrics and steamers quickly subsided and as rural markets replaced urban ones, many New England manufacturers saw their sales dwindle to nothing or faced unfamiliar problems of design and production engineering in trying to switch over to the gasoline-powered car. Michigan and Indiana in particular provided the ideal environment for the manufacture of gasoline automobiles: their excellent hardwood forests had led to their becoming the geographic center for carriage and wagon manufacturing, and they were also important in the manufacturing of the stationary gasoline engines widely used on middle western farms. Michigan and Indiana thus afforded the assembler of gasoline automobiles close proximity to suppliers of bodies, wheels, and internal-combustion engines.[7]

The most notorious example of misplaced optimism and consequent overcapitalization combined with poor technological judgment was the so-called Lead Cab Trust that resulted from the acquisition of the Electric Vehicle Company by William C. Whitney and P. A. B. Widener interests in 1899. In large part also a stock-jobbing venture, the announced aim of this holding company, formed with an inflated capitalization of $3 million, was to place fleets of public cabs on the streets of major American cities. Its manufacturing subsidiary, the Columbia and Electric Vehicle Company of Hartford, Connecticut, for a short time was the leading motor vehicle manufacturer in the United States. It produced some 2,000 electric cabs plus a few electric trucks in 1899, and it formed operating companies in New York, Boston, Philadelphia, and Chicago. The company's ultimate plans for 12,000 vehicles and a $200 million capitalization were squelched by the failing performance of its electric cabs when put into service and by a financial scandal involving a fiscal manipulation that entailed a $2 million loan to a clerk. The operating subsidiaries collapsed, and on June 20, 1900, the Electric Vehicle Company became a manufacturing firm rather than a holding company, which through unwise mergers was again overcapitalized at $20 million by late 1900. The company progressively declined and as a result of the 1907 financial recession went into receivership on December 10, 1907, finally to be reorganized as the Columbia Motor Car Company in 1909 with a more realistic capitalization of $2 million. Strangely enough, the chief asset of this firm turned out to be its ownership of the Selden patent on the gasoline automobile.[8]

The Electric Vehicle Company hedged its bet on the electric car by buying the rights to the Selden patent on November 4, 1899, and began litigation to enforce the patent against the Winton Motor Carriage Company, then the leading manufacturer of gasoline automobiles. Before a decree was entered on March 20, 1903, that the Selden patent was valid and that he had infringed, Winton came to terms with the Whitney interests rather than continue what appeared to be a hopeless legal battle. After Winton's agreement with the Electric Vehicle Company, other prominent manufacturers of gasoline automobiles, who had initially viewed the Selden patent as a threat, began to realize that it might provide a means of regulating competition. The leaders among these manufacturers were Henry B. Joy of Packard and Frederick L. Smith of the Olds Motor Works. Negotiations were concluded with the Electric Vehicle Company on March 6, 1903, to form a trade association under the Selden patent—the Association of Licensed Automobile Manufacturers (ALAM). Licenses to manufacture gasoline automobiles were granted to a select group of thirty-two established companies. They agreed henceforth to pay the association quarterly royalties, amounting to 1.25 percent of the retail price of every gasoline automobile they produced. Concerned about the many fly-by-night entries into automobile manufacturing, the trade journals were initially optimistic that "the association will be beneficial to the trade for the reason that it will prevent the incursion of piratical hordes who desire to take advantage of the good work done by the pioneers to flood the market with trashy machines, made only to sell and not intended to go—at least for any great length of time." [9]

Despite the fact that the licensed companies competed with one another, the ALAM threatened to monopolize automobile manufacturing in the United States. The ALAM tried to exercise arbitrary power over entrances into the industry by granting licenses only to manufacturers that had had prior experience in the automobile business, which theoretically precluded the admission of new firms. It further tried to preserve the status quo in the industry by setting production quotas. The Mechanical Branch of the ALAM was organized in 1905 for the ostensible purposes of facilitating the interchange of technical information and encouraging intercompany standardization of components. But the Mechanical Branch was in fact conceived primarily as a legal tactic in the Selden patent litigation against nonmember companies; it collapsed when the patent was initially upheld by the courts in 1909.

The ALAM threat of litigation proved to be an ineffective deterrent to new entrances, and the Selden patent was widely disregarded. Even though the vast majority of gasoline automobile makers operated without licenses, the ALAM companies accounted for about 80 percent of the industry's total output by 1907. From the consumer's point of view, the influence of the ALAM was regressive because the main interest of the licensed makers was in maintaining high unit profits. The ALAM companies did not seriously attempt to cater to the needs of a broad middle-class market until they were forced to by more responsible so-called independent manufacturers such as Ransom E. Olds, Thomas B. Jeffery, Benjamin Briscoe, and Henry Ford. The outstanding exception among the ALAM companies was William C. Durant of the Buick Motor Car Company, who was considered a maverick within the ALAM fold. As William Greenleaf has pointed out, "In any given year between 1903 and 1911, the ALAM never had more than four makes selling for less than $1,000. . . . In contrast, it was generally agreed that the majority of independent makers produced low-priced cars. Their ranks could . . . cite an average price that was $1,500 below the

ALAM average. In 1909 the independents offered twenty-six models costing $1,000 or less." [10]

Henry B. Joy at the Packard Motor Car Company exemplified the licensed maker who never wavered from producing finely crafted cars for the luxury market. His 1910 Packard "Thirty" limousine sold for $5,450. More typical was Henry C. Leland, who reconciled precision and volume production at the Cadillac Motor Car Company. The 1904 Cadillac Model B, which sold for under $1,000, won the Dewar Trophy of the Royal Automobile Club of London in 1908 for achieving a previously unparalleled interchangeability of parts. But instead of moving toward cutting manufacturing costs on a car of advanced design, Leland conformed to typical ALAM practice and introduced the Cadillac Model Thirty in 1905, a more powerful and expensive automobile that sold for $1,400 in 1908. Thus began the transformation of the Cadillac from a moderately priced to a prestige car. The opposite trend was apparent at the Buick Motor Company, a faltering firm in 1904 that William C. Durant had built into the leading producer of automobiles in the United States by 1908. Durant's emphases upon product improvement, integrated manufacturing operations, and building an efficient national sales network enabled him to sell several models in the $1,000-price range that performed as well as or better than most of the higher-priced cars of his competitors. Like the more responsible independents, Durant aimed at producing a lower-priced, reliable car for the developing mass market.

The trouble with the majority of the independents was that, eschewing quality for low price, they failed to keep abreast of technological improvements and fixed the design of their cars at too early a point in the development of the technological art. Cheaply built cars that sold for only a few hundred dollars were available to the American consumer from the beginnings of the automobile industry in the United States. Several firms, such as the W. H. McIntyre Company of Auburn, Indiana, and the H. K. Holsman

Company of Chicago, continued to build cheap cars essentially similar to the first Duryea and Haynes models instead of switching over to the modern form of the gasoline automobile that had been innovated by Levassor in 1891. These high-wheeled, solid-tired horse buggies equipped with low-horsepower gasoline engines under the seat or in the back could be manufactured to sell for between $250 and $600, and they were very economical to operate. On muddy roads full of ruts and stumps, the high, narrow wheels provided maximum clearance for the chassis; and if the car did get stuck, it was light enough to be easily pushed or lifted out. By 1909, to meet the growing demand for automobiles in the rural Middle West, some fifty firms were turning out "buggy-type" cars. Their problem was that inherent mechanical weaknesses in the surrey design caused them to rattle apart in a short time.

Surrey-influenced design was rapidly abandoned by most manufacturers. Both Ransom E. Olds and Thomas B. Jeffery, who followed Olds into volume production in 1902 at Kenosha, Wisconsin, with his $750 to $825 Ramblers, attempted to mass-produce cars that were soon outmoded. Olds was forced to recognize this after his stubborn insistence on continuing the production of the curved-dash led to his resignation from the Olds Motor Works under pressure from his partners, Samuel and Frederick L. Smith. When Olds reentered automobile manufacturing with his REO Motor Car Company in August 1904, he faced difficulty in getting dealerships established until it became known that he intended to abandon the surrey style of design and emphasize a 1,500-pound, 16-horsepower touring car that sold for $1,250.

The typical 1908 gasoline automobile bore little resemblance to the horseless carriage of 1900. The French practice of placing the engine under a hood in front of the driver was quickly adopted after the turn of the century. The hood was lengthened, and wheelbases became longer as cylinders were added and the engine became larger and more powerful. A lower-slung body resulted from the replacement of high carriage wheels and narrow solid rubber tires with smaller-diameter wheels and wider pneumatic tires. The seats were moved forward in the body; the steering wheel replaced the tiller; and running boards and bumpers were added. Shock absorbers and spring suspension increased riding comfort and reduced strain on the mechanism of the car. Acetylene head lamps made night driving safer. Cape and folding tops with side curtains converted the open car of the period into an all-weather vehicle. Improved engines gave more horsepower for their size and the amount of fuel expended and were capable of generating sufficient power without stalling at a greater range of rpm. Water cooling, forced-feed lubrication by means of an oil pump, mechanically operated valves, and magneto and high-tension ignition systems were other major improvements under the hood. Controls became more sensitive with the adoption of float-feed carburetors that could be throttled and choked, internal expanding foot brakes that operated on the wheel drums, better designed cone or multiple-disc clutches, and either the standard H-slot gearshift with three-speed forward selective transmission or the simpler two-speed planetary transmission. Quick-demountable rims and the power tire pump made tires, the weakest part of the car, easier to change.

These vast improvements meant that the 1908 gasoline automobile was a fairly reliable family car. The problem was to make the cars available at prices the average family could afford, by cutting manufacturing costs or reducing unit profits without sacrificing the quality of the product. Alanson P. Brush made a notable attempt with his Brush Runabout (1907–1912), a light car costing only $500 that combined the body style of the conventional automobile with the solid rubber tires and chain drive of the buggy-type car. However, Brush went too far in reducing construction costs when he substituted wood for metal in his car. Disgruntled owners complained that the Brush Runabout had a "wooden body, wooden axles, wooden wheels, and wooden run."

Henry Ford led the industry in developing the low-priced "car for the great multitude." Ford built his first experimental car in 1896. During two unsuccessful attempts to enter automobile manufacturing, he gained a national reputation as a driver and designer of racing cars. On June 16, 1903, with new backers, he formed the Ford Motor Company to produce cars in the intermediate-price range. A controversy developed in 1905 between Ford and his principal backer, Alexander Y. Malcomson, who wanted to move toward the production of heavier, more expensive touring cars with higher unit profits. The 1906 Ford Model N illustrated Ford's increasing commitment to the volume production of light, low-priced cars. The controversy was resolved when Ford bought out Malcomson on July 12, 1906.

The four-cylinder, 15-horsepower, $600 Ford Model N was one of the better-designed and better-built cars available at any price in 1906. *Cycle and Automobile Trade Journal* called the Model N "distinctly the most important mechanical traction event of 1906. This Ford Model N position of first importance and highest interest is due to the fact that the Model N supplies the very first instance of a low-cost motorcar driven by a gas engine having cylinders enough to give the shaft a turning impulse in each shaft turn which is well built and offered in large numbers." [11] Deluged with orders, the Ford Motor Company installed improved production equipment and after July 15, 1906, was able to make daily deliveries of 100 cars. Henry Ford boasted to reporters: "I believe that I have solved the problem of cheap as well as simple automobile construction. . . . the general public is interested only in the knowledge that a serviceable machine can be constructed at a price within the reach of many." Ford rightly believed that the Model N was "destined to revolutionize automobile construction." At that time he considered it "the crowning achievement of my life." [12]

Encouraged by the success of the Model N, Henry Ford was determined to build an even better low-priced car. At $825 for the runabout and $850 for the touring car, the four-cylinder, 20-horse-power Model T was first offered to dealers on October 1, 1908. Ford's advertising claim about the Model T was essentially correct: "No car under $2,000 offers more, and no car over $2,000 offers more except the trimmings." Committed to large-volume production of the Model T as a single, static model at an ever-decreasing unit price, the Ford Motor Company innovated mass-production techniques at its new Highland Park plant, which permitted prices to be reduced by August 1, 1916 to only $345 for the runabout and $360 for the touring car. Model T production increased from 32,053 units in 1910 to 734,811 units in 1916, giving Ford about half the market for new cars in the United States at the outbreak of World War I.

The Model T was the archetype of a uniquely American mass-produced gasoline automobile. Compared with the typical European touring car, the American-type car was significantly lower priced, was much lighter, had a higher ratio of horsepower to weight, and was powered by a larger-bore, shorter-stroke engine. In addition to the increasingly greater emphasis that American manufacturers gave to producing cars for a mass market, these characteristics of the American car resulted from the lower price of gasoline and the absence of European horsepower taxes. The sacrifice of fuel economy for greater engine flexibility made it possible to build cars that could more readily negotiate steep grades and wretched roads and were easier to drive because they required less frequent shifting of gears. The American car, designed for the average driver rather than for the professional chauffeur, was more apt to withstand abuse and was simpler to repair than the typical European car. However, with a body that sat higher above the roadbed, the American car appeared ungainly and showed less attention to the details of fit, finish, and appointment. That the chassis of a car clear the invariable hump in the center of our unpaved, rutted roads was then more important to the American consumer than style.

At the 1905 Chicago automobile show, twenty independent makers banded together to fight the Selden patent by forming the American Motor Car Manufacturers' Association (AMCMA). Ford, Maxwell-Briscoe, and REO were the most important of the forty-eight manufacturers that ultimately joined the AMCMA. James Couzens, next to Henry Ford the most important executive at the Ford Motor Company, became the AMCMA's first chairman. He explained to reporters: "We manufacturers on an independent basis have simply decided to take the bull by the horns and cooperate for mutual benefit." Henry Ford promised: "I am opposed to the Selden patent first, last, and all the time, and I will fight it to the bitter end." [13] But the other members of the AMCMA lacked Ford's determination. *Automobile* reported in late 1906: "No fight is made against the [Selden] patent by the association, although the members along with some forty other makers, do not believe in it. The Ford Motor Company, one of the leading members of the AMCMA, is fighting the idea single handed, in an effort to disprove the claims made." [14]

American industrial history does not record a more stubborn egotist or better public relations expert than Henry Ford. And in 1903 the ALAM made the mistake of rejecting Ford's application for a license on the ground that he had not demonstrated his competence as a manufacturer of gasoline automobiles. Assured of the support of John Wanamaker, his eastern agent, Ford determined to stay in the automobile business and to contest to the limit of his resources the lawsuit for infringement that was immediately begun against him by the ALAM. The ALAM threatened the purchasers of unlicensed makes with litigation, too. It advertised, "Don't buy a lawsuit with your car." Ford effectively countered this threat with an offer to bond his customers against any suit for damages the ALAM might bring against them. Through a clever propaganda campaign that brought favorable publicity, he turned the Selden patent fight into a great benefit to his business. He gained public sympathy by contrasting his own humble middle western origins and status as a pioneer automotive inventor and struggling small businessman with the image of the ALAM as a group of powerful and parasitical eastern monopolists. The impact of Ford's campaign has been summarized well by William Greenleaf: "By endowing his own struggle for a place in the sun with a luminous appeal to fundamental principles, he translated a wearisome patent suit into one man's struggle for the right to enjoy unhampered opportunity. This was a potent theme in a day when the politics of Progressivism was sweeping the land and the movement for social democracy was still nourished by the hopes and ambitions of the small businessman." [15]

It was appropriate that the industry leader in developing the "car for the great multitude" should also bear the brunt of the battle waged by the independent makers against the ALAM. The Model T and the Selden patent fight were intimately related. The Model T symbolized a victory of the people, who looked upon automobility as a major social reform, over a shortsighted group of budding monopoly capitalists who put short-term higher unit profits ahead of the mass automobility desired by the average person. The Selden patent fight similarly championed the public's beliefs that technological innovation should be unfettered and that businessmen should be able to compete freely in a democratic market place against the ALAM's attempts to preserve the status quo in the auto industry and restrict competition. The Model T and the Selden patent fight were thus major manifestations of the broader pre–World War I crusade to preserve an idealized free enterprise system and the good society from the encroachments of monopoly capitalism.

The ALAM won a fleeting victory when the United States Circuit Court of the Southern District of New York upheld the suit against Ford in 1909. The AMCMA immediately disintegrated, and most of its members sought licenses from the ALAM, swelling its membership to eighty-three. The independent makers who joined were allowed to pay a reduced royalty of 0.8 percent on their production since 1903 for their licenses. Alfred Reeves, the general manager of the AMCMA, became manager of the ALAM with Henry Ford's blessings. The ALAM's liberality in opening its doors to all comers resulted from the recent bankruptcy of the Electric Vehicle Company and the ALAM's anticipation of the expiration of the Selden patent in 1912. The ALAM was making a last-ditch attempt to gain as much revenue as possible from the Selden patent. Ford, too, was now invited to become a licensed manufacturer, but he declined because the ALAM refused to reimburse him for his legal expenses. He decided to continue the fight by appealing the decision in the higher courts.

The collapse of the ALAM followed a written decision of the United States Circuit Court of Appeals for the Second Circuit that was handed down on January 11, 1911. That decision sustained the validity of the Selden patent for motor vehicles that used the Brayton two-cycle engine. But it declared that Ford had not infringed because Ford powered his cars with Otto-type four-cycle engines. Almost all other manufacturers used the four-cycle engine, too. So the decision made the Selden patent worthless. However, the lateness of the decision merely formalized and hastened a bit the imminent breakup of the ALAM, whose exclusive rights under the Selden patent were due to expire in any event in 1912.

In the aftermath of the Selden patent fight, the secondary functions that the ALAM and AMCMA had filled as trade associations were assumed by the Automobile Board of Trade, which became the National Automobile Chamber of Commerce (NACC) in 1914, the Automobile Manufacturers Association (AMA) in 1932, and the Motor Vehicle Manufacturers Association (MVMA) in 1972. To prevent another costly patent controversy from ever again arising in the automobile industry, the NACC instituted a cross-licensing agreement among its members in 1914. Although the Ford Motor Company was not a party to this agreement, Henry

Ford conformed to its principles. The use of Ford patents without payment of royalty fees was liberally extended to competitors, and they reciprocated. Up to the outbreak of World War II, the Ford Motor Company permitted 92 of its patents to be used by others and in turn used 515 outside patents without any cash changing hands.

The patent-sharing arrangement worked out by the automobile industry was undoubtedly the most effective antimonopoly measure that emerged from the Progressive Era. This was recognized and applauded in the late 1930s by the Temporary National Economic Committee (TNEC), a New Deal agency that investigated the significant role the patent system had played in creating monopolistic conditions. A government official testified before the TNEC in 1938 that the effect of the lack of exclusive control over patents in our leading industry was "just to abolish the patent system." William Greenleaf has pointed out that "the arts of negotiation and persuasion replaced the traditional usages of the patent system. . . . The patent policy of the Ford Motor Company and the cross-licensing agreement of other automobile producers are tantamount to radical surgery upon the body of the American patent system. Both patterns have preserved free technology along the frontiers of the automotive industry where conflicts over patent rights might well have hampered it." [16]

The ironic corollary to this thwarting of monopoly as an outcome of Henry Ford's Selden patent fight was that the Model T spelled the end of the era of free competition among many small producers in the automobile industry. The economies of scale and integrated manufacturing operations of a few rising giants led to competitive conditions that could not be borne by the small firms and their suppliers of components. While the large producers could count on their own ability to manufacture parts or on concessions in price on huge orders from independent suppliers, the small automobile makers increasingly were unable to obtain components at reasonable prices and lacked the volume of sales or the capital to manufacture them for themselves. The number of active automobile manufacturers in the United States dropped from 253 in 1908 to 108 in 1920. The saturation of the market for new cars in the 1920s would further reduce the number to 44 by 1929, with about 80 percent of the industry's total output accounted for by Ford, the constituent units of General Motors, and Chrysler.

The main industry-wide effort of the small firms to remain competitive within the industry was made through a standards committee of the Society of Automotive Engineers (SAE). Formed in 1905 as a small but influential group of automotive engineers and trade journalists who wanted to improve the state of automotive technology through the publication of articles, the SAE blossomed into an important force in the industry under the leadership of Howard E. Coffin, the vice-president of Hudson, who was elected president of the SAE in 1910. The standards committee, headed by Henry Souther, a former consulting engineer for the ALAM, was a product of the SAE's take-over of the standardization program of the ALAM Mechanical Branch upon its dissolution in 1909. The committee reflected the interests of the small automobile producers, who made up the bulk of the SAE membership in 1910. These small producers were eager to inaugurate a drive for intercompany standardization of parts that would enable them to buy readily available standard components at much lower prices than they had been paying for small orders of specially designed parts. Howard E. Coffin expressed their sentiment that the lack of intercompany standardization was "responsible for nine-tenths of the production troubles and most of the needless expense entailed in the manufacture of motorcars." [17]

Automotive historians have praised the SAE for carrying out a vigorous standards program that resulted in 224 different sets of standards being adopted in the automobile industry by 1921. But the main point has been missed: the standards program failed miserably in its principal objective of keeping the small producers in a competitive position within the industry. Despite intercompany standardization of components and the NACC cross-licensing agreement, mass-production techniques leading to increased standardization of product at lower unit costs could be effectively implemented only by the large, well-financed firm with a car of superior design. *Scientific American* recognized as early as 1909 that "standardization and interchangeability of parts will have the effect of giving us a higher grade of motorcar at a lower price, but this is dependent in considerable degree upon the production of one model in great numbers and the elimination of extensive annual changes in design that necessitate the making of costly jigs, gauges, and special machinery." [18] Henry Ford grasped this point long before most of his competitors; by the time they came to appreciate it sufficiently, he was so far ahead in design and production engineering that most lacked the capital and talent to catch up.

With half the market for new cars by the outbreak of World War I, the Ford Motor Company might well have moved to monopolize automobile manufacturing in the United States. But, in addition to making some grave errors that allowed General Motors and Chrysler to gain an edge on him by the late 1920s, Henry Ford early recognized that oligopoly was preferable to monopoly. At the pinnacle of the Model T's success, Ford was urged by Charles E. Sorensen, his head of production and chief hatchet man until 1944, to build a near monopoly by shooting for 75 percent of the market for new cars. Ford responded that he did not want more than 30 percent. Sorensen reflected in 1956 on the wisdom of Ford's position: "How right he was! If Ford Motor Company had seventy-five percent of the auto business today, it would be prosecuted as a monopoly. He actually welcomed the competition that loomed before us, though in later years he had suspicion amounting to hallucination that bankers and General Motors were out to ruin him." [19]

Whereas Henry Ford was confident by 1908 that his Model T was the "car for the great multitude," Billy Durant was more uncertain than ever about the best bet in automotive technology. So he decided to play the field and cover all bets. Durant later lamented: "They say I shouldn't have bought Cartercar. Well, how was anyone to know that Cartercar wasn't going to be the thing? It had the friction drive and no other car had it. How could I tell what these engineers would say next? Maybe friction drive would be the thing. And then there's Elmore with its two-cycle engine. That's the kind they were using on motorboats; maybe two-cycle was going to be the thing for automobiles. I was for getting every kind of car in sight, playing it safe all along the line." [20]

Benjamin Briscoe also found conditions in the spring of 1908 "somewhat ominous, especially for such concerns as had large fixed investments in plants, machinery, tools, etc." Briscoe was worried about the "menace to the industry" posed by "concerns which did not have a worthy car or any manufacturing ability, but with large stock issues to sell, and by ingenious exploitation would succeed in stirring up the trade and the public, creating the impression that . . . they, through some newly discovered combination of geniuses, were enabled to sell gold dollars for fifty cents in automobiles." He blamed the parts makers for threatening "demoralization by encouraging into the business undercapitalized concerns and inexperienced makers" that in the aggregate did a large business. But the main problem was that many companies were outright "manufacturing gamblers," and all firms "plunged" by risking unduly large amounts of capital, given the existing technological uncertainties. Briscoe was worried that the bolder companies forced "even the sanest among the manufacturers . . . into business risks which they would not have entered had they not been fearful that some other concern would gain a few points on them." [21]

Briscoe and Durant conceived that the answer to these problems was a horizontal and vertical trust. They decided to try "to form a combination of the principal concerns in the industry . . . for the purpose of having one big concern of such dominating influence in the automobile industry, as for instance, the United States Steel Corporation exercises in the steel industry, so that its very influence would prevent many of the abuses that we believed existed." The easiest way was to merge their own firms, Buick and Maxwell-Briscoe, with several other leading producers of gasoline automobiles. But the merger plan failed when Henry Ford and Ransom E. Olds each demanded $3 million in cash to sell out, instead of accepting the securities offered by Briscoe and Durant.

Another plan was hatched to form an "International Motors Company" around the nucleus of Maxwell-Briscoe and Buick. That fell through, too, when J. P. Morgan and Company, Briscoe's backers in earlier automotive ventures, refused to underwrite the stock issue. During the negotiations with the House of Morgan, Durant correctly prophesied that half a million automobiles would soon be sold annually in the United States. George W. Perkins, who represented the Morgan interests, thought he was dealing with an unbalanced mind and curtly suggested that Durant, when he wanted to borrow money, had better keep such crazy notions to himself. Perkins also believed erroneously that Durant intended to profit personally by enlarging his own holdings and had neglected to inform the other Buick stockholders of the deal. In fact, the Buick stockholders had been aware of Durant's intentions for months.

By this time Briscoe had had enough. He and Durant split up to go their separate ways. Briscoe went on to form the ill-fated United States Motor Company, which in its brief existence came to involve some 130 affiliated companies and an inflated capitalization of $42.5 million. His principal backer in this venture was Anthony N. Brady, a traction magnate who had been associated with the Whitney and Widener interests in the Electric Vehicle Company debacle. Maxwell-Briscoe was the only manufacturing unit in the combination that made money, and its earnings could not support the heavy investment Briscoe and Brady made in too many weak firms producing unpopular automobiles, such as the Brush Runabout. United States Motor went into receivership in September 1912 with liabilities of $12.3 million versus realizable assets of only $9.3 million.

Its reorganization by the banking firm of Eugene Meyer, Jr. and Company brought in Walter E. Flanders at the price of purchasing his weak Flanders Motor Company for $1 million cash and $2.75 million in stock of the reorganized combination. Flanders had been a key figure in an earlier abortive merger of EMF with Studebaker, and he remained general manager of the Studebaker Corporation until early 1912, when he formed the ephemeral Flanders Motor Company. At United States Motor, Flanders followed a severe policy of consolidation and liquidation. Only the Maxwell Motor Company emerged as a going concern. Although Benjamin Briscoe was to found several more automobile companies, his days of prominence in the industry were over. The Maxwell car was to end up as an ingredient in Jack Benny's humor.

William C. Durant fell harder and more spectacularly, but he left a significant heritage in General Motors and Chevrolet. Durant formed the General Motors Company as a New Jersey holding company with a nominal capitalization of only $2,000 on September 16, 1908. The holding company structure allowed Durant, who was short of both cash and bank credit, to finance his combination mainly through the exchange of stock. Cadillac, purchased for a premium $4.5 million, was the most notable of the few companies for which cash had to be paid. General Motors soon acquired control of thirteen motor vehicle and ten parts and accessories manufacturers that varied considerably in strength, prominence, and potential. Within a year its capitalization reached an astonishing $60 million.

General Motors under Durant was in trouble from the start. His attempt at "getting every car in sight, playing it safe all along the line," turned out to be catastrophic. He bought too many weak units that drained off the profits from a few strong companies. Of the thirteen automobile manufacturers in the combination he threw together, only Buick and Cadillac were making money. As Durant dispersed his energies, Buick began to lose money, threatening to leave Cadillac alone among the automobile manufacturing units to support the heavily overcapitalized holding company. His minor mistakes included paying $140,000 for the Cartercar Company to obtain its patent on a poorly designed friction drive and buying the Elmore Manufacturing Company for $600,000 on the slim chance that its outdated two-cylinder, two-cycle engine might prove to be popular in the future. His most spectacular error was purchasing the Heany Lamp Company for $7 million in General Motors stock to obtain a patent on an incandescent lamp that turned out to be fraudulent. Compounding these blunders, Durant was so optimistic about demand that he failed to build up cash reserves, relied on cash from sales to pay his operating expenses, lacked adequate information about the combination's financial condition, and made no attempt to achieve economies through coordinating and integrating the constituent units of General Motors.

The crunch came when sales unexpectedly dropped as a result of a slight business recession in 1910. Durant was unable to meet his payroll and pay his bills from suppliers. General Motors was saved by a $12.75 million cash loan from a banking syndicate composed of Lee, Higginson and Company of Boston and J. & W. Seligman and the Central Trust Company of New York. The stiff price the bankers demanded for this was $6 million in General Motors stock plus $15 million in five-year, 6 percent notes. Durant was forced to retire from active management, and the banking syndicate gained control of the combination through a five-year voting trust. Durant was named one of the trustees, but the other four represented the bankers: James J. Storrow of Lee, Higginson; Albert Strauss of J. & W. Seligman; James N. Wallace of the Central Trust Company; and the ever-present Anthony N. Brady. Storrow, a senior partner in Lee,

Higginson, first took over as the temporary president of General Motors, then directed operations as chairman of the finance committee. Charles W. Nash, who succeeded Durant at Buick in 1910, was moved to the presidency of General Motors in 1912.

The Storrow-Nash regime followed a conservative policy of retrenchment that liquidated all manufacturing units except Buick, Cadillac, General Motors Truck, Oakland, and Oldsmobile. The product was improved, and a program of research and testing was instituted. Great strides were made in attracting top-flight administrative talent and in improving communication and cooperation within the combination. In a few years, banker control thus not only restored General Motors to solvency but greatly strengthened its competitive position in the automobile industry.

As well as being a trustee and a member of the board of directors, Durant was still a substantial stockholder in General Motors. From this strong position he began to make his comeback shortly after the bankers took control. In 1911 he formed the Little Motor Car Company in Flint and the Chevrolet Motor Car Company in Detroit. Then he bought the Republic Motor Car Company of Tarrytown, New York, and converted it into a holding company capitalized at $65 million. The Little and the Republic cars were soon discontinued to concentrate on the Chevrolet, a light, moderately priced car designed by Louis Chevrolet, who had been one of Buick's racing drivers. For the two years ending on August 14, 1915, Durant sold nearly 16,000 Chevrolets and was able to show a net profit of over $1.3 million. He announced that he would bring out a new $490 model to compete with the Ford Model T. On September 23, 1915, he organized the Chevrolet Motor Company of Delaware as a holding company for all Chevrolet activities. Raising its capitalization to $80 million, all in common stock, Durant offered to trade five shares of Chevrolet for one share of General Motors. There were so many takers that the offer was closed on January 26, 1916.

A Chevrolet take-over was imminent when the General Motors

voting trust expired on October 1, 1915. Early that year Durant and Pierre S. du Pont began buying up General Motors stock in the open market with the aid of Louis G. Kaufman, president of the Chatham and Phoenix Bank of New York City. Du Pont and John J. Raskob, treasurer of E. I. du Pont de Nemours and Company, saw General Motors as a large potential customer for du Pont products and as an ideal place to reinvest their mounting profits from World War I munitions sales. Some $27 million of du Pont's money helped push General Motors common stock from a quotation of 82 on January 2, 1915, to a high of 558 for the year. It was summer before the banker-dominated management at General Motors suspected that something was afoot. In fact, the Storrow-Nash regime unwittingly had helped sow the seeds of its own destruction by withholding common stock dividends. This made stockholders anxious to sell out to Durant and du Pont.

At a meeting of the directors and large stockholders of General Motors on September 16, 1915, Kaufman and du Pont were elected to the board of directors, with du Pont as its chairman. A belated attempt by Durant's opponents to mobilize stockholder support for a three-year continuation of the voting trust failed. With the votes of about 40 percent of General Motors common stock in his pocket, Durant called a formal meeting of the board of directors in May 1916 to announce that he controlled the company. He took over again as president with the resignation of Charles W. Nash on June 1, 1916.

Thus by the eve of our first mechanized war, the two giant companies that would henceforth dominate the emerging oligopoly in automobile manufacturing had weathered their first crises. Both Ford and General Motors were firmly in the hands of their egocentric and individualistic founders, corporate brainchildren that had grown like Topsy in what seemed an ever-expanding market for motorcars. World War I, however, was to jostle the automobile industry into a maturity that neither Henry Ford nor William C.

Durant foresaw. The war brought governmental recognition of the industry's importance as well as the development of long-distance trucking and the farm tractor. At the war's end, the sudden conversion to a peacetime economy plunged the industry into a crisis from which neither Henry Ford nor William C. Durant ever fully recovered. The postwar recession showed that the business philosophies and entrepreneurial styles of Ford and Durant were ironically outmoded in the industry they had done so much to shape. Mature market conditions called for a new breed of automotive entrepreneur, exemplified by Walter P. Chrysler and Alfred P. Sloan, Jr.

4 FORDIZATION: AN IDOL AND ITS IRONIES

By May 27, 1927, when the last of over 15 million Model Ts rolled off the assembly line, a new Model T cost as little as $290 and mass automobility had become a reality. The Fordson farm tractor, introduced during World War I, promised to remove the last

No synthesis of American automobility would be complete without an interpretation of Henry Ford and the Ford Motor Company. Yet anyone compelled to write still more about Ford must reckon with Reynold M. Wik's assessment that more has already been written about the subject than any individual could read in a single lifetime. The facts are well known. Most interpretive possibilities have been attempted by one or another Ford admirer, debunker, or apologist.

An adequate interpretation of Henry Ford is difficult not only because one finds many ironic contradictions in his statements and behavior over his lifetime but even more because Ford became a symbol for the differing aspirations of many audiences. Ford the symbol was based on heroic myths that Ford the man unfortunately encouraged and deluded himself into believing. Consequently, most of Ford's many biographers have taken the position that he defies interpretation from any single point of view or consistent set of assumptions. The recent attempt of Anne Jardim, in *The First Henry Ford: A Study in Personality and Business Leadership* (Cambridge, Mass.: M.I.T. Press, 1970), to simplify Ford through a psychoanalytic interpretation must certainly be counted a failure. Yet no one has managed to get a comprehensive handle on the man through more conventional modes of analysis.

Every generation must reinterpret the American past from the perspective of its own values and problems. And this chapter attempts to interpret Henry Ford from the long-range perspective of the disillusioning 1970s. The interpretation inevitably is critical; even more than the mass personal automobility that Ford symbolized, the tenets of entrepreneurial capitalism and the gospel of industrial efficiency that Ford exemplified are increasingly less credible and acceptable social philosophies. Although the interpretation takes a few new twists, the factual information on which it is based will be familiar to anyone steeped in the standard sources on Henry Ford and the Ford Motor Company. Unless otherwise noted, the narrative relies upon the exhaustive three-volume study undertaken by Allan Nevins, in collaboration with Frank E. Hill: *Ford: The Times, the Man, the Company, 1865–1915*; *Ford: Expansion and Challenge, 1915–1933*; and *Ford: Decline and Rebirth, 1933–1962* (New York: Charles Scribner's Sons, 1954, 1957, 1963). To avoid excessive, meaningless notes, only substantial quotations from the standard sources are referenced.

drudgery from farm labor and initiate a new era of agricultural abundance. The introduction of the moving-belt assembly line and the five-dollar, eight-hour day at Ford's Highland Park plant in 1913–1914, in the words of Allan Nevins and Frank E. Hill, "inaugurated a new epoch in industrial society. . . . Mass production furnished the lever and fulcrum which now shifted the globe." [1] Roderick Nash aptly concludes in his study of American culture from 1917 to 1930: "It is possible to think of these years as the automobile age and Henry Ford as its czar. The flivver, along with the flask and the flapper, seemed to represent the 1920s in the minds of its people as well as its historians." [2]

More was written about Henry Ford during his lifetime, and he was more often quoted, than any figure in American history. Theodore Roosevelt complained that Ford received more publicity than even the president of the United States. The *New York Times* reported that Ford's reputation had spread to peasants in remote villages in countries where only the elites had heard of Warren G. Harding or Calvin Coolidge. Will Rogers, probably the shrewdest folk psychologist in our history, said a number of times and in many witty ways that Henry Ford had influenced more lives than any man alive.

The people of what Wik calls "grass-roots America" thought Henry Ford a greater emancipator of the common man than Abraham Lincoln. They made Ford our first, and probably our last, millionaire folk hero. He received several thousand letters a day, ranging from simple requests for help and advice to demands that he solve America's remaining social and economic ills. The newspapers of his day called Ford the "Sage of Dearborn" and made him an oracle to the common man. But beyond this, Wik's analysis of letters to Ford "from farmers and middle-class folks . . . living in the typical small towns of mid-America" reveals "a widespread and simple faith in Ford and the fixed belief that an understanding existed between the writers and this man of immense wealth." [3]

Henry Ford probably could have been elected president of the

United States had he really wanted the office. In 1916 Ford spurned efforts to get him to head the tickets of the American party and the Prohibition party on a platform of peace and prohibition. And, even though he refused to campaign, he won the 1916 Michigan presidential preference primary of the Republican party by a comfortable margin.

President Woodrow Wilson, who was concerned about electing a Senate favorable to the establishment of a League of Nations, induced Ford to run for United States senator from Michigan on the Democratic ticket in 1918. The *New York World* reported on August 22 that "[Ford] hasn't spent a cent, paid for a banner, bought the boys any drinks and cigars, hired a press agent, made any speeches, or kissed a baby since the Democrats endorsed him in June." Michigan was a heavily Republican state; and Truman Newberry, Ford's Republican opponent, spent lavishly, and stooped to a mud-slinging campaign that questioned Ford's patriotism at the outbreak of World War I. (He was convicted in May 1919 of violating the Federal Corrupt Practices Law in the campaign.) Still Ford lost the election by the slim margin of 212,751 votes to Newberry's 217,088.

Ford-for-President clubs sprang up spontaneously across the nation in 1920–1923. In the summer of 1923, both a poll conducted by *Collier's Weekly* and the Autocaster nationwide survey found Ford far ahead of President Warren G. Harding. Probably no potential candidate in American political history has ever had such universal appeal to the voters: blue-collar workers were still impressed by the five-dollar, eight-hour day; farmers suffering from the agricultural depression of the 1920s had confidence in the creator of the Model T and the Fordson tractor; Southerners saw the regeneration of the South in automobility and in Ford's plans to build a nitrate plant at Muscle Shoals, Tennessee. Ford also appealed to middle-class Babbitts who thought that successful businessmen rather than politicians should run the government; his strong advocacy of prohibition made him popular among the drys; and in the disillusion that followed the Versailles Treaty, his early outspoken stand against the war was a plus. Everyone credited Henry Ford with giving America the low-priced, reliable car and recognized that the industry he led was the key to American prosperity.

The Ford-for-President boom was a major expression of the popular discontent of the early 1920s. It ended in October 1924, however, when Henry Ford announced that he would support President Calvin Coolidge, who had assumed office after Harding's death in 1923, if Coolidge would enforce prohibition. The evidence suggests that Ford traded his support for the president's endorsement of Ford's bid to develop Muscle Shoals, which was meeting stiff opposition in Congress. Many voters felt that America had lost her potentially greatest president. Others concluded that Ford, by withdrawing, had "chickened out, leaving us who thought we had a leader for the great Armageddon, the fight between right and wrong, between man and money, between freedom and slavery, between Christ and Satan. We now wonder if we haven't been worshipping a Tin God." [4]

Americans idolized Henry Ford as a symbol of mass personal automobility—a phenomenon uniquely congruent with American values and social conditions. By 1927 the United States had about 80 percent of the world's motor vehicles and a ratio of 5.3 people for every motor vehicle registered. On the criterion of ratio of population to motor vehicles, outside the United States the automotive idea had spread most rapidly in other developing countries with low population densities that had also been settled by European immigrants and had experienced the frontier conditions that Frederick Jackson Turner proclaimed so central in shaping American institutions and character. In 1927 the United States was followed in ratio of population to motor vehicles by New Zealand (10.5:1), Canada (10.7:1), Australia (16:1), and Argentina (43:1). France and the United Kingdom tied for sixth place with ratios of 44:1. [5]

Paradoxically, however, the Ford mystique was most pervasive abroad in the two nations whose totalitarian ideologies were soon to be considered antithetical to the American way of life. Neither Germany, with a ratio of 196 people per motor vehicle, nor the Union of Soviet Socialist Republics, with a ratio of 7,010:1, were likely prospects in 1927 for the development of automobile cultures embodying American ideals. For the Germans and the Russians, Henry Ford symbolized the mass-production and agricultural techniques essential for building self-sufficient national economies and becoming first-rate military powers.

Wik's examination of German newspapers "reveals an obsession with Henry Ford." *My Life and Work*, the autobiography that Ford wrote in collaboration with Samuel Crowther, became a best seller in Berlin in 1925, and the Germans referred to mass production as "Fordismus." "I am a great admirer of Ford," claimed Adolf Hitler. "I shall do my best to put his theories into practice in Germany." [6] Hitler was most interested, of course, in building an industrial system that could mass-produce war materials. Automobility to him primarily meant panzer divisions moving swiftly over the express highways (*autobahnen*) feverishly constructed in Germany after he came to power. Nevertheless, it is interesting to note that the Volkswagen, Hitler's idea of a people's car, was predicated on the philosophy of product first exemplified by the Ford Model T—a static model offering basic transportation at low initial and operating expenses.

Even more incredible than a multimillionaire becoming a folk hero of grass-roots America, the world's most prominent entrepreneurial capitalist was idolized in Communist Russia. The Russians were fascinated with "Fordizatzia" and viewed Henry Ford not as a capitalist but as a revolutionary economic innovator. A visitor to the USSR in 1927 reported that the Russian people "ascribed a magical quality to the name of Ford" and found it incredible that "more people have heard of him than Stalin. . . . Next to Lenin, Trotsky, and Kalinin, Ford is possibly the most widely known personage in

Russia." [7] The 25,000 Fordson tractors shipped to the USSR
between 1920 and 1927 promised the peasant a new agricultural era
free from drudgery and want. Communes and babies born in
communes were named "Fordson." Ford mass-production methods,
widely copied in the USSR, promised an industrial horn of plenty.
Progress in adopting them was chronicled in *Pravda*, and in workers'
processions Ford's name was emblazoned on banners emblematic of
a new industrial era. Translations of *My Life and Work* were widely
read and used as texts in the universities. Wik claims that "people in
Leningrad, Moscow, and Kiev used the word 'Fordize' as a synonym
for 'Americanize.' " [8]

The idolization of Henry Ford as a symbol of differing national
aspirations reflected the universal human tendency to personify the
impersonal forces of history—thus simplistically reducing the com-
plexities of historical processes down to a dramatic parade of
symbolic heroes and villains. Consequently, much of what passes for
history in textbooks as well as in the popular imagination is merely
the perpetuation of culturally meaningful, but misleading, myths.
Henry Ford himself recognized this in the often misquoted, unwit-
tingly sophisticated statement he made to Charles N. Wheeler, a
newspaper reporter, in 1916: "History is more or less bunk."

Henry Ford's views about history were dredged up for public
ridicule to prove that he was "an ignorant idealist" by Elliott G.
Stevenson, attorney for the defense, in May 1919 during the trial of a
million dollar libel suit that Ford had filed against the *Chicago
Tribune* on September 16, 1916. Ford brought the suit against the
newspaper in response to its editorial of June 23, 1916, entitled
"Ford Is an Anarchist." Representing the interests of imperialistic
American corporations who were eager to exploit Mexico's natural
resources, the *Tribune* had lashed out at Ford's opposition to
President Wilson for sending troops to repress Pancho Villa. The
editorial erroneously charged that eighty-nine Ford employees called

to border duty had lost their jobs, and it called Ford "not merely an ignorant idealist, but . . . an anarchist enemy of a nation which protects him in his wealth." Although Ford technically won the suit, he was insulted by being awarded only six cents in damages. He was further embittered by the ridicule that followed from the merciless cross-examination aimed at proving him unpatriotic and ignorant.

It is indisputable that Ford revealed an appalling ignorance of American history in his answers to the fact-laden questions asked by Stevenson. Yet Ford intuitively grasped some of the glaring faults of the prevailing historical synthesis. His main objections were that history was a bastion of tradition rather than a force for change and that history was a collection of esoteric facts that were irrelevant to understanding and solving contemporary problems. Ford explained to Charles N. Wheeler, for example: "That's the trouble with the world. We're living in books and history and tradition. We want to get away from that and take care of today. We've done too much looking back. What we want to do, and do it quick, is to make just history right now. The men who are responsible for the present war in Europe knew all about history. Yet they brought on the worst war in the world's history." [9]

Beyond these very sensible objections, Henry Ford rebelled against a written history dominated by politics, wars, and the careers of great men. The history that Ford remembered was found in books that "began and ended with wars." Roger Butterfield points out that "Ford's matured concept of history as the appreciation and study of 'the general resourcefulness of our people' lives on in the vast collections and more than 100 buildings of the Henry Ford Museum-Greenfield Village-Edison Institute complex at Dearborn. This has become by far the most popular historical preserve in the United States (under nongovernmental operation). Its entertainment features are conspicuous, but its basic purpose is mass education." The idea for the museum complex was hatched by Ford on the ride back to Detroit from the *Tribune* trial at Mt. Clemens, Michigan, as a way to demonstrate his ideas about history. He announced to Ernest Liebold, his secretary, "I'm going to start up a museum and give people a true picture of the development of the country. That's the only history worth preserving, that you can preserve in itself. We're going to build a museum that's going to show industrial history, and it won't be bunk." Butterfield notes that, among the exhibits at Dearborn, "only one major activity of man was slighted—there were no weapons or mementos of war." [10]

The concept of history represented by the Dearborn complex has the obvious grave deficiency that it is predicated on a primitive, visual historicism. The artifacts are assumed to speak for themselves, in Henry Ford's words, about "what actually happened in years gone by." Ford missed the essential point that raw historical data becomes history only when meaningfully interpreted and communicated in literate prose. But Ford did see that history lacking social relevance serves little purpose, that history must emphasize the forces and objects that most influenced the daily life of common people, and that technoeconomic variables are more significant than wars and politics in explaining the historical development of the American people.

The great disservice that Henry Ford did to written history— ironic for a man who complained to reporters as late as 1940 that history "isn't even true"—was that his extreme egocentrism deluded him into becoming the chief progenitor of a cult of personality based upon heroic myths. He lost no opportunity to claim personal credit for both the low-priced reliable car and the mass-production techniques that together revolutionized American life. He also cultivated the public image that the success of the giant Ford Motor Company was entirely due to his individual genius. A Chicago newspaper editor once aptly quipped, "One need not mention Ford—he mentions himself." Ford doted on articles about himself and religiously amassed for posterity what is probably the largest collection of personal data ever accumulated by an American businessman.

The man who most strongly opposed the preposterous claim that George B. Selden invented the gasoline automobile ironically came to fall just short of making the same claim for himself. As late as 1963 the Ford Motor Company advertised: "Henry Ford had a dream that if a rugged, simple car could be made in sufficient quantity, it would be cheap enough for the average family to buy." But the truth is that Ford's idea of "a car for the great multitude" was a generally held expectation, assumed to be inevitable from the introduction of the motor vehicle in the United States. Ransom E. Olds and Thomas B. Jeffery were the most important among several other automobile manufacturers who attempted prematurely to implement the idea while Henry Ford was still absorbed with building racing cars. The basic elements of automotive technology embodied in the Model T were invented and developed by scores of other automotive pioneers. The constituents of mass production—described by Henry Ford in the *Encyclopaedia Britannica* as "the focusing upon a manufacturing project of the principles of power, accuracy, economy, system, continuity, speed, and repetition"—were all well-known aspects of an evolving American manufacturing tradition by the time they were adapted to the Model T.

Recognition that the Ford Motor Company led the industry in developing the mass-produced and, as a consequence, low-priced car should not obscure the fact that Ford's effort to increase output greatly in the 1908–1913 period was far from unique. Many of Ford's competitors attempted to cut manufacturing costs and capitalize on the insatiable demand for motorcars by working out similar solutions to their common production problems. For example, innovations to reduce the time and cost of final assembly similar to those worked out at Ford were independently conceived by Walter P. Chrysler, who replaced Charles W. Nash as the head of Buick in 1910. Buick production was upped from 45 to 200 cars a day by changing outmoded procedures for finishing the body and chassis, which had amounted to "treating metal as if it were wood," and by installing a moving assembly line that consisted of "a pair of tracks made of two by fours" along which a chassis was moved from worker to worker by hand while being assembled. Chrysler recalled that "Henry Ford, after we developed our [assembly] line, went to work and figured out a chain conveyor; his was the first. Thereafter we all used them. Instead of pushing the cars along the line by hand, they rode on an endless-chair conveyor operated by a motor." [11]

Charles E. Sorensen, who was in charge of production at Ford, was keenly aware that the contribution of the Ford Motor Company to mass production lay almost entirely in its refinement of the integration and coordination of the process of final assembly. Sorensen knew that "Eli Whitney used interchangeable parts when making rifles in the early days of the Republic; and in the early days of this century Henry Leland . . . applied the same principles in the first Cadillac cars. Overhead conveyors were used in many in- dustries, including our own. So was substitution of machine work for hand labor. Nor was orderly progress of the work anything new; but it was new to us at Ford until Walter Flanders showed us how to arrange our machine tools at the Mack Avenue and Piquette plants." The only significant contribution that Sorensen claimed for the Ford Motor Company was "the practice of moving the work from one worker to another until it became a complete unit, then arranging the flow of these units at the right time and the right place to a moving final assembly line from which came a finished product. Regardless of earlier uses of some of these principles, the direct line of succession of mass production and its intensification into automa- tion stems directly from what we worked out at Ford Motor Company between 1908 and 1913." [12]

The moving assembly line at Ford was conceived one Sunday morning in July 1908 at the Piquette Avenue plant during the last months of Model N production. The parts needed for assembling a car were laid out in sequence on the floor; a frame was next put on skids and pulled along by a towrope until the axles and wheels were put on, and then rolled along in notches until assembled. However, this first experiment to assemble a car on a moving line did not materialize into a moving-belt final assembly line at Ford until 1913 because the extensive changes in plant layout and procedures "would have indefinitely delayed Model T production and the realization of Mr. Ford's long cherished ambition which he had maintained against all opposition." [13]

There was general agreement in the automobile industry that the sixty-acre Highland Park plant that Ford opened on January 1, 1910, to meet the huge demand for the Model T possessed an unparalleled factory arrangement for the volume production of motorcars and that its well-lighted and well-ventilated buildings were a model of advanced industrial construction. By 1914 about 15,000 machines had been installed. Company policy was to scrap machines as fast as they could be replaced with improved types, and by 1912 the tool department was constantly devising specialized new machine tools that would increase output. The elementary time and motion studies begun at the Piquette Avenue plant were continued and in 1912 led to the installation of continuous conveyor belts to bring materials to the assembly lines. Magnetos, motors, and transmissions were assembled on moving lines by the summer of 1913. After the production from these subassembly lines threatened to flood the final assembly line, a moving-chassis assembly line was installed. It reduced the time of chassis assembly from twelve and a half hours in October to two hours and forty minutes by December 30, 1913. Moving lines were quickly established for assembling the dash, the front axle, and the body. The moving lines were at first pulled by rope and windlass, but on January 14, 1914, an endless chain was installed. That was in turn replaced on February 27 by a new line built on rails set at a convenient working height and timed at six feet a minute. "Every piece of work in the shop moves," boasted Henry Ford in 1922. "It may move on hooks or overhead chains going to assembly in the exact order in which the parts are required; it may travel on a moving platform, or it may go by gravity, but the point is that there is no lifting or trucking of anything other than materials." [14]

The mass-production techniques developed at Highland Park to meet the demand for the Model T became synonymous in the mind of the public with Henry Ford's name. These techniques were widely publicized and described in detail, most definitively by Horace L. Arnold and Fay L. Faurote.[15] Ford's competitors in the automobile industry quickly installed moving-belt assembly lines, too. But the Ford Motor Company set the pace and direction of a new social order based on mass production and mass personal automobility until the early 1920s, when Hudson probably surpassed and other automobile manufacturers began to equal Highland Park's efficiency in production.

The evidence is unequivocal that both the Model T and the Ford mass-production methods, in Wik's words, "represented the efforts of a team of engineers, rather than the inspiration of one man, Henry Ford." C. Harold Wills, the chief engineer, and Joseph Galamb head a long list of Ford employees whose collective efforts were more significant than Henry Ford's inspiration in creating the Model T. Charles E. Sorensen, his assistant Clarence W. Avery, William C. Klann, and P. E. Martin deserve the lion's share of credit for the moving-belt assembly line worked out at Highland Park, while the specialized machinery was designed by a staff of dozens of engineers headed by Carl Emde. "Henry Ford had no ideas on mass production," claimed Sorensen, the man best qualified to know. "Far from it; he just grew into it, like the rest of us. The essential tools and the final assembly line with its integrated feeders resulted from an organization which was continually experimenting and improvising to get better production." Nevins and Hill agree: "It is clear that the impression given in Ford's *My Life and Work* that the key ideas of

mass production percolated from the top of the factory downward is
erroneous; rather seminal ideas moved from the bottom upward." [16]

The business success of the Ford Motor Company depended on
the talents of many other individuals. For, as John Kenneth
Galbraith says, "if there is any uncertainty as to what a businessman
is, he is assuredly the things Ford was not." The marketing of the
Model T was handled by Norval A. Hawkins, a sales and advertising
whiz. Fred Diehl was in charge of purchasing. The Ford domestic
and foreign branch plants were set up by William S. Knudsen. The
man who oversaw the entire operation and provided the main
business brains for the company until his resignation on October 12,
1915, was James Couzens, a minor stockholder as well as vice-president and treasurer. Sorensen called the period from 1903 to 1913 at
Ford the "Couzens period. . . . Everyone in the company, including
Henry Ford, acknowledged [Couzens] as the driving force during
this period." "After Couzens left in 1915, Ford took full command
and the company was never so successful again," Galbraith concludes. "In the years that followed, Ford was a relentless and avid
self-advertiser. And he mobilized the efforts of many others to
promote not the car but the man. Only the multitude remained
unaware of the effort which Ford, both deliberately and instinctively,
devoted to building the Ford myth. . . . He was the first and by far
the most successful product of public relations in the industry." [17]

The image of Henry Ford as a progressive industrial leader and
champion of the common people that Americans clung to during the
1920s was incredibly incongruent with much of the philosophy of
industry expounded by Ford himself in *My Life and Work* (1922),
Today and Tomorrow (1926), and *My Philosophy of Industry* (1929).[18]

Far from identifying with the Jeffersonian yeoman farmer glorified
in Populist rhetoric, Henry Ford looked forward to the demise of the
family farm. As a youth Ford had hated the drudgery of farm labor,
and he longed to rid the world of unsanitary and inefficient horses

and cows. But the Model T was conceived as "a farmer's car" less because Ford empathized with the plight of the small farmer than because any car designed for a mass market in 1908 had to meet the needs of a predominantly rural population. "The old kind of farm is dead," Ford wrote in 1926. "We might as well recognize that fact and take it as a starting point for something better." He looked forward in 1929 to the day when "large corporations . . . will supersede the individual farmer, or groups of farmers will combine to perform their work in a wholesale manner. This is the proper way to do it and the only way in which economic freedom can be won."

Henry Ford viewed the common man with a cynical, elitist paternalism, fundamentally at odds with the equalitarian Populist philosophy he supposedly represented. "We have to recognize the unevenness in human mental equipment," said Ford. "The vast majority of men want to stay put. They want to be led. They want to have everything done for them and have no responsibility." Ford admitted that the thought of repetitive labor was "terrifying to me. I could not do the same thing day in and day out, but to other minds, perhaps to the majority of minds, repetitive operations hold no terrors." He believed that "the average worker . . . wants a job in which he does not have to put forth much physical exertion—above all, he wants a job in which he does not have to think. . . . for most purposes and most people, it is necessary to establish something in the way of a routine and to make most motions purely repetitive— otherwise the individual will not get enough done to live off his exertions."

A journalist asked Ford in 1923, "What about industrial democracy?" "The average employee in the average industry is not ready for participation in the management," Ford answered. "An industry, at this stage of our development, must be more or less of a friendly autocracy." This cynical, elitist paternalism pervaded the Ford Motor Company even during the early years that Ford's admirers peg as its brightest and most progressive. "All economists are agreed," Arnold and Faurote wrote in 1915, for example, "that the only reason why any one man works for another man is because the hired man does not know enough to be the director of his own labor. And, incontrovertibly, the employer being wiser than the employed, the wisdom of the employer should be applied to the benefit of the employed, to some extent at least." [19]

Nevins and Hill credit Henry Ford with running his company "as a semi-public entity" in which workers and consumers shared the benefits of increased productivity at a time when profit maximization was the rule in American industry. But beyond the obvious point that the public had no voice in this "semi-public entity," Henry Ford's business philosophy boiled down to the simple observation that mass production would yield greater profits only if consumer purchasing power was increased sufficiently to enable people to buy what the machine produced. Ford called this the "wage motive" and claimed that "we have discovered a new motive for industry and abolished the meaningless terms 'capital,' 'labor,' and 'public.' . . . It is this thought of enlarging buying power by paying high wages and selling at low prices which is behind the prosperity of this country."

The liberal economist John R. Commons foolishly ranted in 1920 that "prosperity sharing" at Ford was "devoted to faith in human nature" and "good American citizenship" and that Ford was "positively too democratic for this world." [20] More recently, Father R. L. Bruckberger reached such absurd conclusions as that money stood last in Ford's scale of values and that Ford was "infinitely more revolutionary than Marx, who was only an intellectual." [21] The truth is that Henry Ford's philosophy of industry was a pedestrian variation of the conventional business creed that put profits first and foremost, glorified the entrepreneurial capitalist, and accepted as axiomatic the outmoded production ethic of the classical economists' economy of scarcity.

Henry Ford emphatically denied that higher wages and lower

prices should follow from the technological progress of a people as a simple matter of social justice. He held, for example, that "it is untrue to say that profits or the benefit of inventions which bring lower costs belong to the worker. . . . Profits belong primarily to the business and the workers are only part of the business." Lower prices did not come at the expense of profits but resulted from increased industrial efficiency that permitted profit margins to be enhanced. Ford's policy was "to name a price so low as to force everybody in the place to the highest point of efficiency. The low price makes everybody dig for profits." The continual reinvestment of high profits in improved machinery to increase output to make still more profits for reinvestment was indeed what made the "wage motive" a workable proposition for Ford.

So in Ford's philosophy of industry, the key figure remained the entrepreneurial capitalist, whose supposed superior intelligence enabled him to organize production more and more efficiently through the continual reinvestment of his profits in improved machinery. It followed axiomatically for Ford that this industrial superman had the unquestionable prerogative to determine what were fair profits, wages, and prices free from any interference by the government, workers, or consumers. If the superman erred he would be punished by the classical economists' bogeymen, the invisible hand of the market and the unenforceable law of supply and demand.

Ford believed that "business must grow bigger and bigger, else we shall have insufficient supplies and high prices." In a new twist on the Doctrine of Stewardship, which had been the perennial rationalization of American men of wealth since it was conceived by the Puritans, Ford merely urged the men in charge of these industrial giants to consult their enlightened self-interest and "regard themselves as trustees of power in behalf of all the people. . . . It is clearly up to them now, as trustees, to see what they can do further in the way of making our system fool-proof, malice-proof, and greed-proof.

It is a mere matter of social engineering." But in asking for a capitalism stripped of its traditional assumption that self-interest and greed were natural mainsprings of human economic behavior, Ford never went on to call for capitalists free from hypocrisy. Perhaps that would have been too much to expect from a "trustee of power in behalf of all the people" who also declared, "A great business is really too big to be human."

Although the Ford five-dollar, eight-hour day entailed recognition that mass consumption was a necessary corollary of mass production, Henry Ford nevertheless was still committed to most of the beliefs and values of a production-oriented society and economy. He did come to see that mass production made the worker "more a buyer than a seller," and that "the 'thrift' and 'economy' ideas have been overworked." But Ford abhorred waste and remained committed to the central tenet of a production-oriented society and economy—the work ethic. "Thinking men know that work is the salvation of the race, morally, physically, socially," claimed Ford. "Work does more than get us our living: it gets us our life."

Seeing the cure for poverty and want in terms of more efficient production, Ford held that "hiring two men to do the job of one is a crime against society" and that mass production, despite the great increase in output per worker, would always continue to create more jobs than it destroyed. To Ford, overproduction was a theoretical possibility that would mean "a world in which everybody has all that he wants." Ford feared that "this condition will be too long postponed." Nonetheless, he believed that, in the automobile industry, "We do not have to bother about overproduction for some years to come, provided our prices are right." Meanwhile, neither charity nor drones had any place in Henry Ford's conception of the good society and economy: "Fully to carry out the wage motive, society must be relieved of non-producers. Big business, well organized, cannot serve without repetitive work, and that sort of work instead of being a menace to society, permits the coming into production of the aged, the blind, and the halt. It takes away the terrors of old age and illness. And it makes new and better places for those whose mentality lifts them above repetitive work."

Mass production meant that neither physical strength nor the long apprenticeship required to become a competent craftsman was any longer a prerequisite for industrial employment. The creativity and experience on the job that had been valued in the craftsman were considered liabilities in the assembly-line worker. "As to machinists, old-time, all-around men, perish the thought!" reported Arnold and Faurote. "The Ford Company has no use for experience, in the working ranks, anyway. It desires and prefers machine-tool operators who have nothing to unlearn, who have no theories of correct surface speeds for metal finishing, and will simply do what they are told to do, over and over again from bell-time to bell-time. The Ford help need not even be able bodied." [22]

Mass production had two clear benefits from the point of view of the worker. One was that the resulting higher wages and lower prices raised the worker's standard of living appreciably. The other was that new opportunities for remunerative industrial employment were opened to the immigrant, the Black migrant to the northern city, the physically handicapped, and the educable mentally retarded. For the machine did not discriminate and did not demand substantial training, physical strength, education, or intelligence from its operator. Except for the outspokenly anti-Semitic articles published in his *Dearborn Independent*, for which Ford publicly apologized in 1927, no employer was more immune than Henry Ford from the prevailing ethnic, racial, and social prejudices of his day. "Our employment office does not bar a man for anything he has previously done," said Ford. "He is equally acceptable whether he has been in Sing Sing or at Harvard and we do not even inquire from which place he has graduated. All that he needs is the desire to work." [23]

By 1919 the Ford Motor Company employed hundreds of

ex-convicts and 9,563 so-called "substandard men"—a group that included amputees, the blind, the deaf and dumb, epileptics, and about 1,000 tubercular employees. By 1923 Ford employed about 5,000 Blacks, more than any other large American corporation and roughly half the number employed in the entire automobile industry. As at all automobile factories, however, the bulk of the Ford labor force, probably about two-thirds, consisted of immigrants from southern and eastern Europe. The group clearly most under-represented on the Ford assembly lines was the able-bodied, native-born Caucasian. As Nevins and Hill point out, "At the Ford plant the foundry workers, common laborers, drill press men, grinder operators, and other unskilled and semi-skilled hands were likely to be Russians, Poles, Croats, Hungarians, or Italians; only the skilled employees were American, British, or German stock." [24]

Conditions on the assembly line repelled the worker because they were antithetical not only to basic traits of the American character but to man's basic nature. They were grudgingly accepted only by workers accustomed to even more repressive systems of labor or whose opportunities for employment elsewhere at a living wage were almost nil—immigrants, Blacks, "substandard men," and ex-convicts. Even after the inauguration of the five-dollar, eight-hour day at Ford, Arnold and Faurote recognized that "the monotony of repetitive production can be alleviated only by a satisfactory wage-rate, and is, perhaps, much more easily endured by immigrants, whose home wage stood somewhere about 60 cents for 10 hours' work than by native-born Americans." [25]

The demands of the assembly line also put a premium on youth. Nevins and Hill relate that "the bosses had a natural liking for young, vigorous, quick men not past thirty-five. Experienced hands past that age, if they did not possess some indispensable skill, were thus often the first to be dismissed and the last to be re-engaged." [26] The Lynds tied mass production to the emergence of a cult of youth in the 1920s. Noting the trend toward employing younger men in

Muncie, Indiana, factories, for example, the Lynds explained that "machine production is shifting traditional skills from the spoken word and the fingers of the master craftsman of the Middletown of the nineties to the cams and levers of the increasingly versatile machine. And in modern machine production it is speed and endurance that are at a premium. A boy of nineteen may, after a few weeks of experience on a machine, turn out an amount of work greater than his father of forty-five." [27]

"I have not been able to discover that repetitive labor injures a man in any way," wrote Henry Ford. "Industry need not exact a human toll." It is true that mass production shifted many back-breaking tasks from the worker to the machine, and Highland Park exemplified the clean, safe, well-lighted, and well-ventilated factory essential to efficient mass production. Nevertheless, a human toll was exacted if only because mass production meant "the reduction of the necessity for thought on the part of the worker and the reduction of his movements to a minimum." [28] Machines were closely spaced for optimal efficiency, and material was delivered to the worker at a waist-high level so that "wasted motion" was not expended in walking, reaching, stooping, or bending. The worker not only had to subordinate himself to the pace of the machine but had to be able to withstand the boredom inevitable in repeating the same motions hour after hour. A fifteen-minute lunch break, which included time to use the rest room and wash one's hands, was the only break from the monotonous fatigue of repetitive labor, the semihypnotic trance that workers were lulled into by the rhythmic din of the machinery.

The precise coordination of the flow of assembly that mass production demanded meant a new ironclad discipline for industrial workers. "The organization is so highly specialized and one part is so dependent upon another that we could not for a moment consider allowing men to have their own way," Ford explained. "Without the most rigid discipline we would have the utmost confusion. I think it should not be otherwise in industry." Consequently, the easy camaraderie on the job that had been normal in American industry for both unskilled and skilled workers was forbidden at Highland Park. Straw bosses and company "spotters" enforced rules and regulations that forbade leaning against the machine, sitting, squatting, singing, talking, whistling, or smoking on the job. Even smiling was frowned upon. Workers learned to communicate clandestinely without moving their lips in the "Ford whisper" and wore frozen expressions known as "Fordization of the face." "There is not much personal contact," understated Ford. "The men do their work and go home—a factory is not a drawing room." [29]

Mass production influenced many changes in the American way of life that were perceptible by the mid-1920s. Respect for age and parental authority was undercut in blue-collar families as sons became more valued as workers than their fathers. Being male lost some status because, theoretically at least, women could now be employed in industry on the same footing as men. Although the employment of women did not occur on any significant scale until industry experienced grave labor shortages in World War II, the democratization of the American family was furthered by mass production. The role of the housewife changed from that of a producer of many household items to a consumer of ready-made clothes, prepared foods, and electrical appliances, necessitating that she be given more control over the family budget. In addition, the mass-produced family car widened her range of associations beyond the narrow sphere of the home.

From the perspective of traditional American values, the impact of mass production on the worker was debilitating. The individual became an anonymous, interchangeable robot who had little chance on the job to demonstrate his personal qualifications for upward mobility into the echelons of management. Thus the American myth of unlimited individual social mobility, based on ability and the ideal of the self-made man, became frustrating impossibilities for the assembly-line worker. As the job became a boring, dead-ended treadmill to escape from rather than a calling in which to find fulfillment, leisure began to assume a new importance for the assembly-line worker. The meaning of work, long sanctified in the Protestant Ethic, was reduced to monetary remuneration. The value of thrift and personal economy became questionable, too, as mass consumption became an inevitable corollary of mass production.

The first significant recognition by American industry that mass production necessitated mass consumption was the inauguration of the five-dollar, eight-hour day by the Ford Motor Company on January 5, 1914. The minimum daily five-dollar wage was boldly conceived by Henry Ford as a plan for sharing profits with employees in advance of their being earned. Eligible workers consisted of those who had been at Ford for six months or more and were either married men living with and taking good care of their families, single men over twenty-two years of age of proved thrifty habits, or men under twenty-two years of age and women who were the sole support of some next of kin. Almost 60 percent of the Ford workers qualified immediately, and within two years about 75 percent were included in the profit-sharing plan.

The immediate impact of the five-dollar day on the standard of living of Ford employees was dramatic. As Nevins and Hill point out, "When data collected at the beginning of 1916 were compared with materials gathered in the original investigation of employees beginning two years earlier, it appeared that the property of the average Ford employee in bank accounts and real estate equities had risen during that period from $196 to about $750. This figure did not include savings embodied in durable goods, nor in such intangible investments as the better education of children. Nor did the figures fully reflect the effect of the five-dollar wage upon the property of recipients even in the two limited categories named; for the average included many workers who (because of the doubling of the labor force and the six months' service rule) had participated in the plan for less than two years." [30]

The Sociological Department was formed to check on the

qualifications of employees for the five-dollar wage and to ensure that the money was put to uses considered constructive by Henry Ford. A staff of over thirty investigators (headed first by John R. Lee, who was succeeded by the Reverend Dr. Samuel S. Marquis, Ford's Episcopalian pastor) visited workers' homes gathering information and giving advice on the intimate details of the family budget, diet, living arrangements, recreation, social outlook, and morality. Americanization of the immigrant was encouraged by the Sociological Department through mandatory classes in English. The worker who refused to learn English, rejected the advice of the investigator, gambled, drank excessively, or was found guilty of "any malicious practice derogatory to good physical manhood or moral character" was disqualified from the five-dollar wage and put on probation. If he failed to reform within six months, he was discharged and his profits accumulated under the plan were used for charity. Shockingly presumptuous, repressive, and paternalistic by today's standards, the policies of the Sociological Department reflected both the long-standing assumption of American businessmen that the employer had a right to interfere in the private lives of his employees and the most advanced theories of the social workers of the Progressive Era.

In paying roughly twice the going rate for industrial labor for a shorter work day, Henry Ford defied the conventional economic wisdom of the day, which called for wages at a subsistence level. Ford implicitly acknowledged the validity of radical criticisms of income distribution under entrepreneurial capitalism when he told Samuel S. Marquis that five dollars a day was "about the least a man with a family can live on in these days." But Marquis knew that the five-dollar, eight-hour day "actually returned more dollars to [Henry Ford] than he gave out. It was unquestionably a shrewd and profitable stroke. To the credit of Mr. Ford be it said that he personally never maintained that his profit and bonus schemes were a means for distributing charity." [31]

Ford recognized ahead of his fellow industrialists that the worker was also a consumer and that paying higher wages was profitable for several other reasons. Not only did the increased purchasing power stimulate sales; even more important, before the inauguration of the five-dollar, eight-hour day at Ford, the labor force had turned over at an incredibly costly rate. Ford recounted in 1922 that, "when the plan went into effect, we had 14,000 employees and it had been necessary to hire at the rate of about 53,000 a year in order to keep a constant force of 14,000. In 1915 we had to hire only 6,508 men and the majority of these new men were taken on because of the growth of the business. With the old turnover of labor and our present force we should have to hire at the rate of nearly 200,000 men a year—which would be pretty nearly an impossible proposition." Consistent with the primacy of profits in his wage motive, Ford reasoned in 1922 that "the payment of high wages fortunately contributes to the low costs [of production] because the men become steadily more efficient on account of being relieved of outside worries. The payment of five dollars a day for an eight-hour day was one of the finest cost-cutting moves we ever made, and the six-dollar day wage [instituted at Ford in January 1919] is cheaper than the five. How far this will go we do not know." As Arnold and Faurote had tried to explain in 1915, "The Ford Company has no socialistic leanings, and is not making any claim to placing a shining example before the world's employers of labor. It simply has the cash on hand, and it believes it will continue to have the cash on hand, to try to help its own hour-wage earners in its own way. That is the whole story up to date." [32]

The advertising and public relations value of the five-dollar, eight-hour day alone was worth well more than the $5.8 million that the profit-sharing plan cost the Ford Motor Company during its first year of implementation. Henry Ford was roundly denounced as "a traitor to his class" by his fellow entrepreneurial capitalists, especially by his less efficient competitors in the automobile industry. On the other hand, Nevins and Hill conclude that "the public response was overwhelmingly approbatory. Nine-tenths of the newspaper comment was favorable, much of it almost ecstatic. Industrialists, labor leaders, sociologists, ministers, politicians, all hailed the innovation in glowing terms. Not a few commentators perceived the underlying connection which linked high production, high wages, and high consumption, pointing out that a new economic era might find in the Ford announcement a convenient birth date." [33]

Although the eight-hour day, forty-eight-hour week quickly became the norm in automobile plants, Henry Ford's doubling of the daily minimum wage stood for decades as an isolated example of one capitalist's self-interested benevolence. The philosophy underlying the five-dollar, eight-hour day did not become institutionalized in American industry until after World War II. And its institutionalization was due almost entirely to the aggressiveness of the well-organized unions that had arisen during the late 1930s in our major industries, not to enlightened managerial capitalists.

Nor did the experiment in benevolent paternalism last longer than a few years at the Ford Motor Company. By 1918 the inflation of the World War I years had reduced the $5.00 minimum daily wage to only $2.80 in 1914 purchasing power, wiping out the workers' gains. The war also meant greatly reduced profit margins for Ford, and the company only survived the severe postwar recession by adopting stringent economy measures. As the 1920s wore on, the position of the Ford Motor Company in the industry declined as the Model T became outmoded and Ford's competitors became more efficient. Working conditions deteriorated with the speedup of the Ford assembly lines to meet the new competition. After the minimum daily wage of Ford workers was raised to $6.00 in January 1919, giving the workers $3.36 in 1914 purchasing power, there were no further advances in Ford wages during the 1920s. By 1925 the weekly earnings at Ford were $4.21 below the industry average, although cutting the Ford work week to five days in 1926 reduced the gap to $1.37 by 1928.

The Sociological Department folded and its records were burned after the Reverend Dr. Samuel S. Marquis, its head, resigned on January 25, 1921. He later explained: "The old group of executives, who at times set justice and humanity above profits and production, were gone. With them so it seemed to me, had gone an era of cooperation and good will in the company. There came to the front men whose theory was that men are more profitable to an industry when driven than led, that fear is a greater incentive to work than loyalty." [34]

After the Paris taxicab fleet proved indispensable in moving troops to the front to stop the German advance at the Marne, a familiar phrase among military experts was that "in this war the exploding of gasoline is playing a more important part than the exploding of gunpowder." The automobile industry inevitably came to play a key role in American preparedness. The first call upon the industry occurred on August 10, 1915, with the appointment of Howard E. Coffin, vice-president and chief engineer at Hudson, and five other SAE dollar-a-year volunteers to the Navy Department Advisory Committee. Coffin became chairman of the Council of National Defense, which was formed in the spring of 1916 to organize our industrial system for war. Under the council, a Motor Transport Committee, chaired by Alfred Reeves of the NACC, planned for the mobilization of motor vehicles in the event of war, and Roy D. Chapin, the president of Hudson, chaired a Highway Transport Committee to coordinate all highway transportation.

Hundreds of executives of the automobile industry volunteered, and some 463 members of the SAE alone were in government employ by the war's end on November 11, 1918. Automobile manufacturers produced aircraft engines, submarine chasers, tanks, and a variety of other military hardware that ranged from helmets to hand grenades. The industry's principal contribution, however, was made in its normal role of mass-producing motor vehicles, especially trucks. The rapid movement of troops and supplies was essential to victory at the front; and with railroad arteries to our eastern ports clogged, long-distance trucking was being developed as an alternative. By the time the United States entered the war, over 40,000 American-made trucks had been delivered to the Allies. And over half of the 238,000 motor vehicles, mainly trucks and ambulances, that the industry had contracted to make for our own government had been completed by the Armistice. In summarizing the contribution of the automobile industry to the war effort, *Motor* reported in 1919 that Earl Curzon, a member of the British War Cabinet, "said that the war could not have been won if it had not been for the great fleets of motor trucks, and that the Allied cause had been floated to victory on a wave of oil." [35]

Industry support for preparedness and the war effort came mainly from the small automobile manufacturers that dominated the SAE. The position of these companies was deteriorating in the industry. Therefore, they not only had less to lose from a drastic curtailment of civilian production but their much smaller fixed investments in highly specialized plants and equipment made conversion to military production easier and far less costly for them than for the industry giants, Ford and General Motors.

William C. Durant at General Motors opposed undertaking war production less publicly but even more adamantly than Henry Ford. Henry M. Leland and Wilfred C. Leland, for example, resigned from Cadillac to form the Lincoln Motor Company on June 18, 1917, over Durant's vehement refusal to endorse their enthusiastic support of the war effort. When approached by the Lelands the day after war was declared with the proposition that it was a patriotic duty for Cadillac to switch over to the production of airplane engines, Durant had responded: "No! I don't care for your platitudes. This is not our war and I will not permit any General Motors unit to do work for the government." [36] However, no automobile manufacturer could afford the reputation of being a "slacker"; so within a few months, Durant, too, succumbed to the mounting pressures of public opinion in support of the war and undertook token production of the new Liberty aircraft engine at both Buick and Cadillac.

Until the American entry into the war, Henry Ford took an outspoken stand against conscription and preparedness. "I don't believe in preparedness," he said. "It's like a man carrying a gun. Men and nations who carry guns get into trouble. If I had my way, I'd throw every ounce of gun powder into the sea and strip the soldiers and sailors of their insignia." [37] Ford idealistically declared that he would spend half his fortune to shorten the war by one day and joined the American Peace Society, in which he came under the influence of Rosika Schwimmer, a Hungarian pacifist.

To implement Ms. Schwimmer's goals of stopping the war before either side gained a complete victory and establishing an organization for the continual mediation of international disputes, Henry Ford sponsored a "Peace Ship." On December 5, 1915, the *Oscar II* sailed on an abortive fourteen-day voyage to Oslo, Norway, carrying an array of delegates, students, technical advisers, and reporters that Charles E. Sorensen called "the strangest assortment of living creatures since the voyage of Noah's Ark." Newspapers on both sides of the Atlantic stressed the idealistic naïveté of the Peace Ship and seized upon bizarre details in an attempt to discredit "Ford's folly" as an exercise in futility and absurdity. After Ford became ill and left the delegation at Oslo, the peace party went on to Sweden and Denmark, ending up at The Hague in Holland, where it disbanded on January 15, 1916, demoralized and dissension-ridden.

Once diplomatic ties between the United States and Germany were severed on February 3, 1917, Henry Ford abruptly reversed himself, stating that "we must stand behind the President" and that "in the event of war [I] will place our factory at the disposal of the United States government and will operate without one cent of profit." After Congress declared war on April 6, Ford rationalized that "perhaps militarism can be crushed only with militarism. In that case I am in on it to the finish." [38]

On April 8, Ford cabled the British that he would "comply with every request immediately" to help them mass-produce the Fordson farm tractor. Tractors were desperately needed by the British to help alleviate grave food shortages caused by German U-boat attacks on ships importing foodstuffs and by the loss of 80,000 farmhands to the military services. Experiments with a number of makes of tractors conducted by the Royal Agricultural Society had left the British authorities most impressed with the Fordson.

The first commercially successful gasoline-powered tractors in the United States were built by the Hart-Parr Company of Charles City, Iowa, in 1902–1903. By 1907, when Henry Ford began the experiments that led to the Fordson, about 600 gasoline-powered tractors were in use on American farms. These early machines were too heavy, clumsy, complicated, and expensive to meet the needs of the average farmer. Between 1910 and 1915, when the Fordson was announced, several tractor demonstrations in the Middle West drew an estimated 50,000 farmers and showed that there was a large potential market for smaller machines, such as the 4,650-pound, $650 tractor introduced in 1913 by the Bull Tractor Company of Minneapolis, Minnesota. The 2,500-pound Fordson was introduced by Henry Ford personally in August 1915 at a plowing demonstration at Fremont, Nebraska. With a wheelbase of only 63 inches, the Fordson could turn in a 21-foot circle. It was cheap to operate because its four-cylinder, 20-horsepower engine ran on kerosene. And, like the Model T, the Fordson was designed to be mass-produced at low cost. Henry Ford & Son was organized to manufacture the Fordson as a separate corporation from the Ford Motor Company on July 27, 1917.

The Fordson tractor contributed little toward alleviating food shortages during the war. By March 1, 1918, only 3,600 of the 8,000 Fordsons ordered by the British government had been delivered, and privately owned steam tractors were plowing considerably more acres of British farmland than the government-owned Fordsons. Most Fordsons were bought by American farmers, who, faced for the first time in decades with expanding markets for agricultural commodities, were anxious to comply with the patriotic slogan, "Buy Tractors and Win the War." Although it was April 23, 1918, before the first Fordson for domestic use came off the assembly line, by the time of the Armistice 26,817 had been manufactured at Ford's Dearborn tractor plant. Too late to have any significant impact on winning the war, these Fordsons were distributed to the agricultural states in quotas and sold to farmers through permits granted by the County War Boards.

Despite the impression given by Henry Ford that he sold his tractors at cost as a contribution to the war effort, the $750 price of the Fordson included a tidy profit of $182.86 for Henry Ford & Son. The greatest irony was that mass production of the Fordson reached fantastic heights just as the market for American agricultural commodities rapidly evaporated in the postwar period. Some 750 Fordsons a day were being produced by 1924. Total production rose to 486,800 units in 1925 and over 650,000 units in 1927, making Ford responsible for about half the tractors manufactured in the United States up to that time. This proliferation of the Fordson farm tractor was a major factor in creating the ruinous combination of higher fixed costs and overproduction of staple commodities that plagued American farmers during the 1920s.

Even before Henry Ford abandoned his pacifist neutrality to work for the war effort "without one cent of profit," the Ford branch plants in Paris and Great Britain had disregarded Dearborn and turned out thousands of motor vehicles for the Allies. From an initial contract for 2,000 ambulances on May 30, 1917, Ford's American factories went on to produce about 39,000 motor vehicles for the war effort. They also made aircraft motors, armor plate, caissons, shells, steel helmets, submarine detectors, and torpedo tubes. Sixty Eagle

Boats (submarine chasers) were completed by Ford too late to see action, and two tank prototypes developed by the company had just reached the stage where quantity production could begin when peace came.

Although the manufacture of Model Ts for the civilian market never stopped entirely, automotive work was cut back significantly at Ford during the war. By July 31, 1918, no motorcars were being made at the Highland Park plant. However, almost 3,000 a day were still being turned out at the twenty-eight Ford branch assembly plants. These plants had been established throughout the United States at freight-rate breaking points after 1909 because cars could be shipped to their ultimate destinations much more cheaply in knocked-down form. By Armistice Day the Ford branch plants were producing only about 300 cars a day, practically all for the government. The production of Ford motor vehicles declined from a high of 734,800 units in 1916 to 438,800 units in 1918. But conversion back to full civilian production was apparently no problem, for the Ford plants turned out 820,400 units in 1919. The unexpected sharp drop in Ford production to 419,500 units in 1920 shows that the postwar recession had a much greater impact than the war effort on reducing production of the Model T.

Nevertheless, participation in the war effort was costly for the Ford Motor Company in terms of profits. Net income fell from $57.1 million for the fiscal year 1915/16 to $27.2 million for 1916/17 and $30.9 million for 1917/18, and the bulk of the company's profits during the war came from its civilian production. After corporate taxes, the Ford Motor Company made only $4.357 million on its war contracts. As the owner of 58.5 percent of the Ford stock, Henry Ford's share of the company's war profits after paying personal income taxes on them came to a mere $926,780.46—a fraction of what he could have made had civilian production continued uninterrupted. The Dent Act for terminating war contracts was passed by Congress in early 1919. It gave the government until

March 1, 1924, to question all settlements, and the Treasury Department did not complete its careful scrutiny of the Ford settlements until mid-1923. By then Henry Ford was angry about governmental officials probing into his business records, and the Ford Motor Company was facing tougher competitive conditions in the automobile industry. So Henry Ford reneged on his rash promise, repeated as late as his 1918 senatorial campaign, to return all his war profits to the government.

The abrupt termination of war contracts with the unanticipated coming of peace on November 11, 1918, caused little concern in the automobile industry. Automobile plants were quickly converted back to the production of passenger cars—at Highland Park it took only about three weeks—to fill the huge back orders for new cars that had accumulated during the war. Automobile manufacturers began to embark on ambitious expansion programs, confident that the demand for motorcars was insatiable.

These short-lived illusions were shattered with the onset of the postwar recession. General commodity prices continued to rise after the war, reaching a peak in May 1920 of 121.7 percent of the November 1918 level, with automobile prices continuing to rise to a peak of 124.9 percent in August. An illustration of what this meant is that a new Model T touring car that had sold for $360 in August 1916 cost $575 in August 1920. Responding to this sharply rising spiral in the cost of living, some 4.16 million U.S. workers, about 20 percent of the labor force, engaged in 3,630 work stoppages during 1919, making that year a high point of industrial unrest. Except for a major strike at Willys-Overland, the automobile industry experienced minimal direct labor-management strife. But with a million workers out on strike in the steel and coal industries and on the railroads alone, the automobile manufacturers felt the impact of work stoppages in vital ancillary industries. Most important, new car sales slackened with the general decline in purchasing power. This decline was compounded as rural America's demand for new cars, the automobile industry's mainstay for over a decade, began to evaporate. The American farmer returned to hard times with the collapse of foreign markets after 1919. Commodity prices fell rapidly in the summer of 1920. Gross agricultural income dropped from $15 billion in 1919 to only $9.2 billion in 1921 as agricultural exports declined 50 percent. The final puncture that burst the automobile manufacturers' balloon occurred when the Federal Reserve Board, concerned about a rapid expansion in the installment sales of cars, raised the rediscount rate in November 1919. The effect was to up the down payment required on automobile time sales from a fourth or a third to about half the purchase price of the car.

The recession hit Henry Ford in the midst of carrying out plans to develop an industrial colossus on the Rouge River and deeply in debt from a successful drive to buy out his minority stockholders. In the spring of 1915 Ford began buying up huge tracts of land along the Rouge River southeast of Detroit and announced plans for developing a great industrial complex there. John and Horace Dodge, still minority Ford stockholders despite having formed a rival company to build their own car, brought a lawsuit against Ford to stop his diversion of Ford profits into expanding the Rouge plant instead of distributing them as dividends, which the Dodge brothers were counting on to finance expansion at Dodge. On January 6, 1917, the lifting of a restraining order by the court permitted Ford to go ahead with developing the Rouge facilities on the condition that he post a $10 million bond to safeguard the interests of his minority stockholders. But a decision handed down on February 7, 1919, forced the Ford Motor Company to declare a special dividend of $19.275 million plus interest. Although Henry Ford as the principal Ford stockholder received the bulk of this special dividend, the experience left him determined to rid himself of his minority stockholders. Not only had his minority stockholders become wealthy on small investments while contributing nothing to the company,

Ford reasoned, but these ungrateful parasites were now proving to be stumbling blocks to the expansion he deemed essential.

Henry Ford "danced a jig all around the room" when he managed to buy up the options of his minority stockholders for the bargain price of $105.8 million on July 11, 1919. Financing the transaction required a $75 million loan from a financial syndicate composed of the Chase Securities Corporation, the Old Colony Trust Company, and Bond and Goodwin. The reorganized Ford Motor Company's shares were distributed 55.2 percent to Henry Ford, 41.7 percent to Edsel Ford as Henry's only progeny and heir apparent to the throne, and 3.1 percent to Clara Ford. Edsel became titular president of the reorganized company, a position he held until his untimely death on May 26, 1943, from cancer. But no one, including Edsel, doubted that the Ford Motor Company after its reorganization was an autocracy entirely subject to the whims of its aging, egocentric founder.

Turning the giant Ford Motor Company into a family-owned and family-managed business defied precedent, business trends, rational canons of business administration, and simple common sense. Nevins and Hill point out that "never had one man controlled completely an organization the size of the Ford Motor Company. John D. Rockefeller never held more than two-sevenths of the Standard Oil Company certificates, and J. P. Morgan, who presided over the birth of the United States Steel Corporation, owned a much smaller percentage of its shares. Ford wielded industrial power such as no man had ever possessed before." [39] The trends in American industry were toward wider dispersal of ownership among many small stockholders, the separation of ownership from management, the rise of professional managers and salaried experts within the firm, and democratic decision making by committees of executives. At the Ford Motor Company, in sharp contrast, the champion of small business against the forces of monopoly during the Selden patent suit now fastened onto his mammoth corporation the family ownership and one-man rule fit for a mom-and-pop market. By 1920 the Ford Motor Company owned, in addition to its main Highland Park and River Rouge plants, branch plants scattered across the globe, rubber plantations in Brazil, iron mines and lumber mills in Michigan, coal mines in Kentucky and West Virginia, glass plants in Pennsylvania and Minnesota, a railroad, and a fleet of ships. Family ownership and one-man rule of an enterprise of this scope defied sanity, much less Lord Acton's dictum that absolute power tends to corrupt absolutely.

As the full impact of the recession began to be felt in the summer of 1920, Henry Ford still owed $25 million, due in April 1921, on the loan to obtain control of his company; he had pledged to distribute a $7 million bonus in January; and he had to pay between $18 million and $30 million in taxes. Over the past three years $60.45 million had been spent on developing the River Rouge plant and between $15 million and $20 million on purchasing mines and timber tracts. Ford estimated that he needed $58 million, and he had only $20 million in cash on hand. The thought of seeking another loan was abandoned once it became apparent to Ford that the bankers would demand in return a voice in the management of his company. So Henry Ford turned to alternatives that preserved his sovereignty at the expense of the long-range well-being of the Ford Motor Company.

The only progressive move that Ford made was to lead the industry in a long overdue reduction in the price of cars. On September 21, 1920, the Ford Motor Company announced price cuts on the Model T that averaged $148, depending on body style. This reduction theoretically meant a short-term loss of about $20 on every car sold, but the loss was covered by the profit on the $40 worth of parts and accessories sold with every new Model T. Other automobile manufacturers claimed that the drastic Ford price cuts were ruinous for the industry, and some banded together in an attempt to preserve the old price levels. Within a few weeks, however, twenty-three of Ford's competitors followed his lead and reduced prices on their cars.

As the fall wore on, it became evident that the price cuts were failing to check the dwindling sales. By the end of 1920, automobile production was halted at Buick, Dodge, Ford, Maxwell-Chalmers, Nash, Packard, REO, Studebaker, and Willys-Overland; and the automobile plants that remained open were staffed by skeleton work forces. The number of employed automobile workers in Detroit, the geographic center of the industry, dropped from 176,000 in September to 24,000 by the end of the year.

The Ford Motor Company closed its plants "for inventory" on Christmas Eve, December 24, 1920, and remained closed until February 1, 1921, while the company disposed of "stocks on hand." Unlike most of his competitors, Henry Ford maintained full production up to the shutdown of his plants, curtailing only the purchase of raw materials. The strategy implemented at Ford was first to turn the huge inventory of raw materials that had been bought at inflated prices into a reservoir of finished cars, then to stop production until those cars were disposed of at a profit and raw material prices had declined. Consignments of unordered cars were forced on over 6,300 Ford dealers, who had the choice of borrowing heavily from local banks to pay cash on delivery for them or forfeiting their Ford franchises. Henry Ford thus avoided going to the bankers himself and preserved his one-man rule and personal profits by arbitrarily unloading his financial problems onto the backs of thousands of hard-pressed small businessmen.

The shutdown at Ford was accompanied by stringent economy measures that went beyond what was essential for survival and jeopardized the future well-being of the firm. The Ford plants were stripped of every nonessential tool and fixture—including every pencil sharpener, most desks and typewriters, and 600 extension telephones. The sale of this equipment netted $7 million. The company also benefitted from replacing some of it with improved machinery and methods that increased output per man-hour of labor. These gains were canceled out, however, by a ruthless halving of the office force from 1,074 to 528 persons as most departments, including such critical ones as auditing, were overly simplified, merged, or eliminated. Many capable executives were lost to the company. Even more important, the development of the organized bureaucracy essential to a mature corporation in a technologically sophisticated, consumer-goods industry was stultified.

Henry Ford always considered the business end of the company to be nonessential and therefore expendable. So it was inevitable that he took the first opportunity to emasculate the administrative staff after buying out Couzens, who had built it up, with the other minority stockholders. "To my mind there is no bent of mind more dangerous than that which is sometimes described as 'genius for organization,'" Ford explained in 1922. "It is not necessary for any one department to know what any other department is doing." He foolishly boasted that "the Ford factories and enterprises have no organization, no specific duties attaching to any position, no line of succession or of authority, very few titles, and no conferences. We have only the clerical help that is absolutely required; we have no elaborate records of any kind, and consequently no red tape." [40]

The lack of "red tape" amounted to what an increasing number of ex-Ford executives called "Prussianization" as the entrepreneurial team responsible for the success of the mass-produced Model T disintegrated in the early 1920s. A complete list of the Ford executives who were arbitrarily fired or who resigned in disgust between 1919 and Henry Ford's retirement in 1945 would add up to a small town's telephone directory. Although this critical loss of executive talent defies adequate summarizing, after James Couzens the most significant losses were probably William S. Knudsen and Norval A. Hawkins. Both went to General Motors and were instrumental in Chevrolet's sales surpassing Ford's by 1927. Of more symbolic importance were the 1919 departures to build the Wills–

Sainte Claire car of C. Harold Wills, the chief designer of the Model
T, and John R. Lee, the first head of the short-lived Sociological
Department. Charles E. Sorensen, who became Henry Ford's chief
hatchet man, seemed to take a perverse pleasure in the discharges
and resignations of his fellow executives, and he managed to stay in
Ford's favor by saying "yes" longer than any of them. But on March
2, 1944, Sorensen too ended up by resigning—at the request of a
senile Henry Ford, who feared that Sorensen had ambitions to take
over his company.

Citing the Ford Motor Company as the world's outstanding
example of an industrial dictatorship, the *New York Times* on January
8, 1928, called Henry Ford "an industrial fascist—the Mussolini of
Detroit." As the probusiness *Fortune* magazine commented in December 1933, it was well known in the automobile industry that "Mr.
Ford's organization does show extreme evidence of being ruled
primarily by fear of the job." Even Edsel was mercilessly bullied by
the elder Ford, who thought his son too soft and held up as a model
worthy of emulation Harry Bennett, an ex-pugilist with underworld
connections. Bennett enforced discipline in the Ford plants as head
of a gang of labor spies and thugs called the Ford Service
Department. He came to be Henry Ford's most trusted associate and
comrade after the Model A replaced the Model T in 1928 and
production was shifted to the River Rouge plant.

From Edsel Ford on down, the Ford executives came to fear and
despise Bennett as his influence grew, and by the mid-1930s Ford
workers wondered whether Hitler had derived the idea for his
Gestapo from Bennett's Ford Service. "As a rule, Ford's managers,
having more to lose, came to watch their jobs more nervously than
the man at the Rouge who swept the floor," relates Keith Sward.
"On the lower tiers of the Ford organization, Ford Service gave rise
to any number of unmistakable industrial neuroses. These 'shop
complaints' went all the way from mild states of anxiety to advanced
nervous symptoms that were fit material for a psychopathic ward.

Thus conditioned, the personality of any Ford employee was subjected to a process of subtle and profound degradation." [41] Writing during the depths of the Great Depression, Jonathan N. Leonard, an early Ford debunker, claimed that "Detroit is a city of hate and fear. And the major focus of that hatred and fear is the astonishing plant on the River Rouge." Leonard found almost all automobile factories in Detroit "horrifying and repellent to the last degree. But the Ford factory has the reputation of being by far the worst." The main reason was that "over the Ford plant hangs the menace of the 'Service Department,' the spies and stool pigeons who report every action, every remark, every expression. . . . No one who works for Ford is safe from the spies—from the superintendents down to the poor creature who must clean a certain number of toilets an hour." [42]

The Service Department was one manifestation of the Ford Motor Company's deteriorating postion vis-à-vis its competitors in the automobile industry. Except for minor face-liftings and the incorporation of such basic improvements as the closed body and the self-starter, the Model T remained basically unchanged long after it was outmoded. The popularity of the Model T declined in the 1920s as rural roads were improved, consumers became more style and comfort conscious, and the market for new cars shifted from a demand for low-cost, basic transportation by first-time owners to filling replacement demand. Model T owners tended to trade up to larger, faster, smoother riding, and more stylish cars; and the demand for the low-cost, basic transportation that the Model T had met tended increasingly to be filled from the backlog of used cars piling up in dealers' lots. By the mid-1920s, secondhand cars of more expensive makes in good condition could be bought for the same price as a new Model T. In addition, the onset of the market saturation for new cars forced general price reductions in 1925 that, for example, pegged only $200 higher than an obsolete Model T an annually restyled, larger, and far better equipped new Chevrolet.

Henry Ford closed his mind to the advice of his executives, the pleas of his dealers, and mounting complaints about the Model T from his customers. He denounced the new emphasis on style and comfort as extravagant and wasteful and tried to meet the competition by drastically reducing prices—to a low of $290 for the coupe by 1927—and making "everybody dig for profits." The speedup of the assembly line enforced by the Ford Service Department drove workers "to the highest point of efficiency." Ex-Ford executives were the first to testify in their reminiscences that workers were driven harder at Ford than at other automobile plants. Ford dealers, too, were forced "to the highest point of efficiency." As Model T production was cut from 1.8 million units in 1923 to 1.3 million units in 1926, the number of Ford dealerships was increased from about 8,500 to 9,800 in the hope that heightened competition among them would stimulate more aggressive salesmanship. Seven out of ten Ford dealers were losing money by 1926; and as some went bankrupt and others switched to General Motors, about a third of the Ford dealerships turned over that year.

Even Henry Ford was finally forced to recognize that the era of the Model T had ended. Its production was halted on May 27, 1927, and the Ford plants were shut down while its successor, the Model A, was hastily designed. A mild recession in 1927 was attributed in part to hundreds of thousands of automobile owners deferring their purchase of a new car until Henry Ford came out with his new model. Some 400,000 orders were received before the Model A had been seen by the public. At a retooling cost of $18 million, for what was probably up to that time the most extensive changeover of an industrial plant in American history, the assembly lines at River Rouge began to turn out limited numbers of the Model A in November 1927.

The initial response to the four-cylinder, 40-horsepower Model A was enthusiastic. In 1929 Ford briefly regained the industry lead in sales that had been lost to Chevrolet in both 1927 and 1928. Ford production surpassed 1.5 million units in 1929 and 1.15 million units in 1930, compared with Chevrolet's 950,000 and 683,000 units for those years.

But neither the Model A nor the Ford V-8 that replaced it in 1932 could regenerate the Ford Motor Company. Between 1931 and 1970 Chevrolet outsold Ford in every year except 1935 and 1945, and the latter year was an exception only because Ford was the first automobile manufacturer to get back into civilian production following World War II. Plymouth also cut into Ford sales in the low-priced field after it was introduced in 1929. And Ford's cars in the luxury and moderately priced brackets—the Lincoln, acquired from the Lelands in 1921, and the Mercury, introduced in 1939 to compete with Pontiac and Dodge—failed to become popular. Only in the sale of light trucks did the Ford Motor Company enjoy a slight lead over its competitors. In the oligopoly that had come to dominate the automobile industry, by 1936 Ford had dropped to third place in sales of passenger cars, with 22.44 percent of the market versus 43.12 percent for General Motors and 25.03 percent for Chrysler.

The Great Depression, of course, was an even more important impediment to the revivial of the Ford Motor Company than competition from General Motors and Chrysler. Automobile registrations declined for the first time in the United States during the depression, and not until 1949 did the automobile industry equal its record 1929 output of 5.3 million units. Ford production collapsed from over 1.5 million units in 1929 to a low of 232,000 units in 1932 and bounced back to only 600,000 units in 1941, the last full year of civilian automobile production before World War II. During 1931–1933 the Ford Motor Company lost $120 million after taxes. Profits of $17.9 million in 1936 and $6.7 million in 1937, during a brief revival of the economy, went far, however, toward canceling out an estimated total loss of $26 million over the preceding decade.

Henry Ford was one of the few industrial capitalists sufficiently committed to the capitalist system to make a voluntary effort to maintain the economy as it slid into the depression following the stock market crash in October 1929. Hoping to stimulate consumption by increasing purchasing power, Ford lowered prices on the Model A in November and raised the minimum daily wage of his workers to $7 in December. Early in 1930 he announced a $25 million program of branch factory construction.

Ford quickly reneged once the severity of the depression became apparent. He also reduced the profit margins of his dealers on the sale of new cars to the lowest in the industry. And by 1932 the minimum daily wage at Ford was reduced to $6 for skilled workers, $5 for semiskilled workers, and $4 for laborers. Even these rates were illusory because they did not account for the downgrading of many jobs to lower pay scales and an increase in jobbing out components to outside companies that paid lower wages than Ford. The number of Ford employees declined sharply from 170,502 in 1929 to 46,282 by 1932. Those who still had jobs were driven increasingly harder "to the highest point of efficiency." Because Ford, with the help of his Service Department, managed to resist unionization longer than General Motors or Chrysler, the company's wages for 1937–1941 fell a few cents below the average for all industry in the United States and well below the average for the automobile industry.

Outside his company, organized labor, the automobile industry, and the Detroit area, the myths that had built up around the figure of Henry Ford incredibly refused to die. A survey conducted by *Fortune* magazine in 1937 for the National Association of Manufacturers found that 47.2 percent of the respondents still approved of the policies of the Ford Motor Company, versus an insignificant 3.1 percent approval for General Motors and 1.2 percent approval for Chrysler.

Yet the Ford myths were beginning to be shattered, and Henry Ford at least was no longer being deified. In 1932 Jonathan Leonard noted the paradox that "he is hated by nearly everyone who has ever worked for him, and at one time was worshipped by nearly everyone who had not. His story is certainly the most fascinating in all the gaudy tales of American business." Henry Ford's main fault, thought Leonard, was that "he did not consider himself a mere manufacturer, like the Dodges or Chrysler. He was a prophet with a message for the world. That fact that his message was bare, ugly, tyrannical did not keep people from accepting it as long as he was the most successful industrialist in the country. In the United States a record of commercial success makes a man an authority on every subject." Leonard was optimistic that "even if the company does manage to persuade its owner to follow the rest of the industry and keep up with engineering and fashion changes, Henry Ford will never be a prophet again. He will merely be a manufacturer, and since the crash of 1929 the American people refuse to worship without reserve the god of mass production." [43]

Even to the grass-roots Americans who had deified him for a generation, Henry Ford's rhetoric increasingly seemed irrelevant nonsense as the Great Depression wore on. The letters to the "Sage of Dearborn" dwindled and became bitter and resentful. As Wik says, "Instead of writing to Ford, farmers in increasing numbers addressed their remarks to officials in the nation's capitol where the power to affect reform resided. The letters found in the library at Hyde Park, New York, and in the National Archives in Washington, D.C., suggest that farmers believed relief could be found in federal legislation rather than in the good intentions of business leaders." [44]

Henry Ford's mental capacities eroded rapidly after he suffered a severe stroke in 1938. He developed the hallucination that Franklin Delano Roosevelt was a warmonger controlled by General Motors and the du Ponts and that United States involvement in World War II was part of a conspiracy to get control of his company. "His memory was failing as rapidly as his obsessions and antipathies increased," Sorensen recalled. "His pet peeve was Franklin Roosevelt, but any mention of the war in Europe and the likelihood of this country's involvement upset him almost to incoherence. Edsel, who was suffering from stomach trouble, came in for unmerciful criticism." [45]

Ford's delusions were lent substance when Roosevelt appointed William S. Knudsen, then the president of General Motors, Commissioner for Industrial Production of the National Defense Commission on May 28, 1940. Ford was already under attack for his refusal to take British war orders when he reneged on a promise, made to Knudsen at the urging of Edsel and Sorensen, that he would manufacture Rolls-Royce airplane engines, 60 percent to go to the British. Despite Ford's proclaimed neutrality, the Nazis had taken over complete control of his German and French plants. So when Knudsen called for the full cooperation of automobile manufacturers in the defense plans in late November 1940, Edsel and Sorensen recognized that Ford's failure to comply voluntarily would invite the governmental take-over that Henry Ford's paranoia led him to fear.

They managed to obtain Ford's reluctant consent to participate in the aircraft program. On November 1, 1940, the Ford Motor Company signed a contract to make Pratt & Whitney airplane engines for the U.S. Air Force. And on February 25, 1941, the government approved Ford plans for a vast bomber plant at Willow Run, near Ypsilanti, Michigan. Snags in getting "Will-It Run" into production delayed acceptance of the first B-24 bombers completely assembled by Ford until September 1942. By then the Ford Motor Company, along with the rest of the automobile industry, had completely converted over to war production and was playing an indispensable role in the war effort. Henry Ford feared that the military personnel at Willow Run were spies sent by Roosevelt to assassinate him and took to carrying an automatic pistol under the cowl of his car.

Following Edsel's death on May 26, 1943, Henry Ford again became president of the Ford Motor Company. Roosevelt, aware of Ford's mental incompetence, toyed with the idea of removing him and having the government operate the company for the duration of the war. It took the threats of Edsel's widow and Clara Ford to sell their shares of Ford stock out of the family to induce Henry Ford finally to step down in favor of his grandson Henry Ford II on September 21, 1945.

After a generation of gross mismanagement, the Ford Motor Company was losing about $10 million a month when Henry Ford II took over. The Ford Service Department had made fear and demoralization a way of life at Ford. Few executives worth their salt were left. The company lacked both a program of research and development and college-trained engineers. Accounting was so primitive that at least one department estimated its costs by weighing the invoices. There was no coordination between purchasing, production, and marketing. For years the financial statements had been closely guarded secrets even within the firm because of fear that they might damage prestige or prompt an investigation.

This was an ironic inheritance from a founder once worshiped as a deity of progress through industrial efficiency. It was even more ironic that Henry Ford II began the revitalization of the Ford Motor Company by hiring an executive team headed by Ernest R. Breech from General Motors to institute the corporate structure and modern management techniques that the first Henry Ford had sacrificed to maintain family control at Ford. More ironic still, the Ford Motor Company had over $685 million in cash on hand when Henry Ford II began its revitalization. That was not a bad bank balance for a firm that had started in 1903 with only $28 thousand of paid-in capital, that had been mismanaged for a generation, and whose founder claimed in 1916 that "we should not make such an awful profit on our cars."

Perhaps the ultimate irony turned out to be the Ford Foundation, a legal device conceived on February 3, 1936, as a means of avoiding Roosevelt's "soak-the-rich" taxes and maintaining family control of the Ford Motor Company. The Ford Foundation had a 95 percent equity in the Ford Motor Company in nonvoting common stock. A 5 percent equity of all voting common stock was retained by the Ford family. Had it not been for the Ford Foundation, the heirs of Edsel and Henry Ford would have paid federal inheritance taxes estimated at $321 million and would have lost control of the company in selling the stock necessary to raise the money. But by the end of 1955 the Ford Foundation had disposed of some $875 million of the Ford fortune and had announced plans to diversify its investments, which involved selling nearly 7 million reclassified shares of Ford common stock. Thus three-fifths of the Ford Motor Company voting common stock ended up in the hands of key Ford executives and the general public. The family control of the firm that the Ford Foundation was formed to preserve ended less than a decade after Henry Ford's death on April 7, 1947. And in September 1974 the Ford Foundation announced that because of inflation and falling securities markets it might have to reduce its annual grants by 50 percent. It was even considering dissolution.

5 BILLY DURANT AND THE BULL MARKET
(with Glenn A. Niemeyer)

William C. Durant died on March 18, 1947—a few weeks before Henry Ford—leaving a public image that was clouded but untarnished. The colorful founder of General Motors was no longer famous, powerful, or fabulously wealthy. Durant Motors, Inc., his last automotive venture, was liquidated in 1933. Bankruptcy for Billy Durant followed in 1936, when he declared liabilities of almost $1 million versus assets of only $250 (his clothes). After failing as the proprietor of a supermarket in an old Durant Motors salesroom at Asbury Park, New Jersey, he opened a bowling alley in his hometown of Flint, Michigan. His last business venture was backing

This chapter is an expansion and revision of material in James J. Flink and Glenn A. Niemeyer, "The General of General Motors," *American Heritage*, 24:10–17, 86–91 (August 1973). The only comprehensive scholarly article on Durant is John B. Rae, "The Fabulous Billy Durant," *Business History Review*, 32:255–271 (Autumn 1958). The best account of Durant's career by a business associate is probably Jacob H. Newmark, "My 25 Years with W. C. Durant," *Commerce and Finance*, 25:344–346 ff. (May 30–October 17, 1936). Margery Durant's privately printed biography, *My Father* (New York: Knickerbocker Press [G. P. Putnam's Sons], 1929), has been charitably described by John B. Rae as "a work of filial piety" in his annotated bibliography to *The American Automobile: A Brief History* (Chicago: University of Chicago Press, 1965), p. 251. The most detailed and recent compendium of information on Durant is Lawrence R. Gustin, *Billy Durant: Creator of General Motors* (Grand Rapids, Mich.: William B. Eerdmans Publishing Co., 1973), an appreciative, full-length biography authorized by Durant's widow. Gustin's book is an expansion of his newspaper articles, "Billy Durant and Flint," *Flint Journal*, March 19–28, 1972.

There are more Ford scholars than there are scholarly articles about Durant, for research has been handicapped by lack of access to his personal papers and the General Motors archives. All accounts of his career, therefore, have had to rely too heavily on anecdote, newspapers, and a good deal of surmise. On July 31, 1974, the General Motors Institute Alumni Foundation announced that it had acquired Durant's personal papers and was making them available to scholars. Unfortunately, this important breakthrough in access to Durant data occurred after the present account was in press.

a nostrum to prevent baldness and cure dandruff. A stroke suffered in 1942 left him an invalid. That Billy Durant had been the "leading bull" in the great stock market debacle of the late 1920s was already forgotten, as were his foibles during the crisis of 1920 at General Motors.

Billy Durant projected a confusing, contradictory image to the world, and underlying the image were unfathomed depths. The press dubbed the slightly built, indomitable creator of business empires "Napoleonic," a tag that aptly described as well Durant's charismatic charm and his tendencies to be visionary, arbitrary, and impenetrable. Walter P. Chrysler, who resigned in frustration over Durant's arbitrary interference in Buick's operations, wrote that "[Durant] has the most winning personality of anyone I've ever known. He could coax a bird right down out of a tree, I think." Alfred P. Sloan, Jr., objected to Durant's cronyism and intuitive, erratic decision making to the point that Sloan felt that "Mr. Durant was like a dictator." Yet Sloan was "the first to say that William C. Durant was a genius." "When some thought flashed through his mind he was disposed to act on it forthwith, and rarely troubled to consult with the man who had the real responsibility," recalled Sloan. "Yet even when this sort of interference struck as a lightning bolt into your own department, you did not protest, because he was so sweet natured, so well intentioned." One of the few bankers sympathetic to Durant probably best sketched his strengths and weaknesses: "Durant is a genius and therefore not to be dealt with on the same basis as ordinary businessmen. In many respects he is a child in emotions, in temperament, and in mental balance, yet possessed of wonderful energy and ability along certain other well-defined lines. He is sensitive and proud; and successful leadership, I think, really counts with him more than financial success." [1]

Despite his outgoing personableness, Durant has remained one of Earl Sparling's "mystery men of Wall Street." He had few intimate friends and did not encourage familiarity. The diminutive "Billy" was rarely used in his presence. Even to close associates he was "Mr. Durant," while subordinates referred to him as "the boss" or "the man." Typically, Henry M. Leland and Wilfred C. Leland of Cadillac felt that "Durant was a complex personality, exceedingly polite and charming to all, but an enigma even to others much closer to him. The Lelands appreciated his kindness and made no judgment of his operations." His daughter Margery also testified to his reserve in interpersonal relations.[2]

Billy Durant dazzled and amazed the public for a generation with the dramatic boldness of his financial manipulations. However, he was too much the speculator to be immortalized as an industrial statesman, too much the huckster to be idolized as a symbol of automobility. "Some saw him as a reckless gambler, others as a shrewd and ruthless promoter," recalled the *Detroit Free Press.* Billy Durant was the archetype of the supersalesman. He possessed "the power to magnetize men with his belief. But he lacked the pedestrian element. To him the immediate future was remote; the remote future near and vivid." Durant sold automobiles because he believed that the market for new cars would become saturated only "when they quit making babies." But his commitment to the automobile was always secondary to his involvement in the stock market. As Dana L. Thomas says, "William Crapo Durant was drunk with the gamble of America, obsessed with its highest article of faith—that the man who played for the steepest stakes deserved the biggest winnings."[3]

Unlike Henry Ford, Durant neither posed as a champion of progress through automobility and industrial efficiency nor developed a coherent philosophy of industry. The problems of automotive technology and the social issues that intrigued Ford were outside Durant's spheres of competence and interest. To Carl B. Glasscock, who was concerned primarily with the romance and drama of the early automobile industry, "Beside [Durant] Henry Ford was a plodding, insignificant, colorless mechanic, utterly lacking in romance or drama, without distinction, without charm—the tortoise beside the hare. . . . Billy Durant was the comet beside the star of Henry Ford." Durant himself once doubled up in laughter at a lampoon dashed off by Theodore MacManus:

I'm glad I'm not a vacuum
  I'm glad I'm not a myth
I'm glad I'm not the sort of stuff
  They fill pin cushions with.

But most of all I'm glad, O Lord
  You did not make me Henry Ford.[4]

Yet Durant and Ford had much in common. The cardinal values that motivated both men were the risk-taking entrepreneurial capitalist's trinity of power, prestige, and profits. Both were what Alfred P. Sloan, Jr., called "personal types of industrialists; that is they injected their personalities, their 'genius,' so to speak, as a subjective factor into their operations without the discipline of management by method and objective facts. Their organizational methods, however, were at opposite poles, Mr. Ford being an extreme centralizer, Mr. Durant an extreme decentralizer. And they differed as to products and approach to the market." [5]

A minor irony of automotive history is that while the introspective Ford became a major figure in world history, the outgoing, urbane Durant ended up a provincial citizen of Flint, Michigan, where a few amateur historians, collectors, and raconteurs continue to exhibit interest in his importance to local history. Even in Flint, the local automotive museum is named for Alfred P. Sloan, Jr., and the local expressways for David D. Buick and Louis Chevrolet.

When Durant regained the presidency of General Motors on June 1, 1916, he took over a much stronger corporation than he had left to the bankers five years before. Storrow and Nash had paid off the General Motors loan in full and had put GM on a sound financial footing. The internal administration and product had been improved. The du Pont alliance eased the problem of obtaining working capital and assured the supply, at reasonable prices, of many commodities needed for the construction of automobiles. Chevrolet was a moneymaking addition to the General Motors manufacturing units. Strength was also added by the acquisition of the United Motors Corporation, a holding company owning the securities of five leading automobile accessory manufacturers that Durant had put together in the spring of 1916. With United Motors came Charles F. Kettering, the engineering genius, and Alfred P. Sloan, Jr. Recognizing the need to integrate and consolidate his impressive new empire, Durant reincorporated the General Motors Company, a New Jersey holding company, as the General Motors Corporation of Delaware, an operating company, on October 13, 1916.

Some of Durant's moves turned out to be brilliant. The Fisher Body Company was purchased in 1918. Then, recognizing that the automobile industry could not continue on a cash-on-delivery basis, Durant pioneered in time sales for expensive consumer goods with the creation of the General Motors Acceptance Corporation in 1919. Against everyone's advice he paid $56,000 for a faltering, one-man electric refrigerator company that serviced only forty-two customers (on the ground that refrigerators were related to automobiles because both were essentially cases containing motors). He named the company Frigidaire.

Durant lacked the judgment to discriminate among the many ideas about which he became enthusiastic. For every Buick there was a Cartercar; for every Frigidaire there was a Heany Lamp. Durant's idea of "playing it safe all along the line," backing every impulse in the hope that some would pan out, made him an inveterate expansionist who could survive only in flush times. His performance was brilliant when he concentrated his considerable energies upon building up a single company in an expanding market, as at Buick and Chevrolet. But his bents toward indiscriminate dispersal of his energies and one-man rule spelled disaster when times got tight and the profits from a few phenomenally successful bets began to dwindle.

For no apparent reason Durant added two new passenger cars to the General Motors line: the Sheridan and the Scripps-Booth. Both were losers. But even had they proved popular, they would merely have competed in the same general price range with Buick, Chevrolet, Oakland, and Oldsmobile. Durant never bothered to rationalize the various car lines he offered. Sloan objected: "Not only were we not competitive with Ford in the low-price field—where the big volume and substantial future growth lay—but in the middle, where we were concentrated with duplication, we did not know what we were trying to do except to sell cars which, in a sense, took volume from each other." As in 1910, by 1921 only Buick and Cadillac were making money for General Motors.[6]

Durant's enthusiasm for getting into the farm machinery business was more understandable. Impressed by the initial success of the Fordson tractor, he developed an obsession to "lick Henry Ford in the manufacture of tractors" and, while he was at it, to "lick the International Harvester Company in the manufacture of agricultural implements."

In 1917 Durant bought into the Samson Sieve-Grip Tractor Company of Stockton, California, which had invented a tractor called "the Iron Horse" that was guided by reins. He later added the Janesville Machine Company of Janesville, Wisconsin, and the Doylestown Agricultural Company of Doylestown, Pennsylvania, and formed the Samson Tractor Division of General Motors. In addition to "the Iron Horse," which was supposed to be "a man of all work" around the farm, a lighter Samson tractor was developed to compete with the Fordson. Plans for a nine-passenger farmer's car that would sell for only $700 never materialized because it became obvious that there was no way to build it at a profit. The Samson tractor and "the Iron Horse" were returned in droves by irate farmers who demanded their money back. The Samson Tractor Division fiasco cost General Motors over $42 million before it was liquidated in 1920.

Executives were frustrated by Durant's chaotic schedule, inability to recognize priorities, and increasing involvement in the stock market. Walter P. Chrysler was called to New York by Durant. "For several days in succession I waited at his office, but he was so busy he could not take the time to talk with me. It seemed to me he was trying to keep in communication with half the continent; eight or ten telephones were lined up on his desk. . . . 'Durant is buying' was a potent phrase in Wall Street then." [7] Alfred P. Sloan, Jr., recalled that executives lounged around the room watching Durant's barber, Jake, shave him "while our scheduled work was neglected." Sloan remembered twenty telephones and a switchboard in Durant's private office, and it seemed "as if he were always holding a telephone in his hand. . . . In the same minute he would buy in San Francisco, sell in Boston." At executive meetings "the ten or fifteen of us who gathered there would wait all day for the Chief. . . . old friends could not be denied, and so we had to wait. One caller after another would delay him. There would be urgent telephone calls. We scarcely felt like doing anything else until he rang the bell, so tempers soured."

As the stock market came to absorb his attention, Durant relied on cronies and made decisions "right out of his head." Sloan was aghast that a car model was tested on a cross-country trip by the same man who designed it and that Durant waxed enthusiastic over telegraphed reports the man dispatched "by conniving with hotel porters along his scheduled route while he rested nearer home." Sloan was even more aghast at Durant's casual attitude about the location and price of the new General Motors Building in Detroit, a

$20 million project that Durant later opposed as too costly. "He started at the corner of Cass Avenue, paced a certain distance west on West Grand Boulevard past the old Hyatt Building. . . . Then he stopped for no apparent reason, at some apartment houses on the other side of the building. He said that this was about all the ground we wanted, and turned to me and said, as well as I can remember, 'Alfred, will you go and buy these properties for us and Mr. Prentice will pay whatever you decide to pay for them.' " [8]

Charles W. Nash was the first key executive to leave General Motors. Following the Chevrolet take-over, Durant had urged Nash to stay on. But Nash, who had begun his career as a dollar-a-day trimmer at the Durant-Dort Carriage Company and had affection for Billy personally, knew that there could be no security in a corporation that Durant headed. As the *Detroit News* commented many years later, "One day, an associate of Durant's might have hundreds of thousands of dollars in Durant stock. The next day nothing." [9] Nash left with Storrow to form the Nash Motor Company from the faltering Thomas B. Jeffery Company in Kenosha, Wisconsin. The Nash Motor Company was one of the few independents to survive into the post–World War II period. It was merged with Hudson in 1954 to become the present American Motors Corporation, the industry leader in developing the compact car in the late 1950s.

An even greater loss to GM was Walter P. Chrysler, the GM vice-president in charge of operations as well as the president and general manager of Buick. By 1919 Buick was making about half the money that GM earned. But the corporation was spending money at a much faster rate than Chrysler at Buick could make it, and Durant's erratic decision making and arbitrary interference in Buick's operations made Chrysler's job impossible. Chrysler knew that they could never work together when Durant told him, "Walt, I believe in changing the policies just as often as my office door opens and closes." Without consulting Chrysler, Durant sold the lucrative

Detroit Buick branch house to one of his cronies. The last straw for Chrysler occurred when a telegram from Durant was read at a booster luncheon of the Flint Chamber of Commerce promising the city a $6 million frame plant that would cost more in five years than GM would pay for frames from other sources in ten. Chrysler told Sloan, who tried to talk him into staying: "No, I'm washed up. I just can't stand the way the thing is being run." [10]

Walter P. Chrysler has often been called the last great individual constructive force in the American automobile industry. He came out of a brief retirement in 1920 to rescue Willys-Overland from the brink of bankruptcy as its executive vice-president, then took over the reorganization of the Maxwell Motor Company, which was indebted to bankers for $26 million and on the verge of collapse in the post–World War I recession. In 1924 Maxwell introduced the stylish Chrysler Six, the first medium-priced car to use a high-compression engine, and Maxwell made profits of over $4 million that year. Walter P. Chrysler acquired Maxwell in 1925, discontinued the Maxwell line, and reorganized the company as the Chrysler Corporation. By 1928 Chrysler had made some $46 million in profits and held third place in the industry, after General Motors and Ford. Chrysler bought Dodge in July 1928 for $70 million plus the interest payments on Dodge bonds aggregating $56 million. The acquisition of Dodge doubled Chrysler's sales outlets and gave the corporation the plant capacity to bring out the Plymouth and compete in the popular-priced field.

Yet Walter P. Chrysler, unlike Henry Ford and William C. Durant, never saw the corporation that bore his name as an extension of his personal genius. "No matter how proud I feel because it bears the name of Chrysler," he wrote in 1937, "I never fool myself that I did all this. . . . Any great industrial corporation lives and grows only through the devoted services of many who pool their intelligence and energy in a common effort." [11]

Alfred P. Sloan, Jr., the automobile industry's first "gray man," was even more cognizant than Chrysler that the day of the colorful entrepreneurial capitalist was about over, and by 1920 he was on the verge of resigning from GM himself. "If General Motors were to capitalize its wonderful opportunity," Sloan reasoned, "it would have to be guided by an organization of intellects. A great industrial organization requires the best of many minds." His ideal executive was the security-oriented technician who, sensitive to evidence and the opinions of others, worked well as the member of an entrepreneurial team. In the General Motors that he envisioned, there was no place for the one-man rule of an inveterate gambler like Durant, who made decisions on the basis of "some intuitive flash of brilliance." "Eventually this master salesman's optimism, unchecked by facts, became downright disturbing to men who loved him, men whose fortunes he had increased many fold." Sloan asked rhetorically, "Should they blindly, mutely risk loss of those fortunes?"

Sloan took a vacation abroad to think things over in the summer of 1920. When he returned in August, he "sensed something unusual" and decided to "ride along awhile and see what happens." What Sloan "sensed" was that Durant's days at General Motors were numbered.[12]

Durant was then almost sixty, and he did not recognize that the business environment was changing rapidly in the automobile industry. An incurable optimist, he was also banking on an uninterrupted post–World War I boom in automobile sales. He was unprepared, as were Henry Ford and many others, for the sharp recession that accompanied conversion to a peacetime economy. General Motors was caught in the midst of an expansion program that could not have been more ill-timed. The working capital of the corporation had been dissipated. So an issue of $64 million in common stock was offered for underwriting. An English-Canadian banking syndicate picked up $36 million of the issue at $20 a share, but that still left $28 million to be disposed of in a declining market.

As automobile sales slackened, inventories piled up and profits shrank. To compound the situation, Durant's slipshod style of management had encouraged the operating divisions to continue to spend large amounts for new equipment and supplies. As a result, the stock issue that was originally intended for expansion quickly came to be essential to the survival of General Motors.

The expansion program initiated in 1918 was not entirely Durant's error. There is evidence that he urged caution on several occasions when others wanted to push ahead. The du Pont interests, with a view toward diversification and confident of a tremendous postwar market for automobiles, had invested heavily in General Motors. By 1919 they owned 28.7 percent of the GM common stock and, according to an agreement with Durant of December 21, 1917, had responsibility for the financial management of GM. Pierre S. du Pont, chairman of the corporation's board of directors, had supported the expansion program without objection. John J. Raskob, the du Pont treasurer, was chairman of the Finance Committee and was at least as responsible as Durant for enthusiastically promoting the expansion program. Durant and Raskob would later each blame the other for the sorry outcome. According to Sloan, "On the record, both Mr. Durant and Mr. Raskob were strong, optimistic expansionists. They seemed to disagree on occasion only on what to put the money into." [13]

Other large General Motors stockholders, concerned about what was happening, began to unload their holdings. Durant saw that this might collapse the price of General Motors stock, with the disastrous result that it might be impossible to dispose of the remaining $28 million of the new issue. He also wanted to protect the value of his personal holdings, which on paper were worth $105 million. Despite his attempt to snap up large blocks as they were offered for sale, the stock slid from $38.50 to under $30 a share before a syndicate headed by J. P. Morgan and Company agreed to sell the remaining $28 million of the new issue.

On July 15, 1920, the Morgan interests announced that the $28 million in stock had been disposed of. But Durant's troubles were just beginning. The bankers had forced him to agree to let them purchase as a bonus 200,000 additional shares at $10. News of that agreement quickly leaked out to the financial press. Then on July 27, 100,000 shares of General Motors stock were dumped on the market, driving the price down to $20.50. Durant later confided to friends that Edward R. Stettinius, a Morgan partner, was the person who had dumped this huge block of stock that broke the price.

Precisely what happened next remains unclear. Durant had entered into two separate agreements to maintain the price of the stock. One was with the Morgan interests. It bound them not to sell below $20 a share, and they did sell ultimately as low as $9. But Durant was also bound as president of General Motors and Chevrolet that neither of these companies, nor du Pont, nor J. P. Morgan would buy, sell, or borrow General Motors stock on their own accounts. He violated this agreement, at least in spirit, by forming another syndicate of a few close friends and engaging in personal market operations without informing the du Ponts or the House of Morgan.

Perhaps Durant did not think the Morgan interests were acting aggressively enough and saw no harm in helping things out on his own. However, when the bankers found out what Durant was up to, they felt no obligation to uphold their end of the bargain. The only objective of the bankers in the first place had been to prevent the price from deteriorating faster than the general market dropped, not to protect the paper fortunes of Durant and his friends. It seemed foolish to them to try to stabilize the price of the stock with two syndicates operating independently of one another. From the point of view of the Morgan interests, in fact, the main danger to the value of the stock was Durant's using it as collateral for his personal market operations. Durant, on the other hand, believed that he had been sold out by the bankers and that his personal market operations were necessary to protect General Motors, his friends, and himself.

An intriguing possibility, consistent with these motives, is that Durant engaged in personal market operations primarily with a view toward enhancing his power in General Motors vis-à-vis the du Ponts. An egocentric individualist, Durant did not like to share power with anyone. He had already rationalized that Raskob was responsible for the ill-timed expansion program and remembered the many wrangles he had had with Raskob over how to spend the money. Durant certainly did not treat all General Motors stockholders alike in his operations. As early as March 1920 he had John Lee Pratt divide the GM stockholders into three groups. Telegrams were sent out the same day urging group A to hang on to its GM stock because something great was about to happen, group B to buy all the additional GM stock it could afford, and group C to give Durant options on its GM holdings. From this perspective the bankers were right that Durant's second syndicate of friends worked at cross-purposes with the Morgan syndicate, and Durant might have done in the du Ponts had the bankers not gotten suspicious and refused to play his game.

As the stock continued to tumble, Durant bought frantically in a tragic attempt to salvage something. Operating heavily on margin, he supported the stock down to $12 a share before he admitted he was licked. Durant's cash resources were wiped out, and he owed over $20 million to twenty-one brokers and three banks.

The du Ponts, Raskob, and the House of Morgan became afraid that if Durant declared bankruptcy he might drag down with him the brokers, the banks, and General Motors. At a series of meetings in November 1920, they worked out an alternative. They would bail Durant out of the mess on the condition that he hand over to them the control of General Motors. The full extent of Durant's involvement was not suspected by Pierre S. du Pont until November 10. At lunch that day Durant dropped hints to the uncomprehending du Pont that the company and he personally were in the hands of the bankers and that he (Durant) would have to "play the game." But Durant remained evasive and misled du Pont about the true state of his affairs until the du Ponts and the Morgan interests forced him to review his accounts with them on November 18. In many instances the accounts could only be explained orally by Durant or his son-in-law, Dr. Edwin R. Campbell. Durant came out of the deal retaining about $3 million of General Motors stock plus a personal loan of $500,000 from Pierre S. du Pont, which to du Pont and the Morgan interests seemed generous. But Durant later claimed, "There were many things I had forgotten and so when I really cleaned up and protected everybody else, I had nothing left." [14]

Durant resigned as president of General Motors on November 30, 1920. "You knew he was grief-stricken, but no grief showed in his face. He was smiling pleasantly, as if it were a routine matter, when he told us he was resigning," remembered Sloan. The following day Durant cleaned out his desk. When he was leaving the building, he turned to remark: "Well, May first is usually the national moving day, but we seem to have turned it into December first." [15]

The du Ponts gained some 2.5 million shares of General Motors stock, and Pierre S. du Pont reluctantly succeeded Durant as interim president. The job was eventually to go to Alfred P. Sloan, Jr., who became the new executive vice-president. In addition to coughing up $27 million to settle Durant's affairs, the House of Morgan gave General Motors an $80 million loan. To allay fears in Flint about Durant's resignation and the "take-over" of General Motors by eastern bankers, the new management built a $300,000 hotel in Flint and named it the Hotel Durant—the impersonal corporation's final tribute to a founder who had outlived his usefulness to the firm.

The Durant name still had magic. The Goodrich Tire & Rubber Company invited Durant to set himself up in a modest office in their building in New York City. After a brief holiday at White Sulphur Springs, Durant contacted sixty-seven friends, asking them to back a new automobile company that would bear his name. Within forty-eight hours he had raised $7 million, $2 million more than he needed. Durant Motors, Inc. came into being on January 21, 1921.

The enterprise started under propitious conditions. Looking for new business, many accessories and parts manufacturers welcomed the entry of another independent automobile manufacturer. They were willing to extend Durant credit and give him especially low prices to get him started again. Durant's public image was excellent. He was looked upon as an underdog, a self-made man who had been crucified by the du Ponts and the Wall Street bankers. The first model produced, the Durant Four, was an exceptional value at $850—as Durant advertised it, "a real good car."

Durant Motors, Inc. grew by leaps and bounds. Facilities were built in Flint and Lansing, and in Oakland, California. The Sheridan plant in Muncie, Indiana, was bought to produce the Durant Six. The bankrupt Locomobile Company of Bridgeport, Connecticut, was purchased to add a luxury car with a long-standing, prestigious reputation to the Durant line. With the Willys Corporation in receivership, Chrysler and Studebaker were outbid at $5.25 million to acquire the new Willys plant at Elizabeth, New Jersey, the most modern automobile factory in the world, plus the Willys designs for a medium-priced car that became the "Flint." Then, on February 15, 1922, Durant announced that he would bring out the "Star," which at a price of $348 would compete with the Ford Model T. Aware of Ford's blatant anti-Semitism, Durant thought the Star car would have a special appeal to Jewish buyers. Some 60,000 people flocked to see the Star at its first showing in New York City, and by January 1, 1923, Durant had accepted cash deposits on orders for 231,000 Star cars, a full year's production. The Durant Motors Acceptance Corporation was formed to finance time sales and to help dealers store cars over the winter for spring delivery.

Shortly after the organization of Durant Motors, Durant hit upon a novel scheme to finance its expansion. The Liberty Loans of World War I had demonstrated for the first time that large blocks of securities could be marketed directly to small investors. While at General Motors, as a sideline, Durant had organized the Durant Corporation as a device for selling on the installment plan the stock of General Motors, the Fisher Body Company, the United States Cast Iron Pipe Company, and other firms. After his bitter experience at General Motors, Durant was thoroughly convinced that the safety of management depended upon the widest possible dispersal of stock among small investors. So he revitalized the Durant Corporation to raise large amounts of money for Durant Motors through popular subscription.

The stock of Durant Motors was listed on the New York Curb Exchange. Since there was very little stock outstanding, the price could easily be maintained at between $15 and $20 a share. Durant Corporation salesmen offered limited numbers of shares to individuals at four to six points below the Curb quotation. The catches were that the stock had to be purchased on the installment plan and that, even after it was paid for, the stock was escrowed so that it could not be sold by its owner for two years. The public bought up everything that the Durant Corporation offered. With 146,000 shareholders by January 1, 1923, Durant Motors had more stockholders than any American company except American Telephone & Telegraph, a much larger enterprise.

To raise still more money, Durant formed the Liberty National Bank. He called it "the most democratic bank in the United States." Its officers and board of directors worked without salary. Anyone could purchase stock in it, but only the directors were allowed to own more than 1 of its 300,000 shares, which could be purchased on the installment plan.

Feeling his oats again, Durant tried to achieve another take-over of General Motors. As he had done earlier with Chevrolet stock, he hatched a plan to trade Durant Motors stock for General Motors stock, which was then priced below Durant. However, General Motors had increased its common stock to some 43 million shares, and he soon realized that the task was insurmountable.

Despite its promising start, Durant Motors never amounted to much. In its best years it was unable to capture more than a fifth of the market for new cars. Henry Ford effectively crushed the threat of competition from the Star car by unexpectedly lowering his prices for the Model T. The Flint and the Durant Six never caught the fancy of the buying public, and the Locomobile could not regain its lost luster. The Durant Four was soon outmoded by competing models. Beyond these considerations, by the mid-1920s the market for new cars was rapidly approaching the saturation point. In 1927, replacement sales would for the first time exceed sales to initial owners and multiple-car sales combined. The average life of a passenger car was then pegged by the industry at seven years.

A well-managed firm might have pulled through. However, Durant failed in recruiting topflight managerial talent. Few of his more capable associates at General Motors had left with him. They knew that security with Durant was a roller coaster ride that was apt to end in a crash. And in the automobile industry the word had gotten around that he was difficult to work for. That put the burden of managing Durant Motors squarely on Durant's shoulders. He might have succeeded if he had applied his energies fully to the task. But he began to see that there was bigger game to be shot on Wall Street, and he soon started to treat Durant Motors as a sideline.

After World War I the dominating power that the eastern investment bankers historically had wielded on Wall Street increasingly came to be shared with a new group of self-made millionaires who came mainly from the Middle West. Less cautious and conservative than their predecessors, these new speculators became the prime movers in the runaway bull market of the late 1920s. By far the most important figure among them was Durant, who after 1924 was widely referred to by the press as "the leading bull." [16]

The "bull consortium" that Durant led was estimated at various times to include between twenty and thirty millionaire investors, who were known as "Durant's prosperity boys." It was said that Durant himself had $1.2 billion in the market by 1928 and that he directly controlled about $4 billion in investments. He had accounts with at least fifteen brokers, and his commission fees to brokers were rumored to run as high as $6 million a year. Telephone bills of $20,000 a week were supposedly not uncommon. The financial press regularly reported the multi-million-dollar killings he made in individual pools. Through an investment trust formed in 1924 and administered by the Liberty National Bank, he sold bonds secured by the stock of ten corporations to the public. He also sold the securities of the Goldman Sachs Trading Corporation to the public after the Goldman Sachs insiders quit buying their stock themselves in March 1929.

The insiders most closely associated with Durant's stock market activities were an odd lot. The seven Fisher brothers were probably the least colorful members of this unholy alliance of unkindred spirits. Sons of an Ohio blacksmith, the Fishers had stuck together and accumulated fortunes totaling $200 million in the automobile industry.

Arnold W. Cutten, quickly dubbed "the novice with a bag of tricks," was a reserved, lone-wolf Canadian who had worked his way up from salesclerk to the most successful commodities trader in the Chicago grain pits. He managed this by carefully scrutinizing weather maps, the behavior of a plant louse called the grain aphis in endless bottles of wheat, and the peculiar mannerisms of his fellow traders. Cutten came to Wall Street a multimillionaire in the early twenties, after the Federal government instituted closer supervision of grain trading that would have forced him to open his trading records for inspection.

Jesse L. Livermore, a steel-nerved, chain-smoking, New England farm boy, rose from being a small-time gambler in the "bucket shops"—the market equivalent of bookie joints—to a power on the Street after a psychic premonition led him to sell Union Pacific heavily short just before the 1906 San Francisco earthquake. Ten-strikes made by selling short again in anticipation of the panic of 1907 and in the recession after World War I earned Livermore the title "king of the bears." A strange bedfellow for the "bull consortium," Livermore was widely feared and despised as a vulture who grew fat on national calamities. He was a mastermind equally adept at reading the hidden nuances of a ticker tape and the secrets of a man's inner soul.

A latecomer to the inner circle of speculators was Michael J. Meehan, a cherubic, redheaded, Irish specialist in stocks who was superstitious about wearing green ties at the exchange. His favorite saying was, "There are no pockets in shrouds." Meehan had progressed from managing a theatrical ticket agency to heading an important brokerage business that pioneered in putting offices on Atlantic steamers for the convenience of customers. He was the leading promoter of RCA, the number one glamour stock of the decade. His stock-selling career was to end up in a swank asylum, where he was one of the few inmates trusted to keep his own matches.

The stocks bulled up to new heights by the Durant group included United States Cast Iron Pipe, Studebaker, International Nickel, American Smelters, and Baldwin Locomotive. The most impressive operation of the "bull consortium" involved Radio (RCA). Although only 400,000 shares of Radio were officially available, there were days when 500,000 shares were traded, and in March 1928 Radio was forced into a technical corner, jumping its price 61 points in four days. Radio had never paid a cent in dividends and had been overpriced at $85. Yet the stock was bulled to $420 a share in 1928 and, on a split, to $570 in 1929. When the insiders began taking profits, Radio dropped some 300 points within a few weeks.

While he was involved in bulling up RCA, Durant announced on August 27, 1928, that he was offering a $25,000 prize "for the best and most practicable plan to make the 18th Amendment effective," to be awarded and paid December 25. In addition, he offered a $5,000 prize for the best and most practicable plan submitted by a high school student. A committee of fifteen people "of national prominence and unquestioned integrity" was chosen to judge the contest. The best essays were published, along with an introduction by Durant, in early 1929 as a book titled *Law Observance: Shall the People of the United States Uphold the Constitution?* (New York: Durant Award Office, 1929).

Old friends wondered why Durant became publicly involved in the prohibition movement at this late date, when most other businessmen were getting off the prohibition bandwagon. It was true that Durant had never been fond of saloons or alcohol. However, as he himself said, he was "no fanatical dry," and it was well known that he enjoyed an occasional weak scotch or glass of champagne. There seemed to be no good reason why Durant so belatedly started to preach, in his introduction to *Law Observance*, that the bootlegger was "our country's greatest enemy" and that "for the widespread disobedience to the liquor law as embodied in the Constitution the business leaders of the country are very largely responsible."

Jacob H. Newmark, the advertising manager at Durant Motors, guessed later that the main motive for the contest might have been publicity. It is more probable that Durant wanted to divert public attention away from the market in order to lay a solid foundation from which to launch an attack against the Federal Reserve Board, whose restrictive financial policies had irked him since 1919. The list of judges for the contest included Jane Addams, a nationally prominent social worker and reformer; U.S. Senator William E. Borah, a long-standing foe of the trusts and special business interests; Bruce Barton, the author of a best-selling biography that portrayed Jesus Christ as a supersalesman; Major General James G. Harbord, the president of RCA; William G. McAdoo, secretary of the Treasury during the Wilson administration; and U.S. Senator

Carter Glass, sponsor of the legislation that had established the Federal Reserve Board.

During the last six months of 1928 Durant, like many other speculators, became increasingly worried that Calvin Coolidge's successor in the White House might tend to curb the runaway bull market through a tighter monetary policy. Brokers steadily became more cautious and by early 1929 had raised margin requirements to about 50 percent. After the inauguration of Herbert Hoover in March, substance was given to the speculators' fears when the Federal Reserve Board met behind closed doors for almost a month. The stock market went into a minor, but sharp, decline.

On April 3, 1929, Durant took an evening train down to Washington, D.C., to discuss some urgent business with the new president of the United States. He went alone and rode in taxicabs to and from the train to avoid arousing suspicions that might further disrupt the market, arriving at the White House at ten o'clock that night. Despite the late hour, Hoover saw him. The president was told that more stringent monetary controls could have disastrous consequences for the nation as well as for the stock market. Durant asked Hoover to issue a strong statement calling off the Federal Reserve Board and made thinly veiled threats that, unless this were done, he and his associates might find it necessary to unload some $4 billion worth of stock on the market. Herbert Hoover remained noncommittal. Perhaps the reason was that Hoover, before his inauguration, had been informed by Mabel W. Willebrandt that Durant was allied with the president's opposition within the Republican party in an attempt to embarrass him over the Federal Reserve Board issue.[17]

News of the meeting leaked to the press, but it was given only minor attention. Durant also took the Federal Reserve Board to task as speaker at a businessmen's luncheon in New York City. But that, too, stirred little comment. Then, in a radio broadcast over WABC on April 14, he called upon the Federal Reserve Board to stop curbing speculation through restrictions on brokers' loans and to "keep its hands off business."

The "prosperity boys" divested themselves of their huge holdings during May and June. The *New York Times* reported on June 2 that, according to Wall Street gossip, Durant had "liquidated large portions of his holdings at substantial losses in the last few weeks. His present losses are said to reach many millions. . . . Rumors of selling by Durant have hung over the market like a pall."

Two United States senators assailed Durant's tactics. James Couzens, who had become a senator from Michigan, said that "when men like Durant, who have made their great fortunes by speculative methods, come out and find fault with whatever measures the Federal Reserve banks may take to suppress the orgy of speculation, it is perfectly obvious that he is doing it for speculative purposes." Senator Carter Glass of Virginia replied, "Yes, and he [Durant] has lured more innocent amateur gamblers into the market than any other forty individuals in the United States." [18]

Durant sailed for Europe on April 18. He did not return to the United States until June 15. On Friday, May 31, he delivered an address at a luncheon of the American Club in Paris, titled "American Prosperity and the Federal Reserve Board." Durant told the audience that American prosperity during recent decades had been based upon three things: the dynamic growth of the automobile industry, the high wages paid to American labor, and the willingness of American investors to risk capital in large amounts. The Federal Reserve Board, he warned, threatened American prosperity because its policies were undermining the incentive of investors to take risks.

Analysis by others in hindsight would, of course, spell out the threats to American prosperity differently. The house of cards that had been built in the stock market rested on an economic foundation riddled with weaknesses. Contrary to Durant's sentiments, within a decade it was generally agreed that governmental supervision of trading on the stock exchanges during the 1920s had been inadequate and that more stringent monetary controls should have been applied much earlier to curb the boom. It also came to be recognized that weak banking and corporate structures and international monetary problems contributed to bringing about the crash. Most important, it became textbook knowledge among economic historians that the collapse of the stock market in October 1929 was merely a symptom of more fundamental problems faced by the American economy in the late 1920s.

Durant isolated the right variables in his Paris speech, but his interpretation was faulty. Although real wages rose to a new high during the twenties, they did not rise fast enough to keep pace with a mushrooming technology that vastly increased the output of consumer goods per man-hour of labor. And income distribution was inequitable: the top 5 percent of the population in income received approximately one-third of all personal income in 1929. The great extension of consumer credit that the twenties witnessed provided no satisfactory long-term answer to the resulting problem of market saturation. A strong labor movement during the decade might have helped, but one never developed, in part because employers, still wedded to many of the beliefs and values of a production-oriented economy, did everything possible to discourage unionization. Both Durant Motors and General Motors, for example, like the Ford Motor Company, employed labor spies to ferret out union organizers and radical agitators.

Nor was Durant correct that it was crucial to prosperity to maintain the incentive of investors and that a loose monetary policy could do this. During the twenties, corporate profits and dividends had risen between eight and nine times faster than real wages. The trouble was that the resulting excessive savings by corporations and individuals in the upper-income brackets could not find sufficient productive outlets. Once markets began to become saturated, there was no incentive to invest money in plant expansion and new equipment. The money ended up instead in diversified stock portfolios, where it accumulated paper profits. Lacking borrowers, the banks put their money in the same place. It was this large volume of capital that could not find a productive use that skyrocketed stock prices from reasonable bets on the future into fantastic gambles on the hereafter.

For all the wrong reasons, then, the Durant group reached its decision to unload in the spring of 1929. The impact of this decision on the subsequent crash in October should not be underestimated. While even $4 billion was not an appreciable sum compared with the total amount of money Americans had plunged into securities by 1929, once the word got around that the "bull consortium" had abandoned the pasture, the impact on other large investors was tremendous. Long before this, it had been apparent that Durant's personal vicissitudes were reflected in the market. When news reached the Street in January 1926, for example, that Durant had been injured in a train wreck, the prices of several key stocks declined sharply, only to rally again once Durant started putting in buy orders from his hospital bed. Several European vacations had to be postponed and buying campaigns initiated by Durant to reverse drops in the market caused by rumors that he was selling out and going abroad.

By October 1929 the market was being held up by the many small investors. And the bulls had done such a good job of killing off the perennial bears in the market during the late twenties that, when prices started to tumble, there were few bears left around to cushion the fall through buy orders to cover their short lines. Thus the worst financial disaster in American history became inevitable.

Shortly after the collapse of the market on Tuesday, October 29, 1929, Earl Sparling, a financial writer, visited Durant to get his opinion on what it meant to have some $40 billion in security values wiped out overnight. Durant did some quick calculations on a pad of paper, smiled, and announced that if the loss were translated into a stack of silver dollars it would reach 100,000 miles into the sky.

Like many other insiders who had managed to unload before the initial disaster struck, Durant assumed that the worst was over. He plunged back into the market to pick up stocks at what he thought were bargain prices, only to find that the market kept deteriorating. His brokers sold him out in 1930.

Durant scraped together his remaining resources and plowed them into Durant Motors. Conceiving that the American market was ripe for a small car with low initial and maintenance costs, he started to manufacture the French "Mathis" in New Jersey. Ultimately, the Volkswagen was to prove him right, but at the outset of the Great Depression not even Billy Durant could revitalize the corpse that Durant Motors had become. It was liquidated in 1933.

A short time after Durant declared bankruptcy in 1936, some reporters, acting on an anonymous tip, found him washing dishes in a five-cent hamburger joint attached to a supermarket that had recently been opened in an old Durant Motors salesroom at Asbury Park, New Jersey. Looking at least two decades younger than his seventy-five years, Billy obligingly posed for pictures. It was a publicity stunt. Durant owned both the supermarket and the lunch counter. His nephew confided to the reporters: "Mr. Durant is just as enthusiastic over building up the Food Market as he ever was over automobiles. In fact he no longer can bear the thought of an automobile." [19]

Disgusted with Hoover's failures to curb the Federal Reserve Board and enforce the Eighteenth Amendment, Durant supported Franklin Delano Roosevelt in 1932. He lived to regret this move. In March 1939 Secretary of Agriculture Henry A. Wallace charged Durant and his wife, along with several associates, with violating the fraud provisions of the Commodity Exchange Act in grain trading. The government's case was so flimsy that the charge was dropped in May. To Durant it seemed "incredible that any department of the New Deal government would lend itself to any action that would have for its purpose the destruction of a business honestly conducted, or the reputation of the individuals engaged therein." [20]

Durant's interest in taking another flier never failed. Looking forward to the post–World War II boom, in late 1943 Durant wrote to W. H. Washer, a Flint inventor: "When you have developed anything novel that appeals to you, don't be afraid to give 'Uncle Bill' an opportunity of joining the workers' ranks." At the war's end, Durant told the *Flint Journal*, in a formal statement through his secretary: "The consumer market needs everything at home and abroad. The demand is so great there virtually is no competition and no sales resistance." He predicted a three- to seven-year boom.[21]

A eulogy in the *Detroit Free Press* claimed: "There was nothing of the ruthless pirate in Durant for all of his financial manipulations. Despite his fortunes and his power he was always a simple, human person, with a consciousness of the problems of the little fellow. . . . W. C. Durant typified the courage of American business, of free enterprise and initiative. If all of his principles are no longer acceptable, there are elements in his character that America badly needs today." Billy Durant himself is reported to have declared: "Money? What is money? It is only loaned to a man. He comes into the world with nothing and he leaves with nothing." To the end, Durant insisted that he had gone broke trying to protect his friends, that his fondest hope was to repay his creditors in full, and that he had never sold America short. The myth persists that Billy Durant held "an attitude not uncommon among men of big money—he always tried to protect the people who invested with him, even if this protection would break him. Finally it did. And when at last he was unable to save his investors, he himself plunged from millionaire to bankruptcy." [22]

Yet the legend falls a good deal short of the truth. "Folklore has it that Durant died broke. He didn't. While by no means one of the wealthiest Americans, he was living comfortably, attended by three maids, on New York's fashionable Gramercy Park when visited by a *Newsweek* reporter a year before he died in March 1947." One reason that no monuments have been dedicated to Billy Durant's memory even in his home town of Flint is that "a lot of Flint people lost their savings in his last automotive venture, Durant Motors." [23] Neither Durant's stock market operations nor his record as an automobile manufacturer reveal "a consciousness of the problems of the little fellow." Any illusions about the social and economic outcomes of "the courage of American business, of free enterprise, and initiative" that Durant typified should have been dispelled by the stock market crash of 1929 and the Great Depression of the 1930s. Durant's main brainchild, General Motors, has come to symbolize much that is wrong with contemporary American institutions and values, and it is difficult to see what "elements in his character . . . America badly needs today." [24]

6 THE AUTOMOBILE CULTURE: PROSPECTS AND PROBLEMS

With his characteristic flair for understating the spectacular, President Warren G. Harding said in his April 12, 1921, message to Congress that "the motorcar has become an indispensable instrument in our political, social, and industrial life." An anonymous resident of Muncie, Indiana, was more accurate when he exclaimed to the Lynds, "Why on earth do you need to study what's changing this country? I can tell you what's happening in just four letters: A-U-T-O!" A Middletown Bible class teacher was told by her class that the only animal God created that man could get along without was the horse. "Ten or twelve years ago a new horse fountain was installed at the Courthouse square; now it remains dry during most of the blazing heat of a Mid-Western summer, and no one cares," wrote the Lynds in 1929. "The 'horse culture' of Middletown has almost disappeared. Nor was the horse culture in all the years of its undisputed sway ever as pervasive a part of the life of Middletown as is the cluster of habits that have grown up overnight around the automobile." [1]

During the 1920s automobility became the backbone of a new consumer-goods-oriented society and economy that has persisted into the present. By the mid-1920s automobile manufacturing ranked first in value of product and third in value of exports among American industries. In 1926 United States motor vehicle factory sales had a wholesale value of over $3 billion and American motorists spent over $10 billion that year in operating expenses to travel some 141 billion miles. The automobile industry was the lifeblood of the petroleum industry, one of the chief customers of the steel industry, and the biggest consumer of many other industrial products, including plate glass, rubber, and lacquers. The technologies of these ancillary industries, particularly steel and petroleum, were revolutionized by the new demands of motorcar manufacturing. The construction of streets and highways was the second largest item of governmental expenditure during the 1920s. The motorcar was responsible for a suburban real estate boom and for the rise of many new small businesses, such as service stations and tourist accommodations. In 1929, the last year of the automobility induced boom, the 26.7 million motor vehicles registered in the United States (one for every 4.5 persons) traveled an estimated 198 billion miles, and in that year alone government spent $2.237 billion on roads and collected $849 million in special motor vehicle taxes. The eminent social and economic historian Thomas C. Cochran noted the central role of automobility and concluded: "No one has or perhaps can reliably estimate the vast size of capital invested in reshaping society to fit the automobile. Such a figure would have to include expenditures for consolidated schools, suburban and country homes, and changes in business location as well as the more direct investments mentioned above. This total capital investment was probably the major factor in the boom of the 1920s, and hence in the glorification of American business." [2]

The automobile culture became truly national in the 1920s as significant early regional differences in automobility lessened. California led the nation in 1929 as it had in 1910 in ratio of population to motor vehicle registrations. It remained true as well that the leading regions in motor vehicles per capita were still the Pacific and West North Central states and that the South continued to lag behind the rest of the country in adopting the automobile. But the gap among the various regions of the United States had closed appreciably by 1920. During the decade 1910–1920 automobile registrations per capita increased more rapidly in the Mountain states and in the South, the early laggards in adopting the automobile, than in the East North Central, Middle Atlantic, and New England states. Although the agricultural states of the trans-Mississippi West continued to be the best market for new cars, and

California remained known in the industry as "a bottomless pit" for automobile sales, there was evidence that regional differences in the diffusion of the motorcar were becoming less significant. With a United States average of 10.1 persons for every motor vehicle in 1921, California ranked first with a ratio of 5.2:1 and Mississippi last with 27.5:1. By 1929 the United States average was 4.5:1. California still led the states with 2.3:1, and Alabama ranked last with 9:1. Probably the range of variation would be less among the states if one adequately adjusted for such crucial demographic variables as family size, age, and sex distribution.[3]

Another indication that the automobile culture had become national by 1920 was that automobile ownership was beginning to approximate the distribution of population along a rural-urban dimension. By 1924 the 53.1 percent of the population that lived on farms and in cities and towns under 5,000 population owned 50.3 percent of the motor vehicles; the 21 percent in cities between 5,000 and 100,000 population owned 28.2 percent; and the 25.9 percent in cities over 100,000 population owned 21.5 percent. A survey of car ownership among over 4.1 million American families conducted in 1927 by the General Federation of Women's Clubs showed only slight differences in the percentage of families owning automobiles in cities of various sizes. The range was from a low of 54 percent of families owning cars in cities of 100,000 population and over, to a progressively increasing percentage as cities got smaller, which peaked at 60.5 percent for towns under 1,000 population. The survey showed that 55.7 percent of the 27.5 million families in the United States in 1927 owned automobiles and that 2.7 million of these families (18 percent of those owning automobiles) owned two or more cars.[4]

The only thing that prevented the American automobile culture of the 1920s from being universally shared was the inequitable income distribution of Coolidge prosperity. It seems significant, although to my knowledge it has never before been stressed, that almost half of American families still did not own a car in 1927, the year when the market for new cars became saturated and the replacement demand for cars for the first time exceeded the demand from initial purchasers and multiple-car owners combined. *Motor* calculated in 1921 that ownership of a $600 automobile necessitated an annual income of at least $2,800 if one lived in a city and at least $1,936 if one lived in the country. In 1924 the National Automobile Chamber of Commerce (NACC) estimated that "the entire field of those receiving under $1,500 [in income] yearly is still unsupplied with motor transportation." The NACC thought that "the growth in the motor vehicle market depends on the ability of the lower income brackets to purchase *used cars*, not necessarily new ones" and that industry policy ought to be "pouring [new cars] in at the top, with the used cars being traded in and going to a secondary market." [5]

The market for automobiles among the lower-income brackets by 1924 was thus conceived by the industry's main trade association primarily as a dumping ground to solve what was known as "the used car problem." From the beginnings of the industry, most automobile manufacturers and dealers had encouraged owners to trade up to higher-priced models or to keep up with technological improvements and changing fashions by replacing their cars long before they were ready for the junk heap. Owners in turn expected a generous trade-in allowance. The problem was that the depreciation was great because used car prices were fixed at the maximal amounts that new, less affluent classes of purchasers could afford to pay. As early as 1906 *Motor World* observed that "the car that sold for $2,000 when new will seldom bring much more than half that price when a year old and at the end of its second year this will practically be halved again despite the fact that as a well-built piece of machinery it may have several years of efficient life before it." The automobile dealer was therefore increasingly faced with having to sell several used cars at a loss in order to make one new car sale. By the mid-1920s, when the market for cars was becoming saturated, most dealers were selling more used cars than new models. Used car prices had been standardized as early as 1914 by the "Used Car Central Market Report," published by the Chicago Automobile Trade Association, which was the forerunner of the now familiar dealers' "Blue Book." By the early 1920s the public had been educated "that they must charge off depreciation to transportation and not expect too much for their old cars." But the trade-in remained a losing proposition until the Ford Motor Company in 1925 and General Motors in 1928 inaugurated plans to help their dealers dispose of used cars at a slight profit.[6]

Although even used cars that brought a mere $10 to $25 profit to the automobile dealer were beyond the reach of almost half of all American families in 1927, still other households operating on marginal incomes skirted insolvency and sacrificed essentials for personal automobility. *Motor* noted that only 357,598 Americans in 1914 earned enough money to pay federal income taxes, but 1,287,784 Americans owned motorcars. As early as 1907 *Horseless Age* had expressed concern that "extravagance is reckless and something must be done before utter ruin follows in the wake of folly. . . . Many owners of houses worth from $5,000 to $15,000, which they have acquired after years of toil, are mortgaging them in order to buy automobiles." The Lynds found in 1929 that many working-class families in Middletown were mortgaging homes to buy cars, that "a working man earning $35.00 a week frequently plans to use one week's pay each month as payment for his car," and that "the automobile has apparently unsettled the habit of careful saving for some families." "We'd rather do without clothes than give up the car," a working-class mother of nine told the Lynds. "I'll go without food before I'll see us give up the car," said another working-class wife emphatically. "Meanwhile," observed the Lynds, "advertisements pound away at Middletown people with the tempting advice to spend money for automobiles for the sake of their homes and families." One such automobile advertisement urged Middletowners: "Hit the trail to better times!" [7]

Advertising undoubtedly played an important role in booming automobile sales beyond the bounds of sanity in the 1920s. The automobile industry during the decade became "one of the heaviest users of magazine space as well as of newspaper space and of other types of mediums. . . . the expansion in the advertising of passenger cars and accessories, parts and supplies in 1923 being particularly noteworthy." Expenditures for automobile advertising in magazines alone climbed from $3.5 million in 1921 to $6.2 million in 1923 and to $9.269 million in 1927.[8]

Automobile advertisements incredibly managed to make irresistible to an increasing number of American families in the 1920s a combination of time payments on the family car, a mortgaged home on the outskirts of town, and the inevitable traffic jam that accompanied the Sunday afternoon drive. As the utilitarian virtues of the product came to be taken for granted by the consumer, automobile advertisements gave more emphasis to making the consumer style conscious and to psychological inducements to buy cars. Especially potent and pervasive themes remained the fusing of rural and urban advantages and family togetherness. The first played on deep internalization of the agrarian myth among Americans. As *Automobile* explained, "Holding the family together is with many families one of the strongest arguments that can be advanced in these days when the divorce mill is grinding overtime. . . . It is an argument that has sold thousands of cars and will continue to sell tens of thousands more, even if salesmen never mention it. Any force that makes stronger the family ties is bound to be a potent force; it is bound to be an enduring force. With the middle classes it is a very strong force." [9]

Paying for mass personal automobility presented problems. By 1910, conservative country bankers were beginning to complain about the growing tendency of farmers to withdraw their savings to purchase motorcars. "Who made the banks dictators?" responded *Motor Age.* "If bank presidents and cashiers are to criticize every so-called luxury or pleasure that to some extent depletes their deposits, it would perhaps be best for Congress to make them guardians of the public funds and permit them, as some do at present, to invest their deposits in most questionable enterprises." *Motor World* was also incensed in 1910 that the big bond houses were refusing to bid on municipal bonds of cities in the Middle West that had "too many automobiles in proportion to population." The New York bond house of Spencer Trask & Company explained in a bulletin, however, that "our people, never of a particularly economical disposition, have been carried away by the automobile craze, and thousands are running cars who cannot afford to do so without mortgaging property, while thousands of others are now investing in motors who formerly invested in bonds. It is calculated that upward of $300,000,000 will be absorbed by the automobile industry this year [1910], which represents the interest on about two-thirds of our entire prospective crops of the present year. This is a phase in our political economy which deserves more consideration than is usually given it." [10]

The early so-called "mortgage on the farm to buy a car scare" was most effectively countered by Benjamin Briscoe. He sent out a questionnaire to some 24,000 bankers across the country and received 4,830 replies. The results showed that, of the total 198,216 motorcars in the bankers' towns, mortgages had been placed to buy only 1,254 cars and money borrowed without mortgage to buy another 7,475. What the trade journals' analyses of these data underplayed, however, was that the market for new cars in 1910 was still far from being saturated among people who could well afford personal automobility. *Horseless Age* estimated, for example, that although only about 400,000 automobiles had been produced up to that time, almost a million American families had incomes above $3,000 a year.[11] With the coming of the mass-produced car in the next decade, this market would become saturated, the industry would begin to encourage less affluent classes of purchasers to become automobile owners through the extension of consumer installment credit, and the worst fears of the conservative bankers would come to be realized.

The Morris Plan banks began financing time sales of automobiles in 1910. In 1911 the Studebaker Corporation announced that it would accept notes endorsed by its dealers on the purchases of EMF and Flanders cars. Walter E. Flanders, the Studebaker general manager, explained, "We have in view the future rather than the immediate present. . . . We have considered the advent of the credit in this business as inevitable and our move is but the consummation of a plan long since laid." [12] By 1912, commercial vehicles were commonly sold on time, and a few large automobile dealers had inaugurated their own plans for the installment selling of passenger cars.

The manufacturers of moderately priced cars, under pressure from their dealers, by 1915 came to see installment selling as an alternative to Henry Ford's strategy of progressively lowering the price of the Model T. On November 8, 1915, the Guaranty Securities Company was formed in Toledo, Ohio, with John N. Willys and Alfred P. Sloan, Jr., among its directors, to finance time sales of Overland and Willys-Knight cars. Reorganized as the Guaranty Securities Corporation of New York City, by April 1, 1916, the company was financing time sales of twenty-one makes of car, including all General Motors lines, Dodge, Ford, Hudson, Maxwell, REO, and Studebaker. General Motors, as noted, was the first automobile manufacturer directly to finance time sales of its products with the creation of the General Motors Acceptance Corporation on March 15, 1919. By the spring of 1921, over 110 automobile finance corporations were in existence, and about 50 percent of all automobiles were being sold on some form of deferred payment system.

Bankers continued to oppose the installment selling of automobiles. At a meeting of the Chicago Central Automobile Credit Association on March 20, 1922, for example, the principal speaker focused on the "widespread conviction on the part of the bankers that the financing of automobile purchases was a more or less hazardous business and that furthermore the operation of the financing companies had a tendency to encourage extravagance and was contrary to the thrift ideas which the bankers were so anxious to establish in the minds of the public." Ironically, Henry Ford, who generally had little respect for bankers, agreed with them on this point. He advised the Wisconsin Bankers' Association at its 1915 annual convention to adopt the slogan, "Get Cash, Pay Cash." It was brought out that 90 percent of a $70 million dollar investment in motorcars in Wisconsin represented money withdrawn from savings, money borrowed, or notes purchased. "It has always seemed to me that this putting off the day of payment for anything but permanent improvements was a fundamental mistake," said Ford. "The Ford Motor Company is not interested in promulgating any plan which extends credits for motorcars or for anything else." Ransom E. Olds felt the same way. Upon his resignation as president in 1923 to become chairman of the REO Motor Car Company board of directors, Olds assailed the installment selling plan adopted by other automobile manufacturers. "I believe that the plan is dangerous and a menace to the business," said Olds. "I further believe that eventually this plan will prove to be bad for this country. The automobile industry has become of such tremendous importance and such gigantic proportions, that anything that affects it affects the country as a whole." [13]

Although some expensive items, such as pianos and sewing machines, had been sold on time before 1920, it was time sales of automobiles that set the precedent during the twenties for a great extension of consumer installment credit. By 1926 time sales accounted for about three-fourths of all automobile sales. And as the market for automobiles approached saturation after 1925, the finance companies, fearing they had overextended credit for automobile purchases and wishing to diversify their risks, played an active role in encouraging installment purchases of many other types of merchandise. The Hoover Committee on Recent Economic Changes reported in 1929 that, "simultaneously with the advance in the use of the automobile there has been a marked advance in the purchase of many commodities that a decade ago would have been described as luxury goods, but which have since entered so universally into the average budget as no longer to be regarded as such." A 1926 survey made by the Eberle and Riggleman Economic Service of Los Angeles showed that the automobile installment commitments of California car buyers averaged 18 percent of monthly income. Walter Engard, a Warren, Ohio, automobile dealer, gave a typical simple-minded assessment of how time sales supposedly benefitted America's society and economy. "Higher standards of living are built up through the millions of individual extravagances," wrote Engard in *Motor*. "To keep America growing we must keep Americans working, and to keep Americans working we must keep them wanting; wanting more than the bare necessities; wanting the luxuries and frills that make life so much more worthwhile, and installment selling makes it easier to keep Americans wanting." [14]

John C. Burnham, the leading authority on the gasoline tax, is amazed at the extent to which "Americans were willing to pay for the almost infinite expansion of their automobility." Public support for heavy motor vehicle special use taxes is a case in point. Motorists early came to support higher and annual registration fees as one means of securing better roads. For the same reason, there has consistently been almost no public opposition to the gasoline tax. The gasoline tax was innovated in Oregon, New Mexico, and Colorado in 1919 as a means of raising money to meet matching funds for road construction that the federal government made available to the states after World War I. By 1925 gasoline taxes had been imposed by forty-four states and the District of Columbia. By 1929 all states collected gasoline taxes, which amounted to some $431 million in revenue that year, and rates of three and four cents a gallon were common. In 1921 road construction and maintenance were financed mainly by property taxes and general funds, with only about 25 percent of the money for roads coming from automobile registration fees. By 1929 gasoline taxes were the main source of revenue for highway expenditures, and twenty-one states no longer used any general property taxes for main roads. The reasoning was that "the gasoline tax was superior as a user tax because the amount of gasoline consumed in a vehicle was a good measure of the use of the road and also of the damage that a vehicle did to a road. . . . the tax was 'equitable' in itself and also that those who paid it benefited directly." The chief collector of the gasoline tax in Tennessee exclaimed in 1926, "Who ever heard, before, of a popular tax?" And Burnham has pointed out that "never before in the history of taxation has a major tax been so generally accepted in so short a period." [15]

"Among the many factors which contributed toward the expansion of local taxes [between 1913 and 1930], probably no single one, price inflation aside, exercised a more potent influence than did the automobile," reported the President's Research Committee on Social Trends in 1933. "This taking to wheels of an entire population had a profound effect on the aggregate burden of taxation." Staggering highway expenditures, the bulk of which came directly out of the motorists' pockets in use taxes, accounted for only part of this increased tax burden. The committee found that "it was not merely in its influence on highway costs that the automobile affected the size of the tax bill. Its use in cities created serious problems of traffic congestion and increased crime. Motorized police and traffic control became important items of increased expenditure. Moreover, . . . the motorcar was responsible for a spreading out of the population of cities toward the peripheral or suburban areas. This movement helped to swell the volume of local taxation, since schools and other public facilities had to be provided anew in these outer areas, despite the under-utilization of such facilities in older areas where population declined. In the rural sections of the country, good roads and the motor bus stimulated the growth of the consolidated school, thus putting within the reach of farm children an educational offering which approached the urban standard. In terms of educational returns per dollar spent, it was much more economical than the little one-room school. Nevertheless, it involved a larger absolute amount of expenditure and rural tax rates rose accordingly." The committee concluded that, "since the changes which came with the motor era are inextricably bound up with other types of change, it is impossible to state in dollars and cents just how much the automobile has cost the taxpayers of the country." [16]

This was indeed an ironic outcome from the adoption of an innovation whose proponents had claimed, less than a generation before, would lower the cost of living. Thomas L. White had spoken the mind of the public as well as of the experts when he predicted in 1910 that by relieving "the situation arising out of the diminished fertility of the soil, the depopulation of the rural districts, the growing congestion of the cities, and the decreasing food value of the dollar . . . the self-propelled vehicle will justify from a national standpoint the expenditure of brains and money hitherto so freely lavished on its development." [17] But by the late 1920s our historical experience was proving that these and most other early predictions about the benefits of mass personal automobility were erroneous.

The President's Research Committee on Social Trends noted that "car ownership has created an 'automobile psychology'; the automobile has become a dominent influence in the life of the individual and he, in a very real sense, has become dependent on it." Blaine A. Brownell has recently made a well-phrased assessment of the motorcar's cultural meaning in the 1920s. "It was clear to almost all observers in the 1920s that technology was a highly significant factor in altering the past and shaping the future," he writes. "Whether technology was to be welcomed as symbolic of a new and more prosperous age, or damned as subversive of age-old values and mores is perhaps less important than the fact that all observers tended to see technology as a fundamental force in American life, and the automobile as probably the most significant of the technological innovations appearing in the period. The motor vehicle was a more impressive piece of machinery than a radio, more personal in its impact than a skyscraper or dynamo, and certainly more tangible than electricity. Thus it was generally more legible as a symbol and more apparent in its consequences." [18]

Brownell's work on the automobile in southern urban areas in the 1920s stands as a model of what needs to be done for American culture as a whole. Even though the South lagged behind the rest of the nation in adopting the automobile, "the motorcar's overall influence on the South was massive. The region's transportation system was probably revolutionized to a greater extent by the motor vehicle than was the case elsewhere, and the traditional provinciality of the rural South was radically altered by new highways." By 1929 the percentage of retail businesses listed in the automotive category by the Bureau of the Census for major southern urban areas ranged from 14.2 in New Orleans to 20.7 in Birmingham, Alabama. "Its total economic significance is virtually impossible to compute with precision, but it would probably be measured in the billions of dollars in major southern cities alone." Sunday blue laws gave way to automobility, and problems caused by the automobile became the most time-consuming item on the agendas of southern city councils. As the historian Thomas D. Clark observed in 1961, "Detroit automobile makers set off the most effective Yankee invasion that ever disturbed southern complacency," an invasion that "had more long-range economic meaning for the South than all the Civil War generals combined. The established way of life in the South was shaken to its very foundation by this new Yankee machine." [19]

"Highly favorable reactions to the automobile were frequently voiced in the major daily newspapers in southern cities," finds

Brownell. "General community sentiment, to the extent that it was mirrored in these editorial columns, was that the motorcar contributed to 'progress' and to the prospects for material prosperity. An era marked by widespread automobile travel was welcomed as one both modern and affluent." He notes further that "the opinions of all groups toward the motor vehicle are, in the final analysis, impossible to fully determine, largely because most such opinions were never preserved in the historical record. . . . and because many black and labor union publications were at best but partially representative of the sentiments prevailing in either the black community or among white workingmen. On the basis of the existing evidence, however, attitudes toward the automobile cannot be differentiated along racial or class lines." Among the groups for which adequate data exist, "the motor vehicle was especially lauded by the southern urban business community, largely because it promised to open up new channels of commerce, expand the pool of customers for downtown merchants, and make available large expanses of outlying territory for urban growth and economic development."

A major contribution of Brownell's work is that he demonstrates for the first time that, as the 1920s wore on, many problems of mass personal automobility began to become apparent. He believes that "the notion advanced by some historians that the motor vehicle was accepted uncritically and with little awareness of its potential consequences is a false one." According to Brownell, the seeds of our contemporary discontent with the motorcar were already beginning to germinate by the late 1920s. "Then as now, ownership of automobiles did not necessarily reflect a complete and unquestioning acceptance of their consequences. The views expressed about the motor vehicle in the 'circulating media' in southern cities during the decade . . . suggest a much more complex pattern of response. Such views ran the gamut from complete acceptance of the automobile to rather deep suspicions concerning its impact on American life. Not surprisingly, most conceptions of this significant technological innovation were highly ambiguous. The vehicle that promised to infinitely expand the radius of individual mobility also seemed to threaten the tightly knit family unit and prevailing moral standards; the same automobile that was supposed to decentralize the city and improve urban access to the countryside acted paradoxically to render the city even more congested; and the motor vehicle that epitomized freedom from restraint was to impose new restrictions on the possibilities and style of urban living." Although atmospheric pollution by the motor vehicle was not yet recognized as a problem, "as the decade progressed many business-oriented publications and organizations expressed a rising concern about the motorcar's threat to streetcar lines and the growing toll of deaths and injuries for which it was responsible. Downtown merchants were especially worried over the motor traffic congestion that plagued most central cities throughout the period. . . . Many writers, especially clergymen, lamented the auto's allegedly unfavorable impact on traditional moral standards and the family unit, though most of these observations were apparently jeremiads aimed at undesirable secular forces that seemed to be undermining older values—and which the automobile seemed to symbolize perfectly." [20]

The most comprehensive contemporaneous analysis of the automobile culture in the 1920s and the 1930s is in the Lynds's Middletown series. "As, at the turn of the century, business class people began to feel apologetic if they did not have a telephone, so ownership of an automobile has now reached the point of being an accepted essential of normal living," the Lynds wrote in 1929. They found in the depths of the Great Depression, however, that "if the word 'auto' was writ large across Middletown's life in 1925, this was even more apparent in 1935, after six years of depression. One was immediately struck in walking the streets by the fact that filling stations have become in ten years one of the most prominent physical landmarks. . . . In 1925 Middletown youngsters, driven from street play to the sidewalks, were protesting, 'Where can I play?' but in

1935 they were retreating even from the sidewalks, and an editorial, headed 'Sidewalk Play is Dangerous,' said, 'It is safe to say that children under the age of eight years should not be permitted to play on sidewalks.' . . . While some workers lost their cars in the depression, the local sentiment, as heard over and over again, is that 'People give up everything in the world but their car.' According to a local banker, 'The depression hasn't changed materially the value Middletown people set on home ownership, but *that's* not their primary desire, as the automobile always comes first.' " It was apparent to the Lynds in 1937 that, "to a considerably greater extent than in 1925, Middletown's life is today derived from the automotive industry—and the city is aware of it to its marrow!" [21]

During the depression the Middletown car culture if anything had more symbolic meaning to the working class than to the business class. "If the automobile is by now a habit with the business class, a comfortable, convenient, pleasant addition to the paraphernalia of living, it represents far more than this to the working class; for to the latter it gives the status which his job increasingly denies, and, more than any other possession or facility to which he has access, it symbolizes living, having a good time, the thing that keeps you working." Indeed, automobility was probably the main barrier to the development of class consciousness among workers in the 1920s and 1930s. "Working in an open-shop city with its public opinion set by the business class, and fascinated [even in the depression!] by a rising standard of living offered them on every hand," noted the Lynds, "[workers] do not readily segregate themselves from the rest of the city. They want what Middletown wants, so long as it gives them their great symbol of advancement—an automobile. Car ownership stands to them for a large share of the 'American dream'; they cling to it as they cling to self-respect, and it was not unusual to see a family drive up to a relief commissary in 1935 to stand in line for its four- or five-dollar weekly food dole. 'It's easy to see why our workers don't think much about joining unions,' remarked a union official in 1935. He went on to use almost the same words heard so often in 1925: 'So long as they have a car and can borrow or steal a gallon of gas, they'll ride around and pay no attention to labor organization; and if they can't get gas, they're busy trying to figure out some way to get it.' " [22]

Automobility was undoubtedly the major force unifying Americans in the period between the two world wars. Despite comments in the automobile trade journals in the early 1920s recognizing that "illiterate, immigrant, negro and other families" were "obviously outside" the market for motorcars, there was agreement that "every clear-thinking American, be he rich or poor, realizes that in a measure, the automobile and its manufacturers are helping to solve the labor and social problems of the future," as well as "the tendency of the automobile to bring into intimate and helpful contact sections of our population which normally would never meet." [23] The automobile outing and the automobile vacation became national institutions in the 1920s. By 1926 some 5,362 "motor camps" dotted the American countryside, and an avalanche of tourists who never before had traveled more than a few miles from home began to descend on distant national parks, forests, and points of historic interest. The new mobility of the labor force and long-distance trucking decentralized the location of industrial plants, opened up the Pacific Coast and the Southwest to commercial development, knit regional economies more tightly together, and promised eventually to abolish class and ethnic, as well as sectional, differences. "Scarcely ever before have rich and poor, educated and ignorant, self-styled superiors and acknowledged inferiors, landlords and landless, white folks and black, ridden in the same type of vehicle; and never before have they ridden so fast that they could not see who was approaching," said Arthur Raper in a 1936 study of two rural Georgia counties. "The opportunities afforded by the automobile provide a basis for a new mobility for whites as well as Negroes, based upon personal standards rather than upon community mores

—upon what the individual wants to do rather than what the community does not want him to do." [24]

There was ample evidence by the 1920s that the national, individualized automobile culture was destructive of the beneficial as well as the repressive aspects of "community." "The mobility afforded by new modes of transportation combined with . . . periodic waves of employment, unemployment, and reemployment to diminish the tendency for the workers in a given factory to live together immediately about the plant," observed the Lynds. "The trend towards decentralization of workers' dwellings means that instead of a family's activities in getting a living, making a home, play, church-going, and so on largely overlapping and bolstering each other, one's neighbors may work at shops at the other end of the city, while those with whom one works may have their homes and other interests anywhere from one to two-score miles distant." The breakdown of the neighborhood was also evident in that "the housewife with leisure does not sit so much on the front porch in the afternoon after she 'gets dressed up,' sewing and 'visiting' and comparing her yard with her neighbors', nor do the family and neighbors spend long summer evenings and Sunday afternoons on the porch or in the side yard since the advent of the automobile and the movies." A Middletown housewife explained, "In the nineties we were all much more together. People brought chairs and cushions out of the house and sat on the lawns evenings. We rolled out a strip of carpet and put cushions on the porch step to take care of the unlimited overflow of neighbors that dropped by. We'd sit out so all evening. The younger couples perhaps would wander off for half an hour to get a soda but come back to join in the informal singing or listen while somebody strummed a mandolin or guitar." [25]

E. C. Stokes, a former governor of New Jersey and the president of a Trenton, New Jersey, bank, claimed in 1921: "Next to the church there is no factor in American life that does so much for the morals of the public as does the automobile. . . . Any device that brings the family together as a unit in their pursuit of pleasure is a promoter of good morals and yields a beneficent influence that makes for the good of American civilization. If every family in the land possessed an automobile, family ties would be closer and many of the problems of social unrest would be happily resolved. . . . The automobile is one of the country's best ministers and best preachers." [26]

Contrary to Stokes's widely shared expectations, by 1929 it was evident to the Lynds and many others that any tendency of automobility to bring the family together was "a passing phase"—although an increasing number of people did tend to find the Sunday drive preferable to attending church. "No one questions the use of the auto for transporting groceries, getting to one's place of work or the golf course, or in place of the porch for 'cooling off after supper,'" the Lynds found. "But when auto riding tends to replace the traditional call in the family parlor as a way of approach between the unmarried, 'the home is endangered,' and all-day Sunday motor trips are a 'threat against the church'; it is in the activities concerned with the home and religion that the automobile occasions the greatest emotional conflicts." Although no one has ever proved that the back seat of a Model T was more convenient or comfortable than a haystack, of thirty girls brought before the Middletown juvenile court for so-called "sex crimes," nineteen named an automobile as the place where the offense occurred, and a Middletown judge explained a dwindling red-light district by pointing out that "the automobile has become a house of prostitution on wheels." " 'What on earth *do* you want me to do? Just sit around home all evening!' retorted a popular high school girl . . . when her father discouraged her going out motoring for the evening with a young blade in a rakish car waiting at the curb." [27]

John B. Rae may well be right in his claim that such criticisms of the automobile simply "exemplified man's propensity to blame his technology rather than himself for whatever evil consequences it might produce." Yet Rae dismisses too facilely the fact that automobility undermined the family as an institution. Although in theory the family car could bring husbands, wives, and children together in their leisure-time activities, the divorce rate continued to climb in the 1920s, and intergenerational conflicts between parents and children reached a new height during the decade. There is no evidence that the motorcar contributed to the divorce rate, but then neither did it, as early proponents of automobility expected, stop the divorce mill from grinding. That the motorcar undercut parental authority, on the other hand, is unequivocal. The Lynds pointed out, for example: "The extensive use of this new tool by the young has enormously extended their mobility and range of alternatives before them; joining a crowd motoring over to a dance in a town twenty miles away may be a matter of a moment's decision, with no one's permission asked. Furthermore, among the high school set, owner-ship of a car by one's family has become an important criterion of social fitness: a boy almost never takes a girl to a dance except in a car; there are persistent rumors of the buying of a car by local families to help their children's social standing in high school." [28]

Mounting automobile registrations are undoubtedly the best indication that Americans in the 1920s continued to view automobil-ity on balance as highly beneficial. Automobile sales dropped sharply in the Great Depression. "Car ownership in Middletown," nevertheless, "was one of the most depression-proof elements of the city's life in the years following 1929—far less vulnerable, appar-ently, than marriages, divorces, new babies, clothing, jewelry, and most other measurable things both large and small. . . . The passenger-car registrations in Middletown's entire county not only scarcely registered any loss in the early years of the depression but, both in numbers and in ratio to population, stood in each of the years 1932–35 above the 1929 level. Along with this tough resistance of Middletown's habit of car owning to the depression undertow, went a drop of only 4 percent in the dollar volume of gasoline sales in Middletown between 1929 and 1933." For the nation as a whole, motor vehicle miles of travel increased from 198 billion in 1929 to 206 billion in 1930 and 216 billion in 1931. Their depression low of 201 billion occurred in both 1932 and 1933. Special motor vehicle tax receipts progressively mounted through the depression from $849 million in 1929 to $990 million in 1932, the trough of the depression, reaching $1.693 billion in 1940. Highway expenditures were significantly greater throughout the depression than they had been in the supposedly prosperous 1920s. Motor vehicle registrations decreased from 26.75 million in 1930 to a low of 24.159 million in 1933, then bounced back to 32.453 million in 1940. "While, therefore, people were riding in progressively older cars as the depression wore on, they manifestly continued to ride." [29]

Other data, however, indicate that for the bulk of the population the benefits of automobility, even by the early 1920s, were probably mainly symbolic. A questionnaire mailed by the National Automobile Chamber of Commerce in 1920 to a random sample of automobile owners in "ten widely selected states" showed scant evidence that automobility was improving the quality of car owners' lives. Of the owners who responded, 90 percent said their cars were "used more or less for business," and 60 percent of the mileage driven was "for business purposes." The NACC estimated a 57 percent "gain through car use over previous income or efficiency." The rank order of gains reported, by occupation, was real estate and insurance agents (113 percent), medical doctors (104 percent), salesmen (103 percent), clergymen (98 percent), school supervisors (72 percent), farmers (68 percent), contractors (51 percent), and manufacturers and bankers (33 percent). The most signficant point was that only 37 percent of the owners reported "improving living conditions through use of the car (suburban life, etc.)," meaning that almost two-thirds of the automobile owners who responded found that the quality of their lives either had remained about the same or had deteriorated with automobility. There was thus much more ironic truth than its author could have recognized in a 1923 quip in

Motor: "It may be that Kipling is right, and that we have lost our national soul if we ever had one. We may be a nation of mechanical, money-grubbing 'robots.' But certainly the automobile touched either a soul or some controlling springs and gears in our national life." [30]

The main things that automobility symbolized were material prosperity through a higher standard of living, individual mobility, and an improvement in the quality of life through a fusing of rural and urban advantages. If one excludes the obviously great payoff for such economic interest groups as the automobile and oil industries, real estate developers, and contractors, the realities of the automobile revolution fell far short of its proponents' promises for most Americans. As we have already seen, what the individual gained from automobile ownership was at the expense of undermining community and family, and it invited anonymity and anomie. Improvements in the quality of life through a fusing of rural and urban advantages also proved illusory.

Reynold M. Wik's "grass-roots Americans" undoubtedly benefitted more than the urban masses from personal automobility. The motorcar and improved roads increased rural land values, lessened the drudgery of farm labor, ended rural isolation, and brought the farm family the amenities of city life, the most important being far better medical care and schools. In a day when "busing" has come to be associated in the minds of many Americans with an alleged lowering of educational standards, it seems particularly pertinent to point out that in the 1920s and 1930s the daily busing of farm children long distances to consolidated schools was hailed as a significant forward step in achieving educational parity between rural and urban schools.

These benefits of the school bus and the Model T notwithstanding, the cityward migration of farm youth was not stemmed, as auto enthusiasts promised it would be. Even more important, the family farm was already being killed off in the 1920s by a combination of the farm tractor, corporate agriculture, and the propensity of bankers to foreclose mortgages that had been incurred to finance the farmers' automobility. One of the main symbols of the dispossession of rural Americans in the 1930s, chronicled so eloquently in John Steinbeck's *The Grapes of Wrath*, was "the machine man driving a dead tractor on land he does not know and love . . . contemptuous of the land and of himself." And in Steinbeck's novel, automobility ended up as the frustrating search for daily subsistence of the migrant agricultural worker.[31]

Proponents of automobility were right about the necessity of banishing the unsanitary horse from cities, and they were right that a viable urban transportation system could not run entirely on rails but also required great dependence on the more flexible motor vehicle. From the perspective of rational hindsight, however, the best solution to urban transportation problems would have been a balanced commitment to motortrucks and motor buses, along with rail transportation, rather than the mass ownership of private passenger cars in cities. By the 1920s it was obvious, contrary to the predictions of early proponents of automobility, that mass dependence on passenger cars had compounded urban traffic congestion and parking problems. Although it was not yet recognized, the urban neighborhood as a community was already being destroyed by the decentralization and segregation of activities encouraged by automobility and by the longer blocks, combined with widened streets and narrower sidewalks, that accommodation to the motorcar demanded. Nor was it foreseen that auto exhaust in the antiseptic, horseless city was going to prove even more detrimental to public health than horse exhaust once had been.

As early as 1913 a spokesman for the Merchants Association of New York complained to that city's Motor Truck Club at its October 15 meeting: "The growth of the automobile industry and automobile traffic has gone on faster than our ability to care for it properly. The automobile manufacturer and dealer has been so busy selling automobiles that he hasn't even taken the time to give his customers proper treatment or his broken-down machines the proper kind of convalescent care, let alone giving attention to traffic conditions, which are primarily municipal and interest him only indirectly." By the end of 1916 even the editors of *Automobile* were overwhelmed that "every day in big cities the parking problem grows more acute. If it is bad today, and indeed it is so, what will be the situation in 3 years? We are facing something which was never foreseen in the planning of our towns, a thing which has come upon us so swiftly that there has been no time to grasp the immensity of the problem till we are almost overcome by it." The situation had become so grave by 1920 that *Motor Age* felt that "the collapsible wheelbase seems to be about the only solution of the traffic problem as it exists in our larger cities today. There is an alleged joke in vaudeville about the manufacturer of a certain well known car [Ford] who is considering putting wheels on the rear end of his cars so that he can run them on end and so get more of them on the streets. But if you watch the stream of motor traffic in any of our large cities at the 'rush hours,' you will realize that that joke isn't so all-fired funny after all." By 1923 the automobile trade journals considered the urban traffic problem "one of the great problems of the day." Articles in *Motor*, for example, warned, "Stop! You Are Congesting the Streets," and asked, "Will Passenger Cars Be Barred from City Streets?" [32]

"The only means of affording substantial relief from this burden [of urban traffic problems] as far as most city leaders were concerned was city planning—a concept that was advanced as a virtual panacea for a whole range of urban ills, but was always fundamentally tied to the demands posed by motor vehicles," Brownell concludes. "The ultimate failure to significantly ease the impact of the automobile occurred even though the responses of city governments and local leaders to the automotive challenge was in the best American pragmatic tradition. As the numbers of automobiles mounted, so did the governmental response: new taxes, improved roads, expanded parking facilities, extensive surveys, and a vast system of regulations enacted to guarantee the auto's operation in the public interest and welfare." Thus, instead of attempting to discourage the use of private passenger cars in cities, politicians and city planners adopted the expensive and ultimately unworkable policy of unlimited accommodation to the motorcar. That American urban life would conform to the needs of automobility rather than vice versa was obvious by the early 1920s. In 1923, for example, the Chicago Automobile Trade Association was shown plans drafted by the Chicago Plan Commission for "vast projects . . . to widen streets and extend boulevards, open more through streets, eliminate jogs, straighten the Chicago river, and connect up the whole street system so that automobile traffic may be conducted with convenience." The association's president thought it "imperative that something be done to make room for the hundreds of automobiles being put on the streets by the dealers each week." And he stressed that "of all the business interests of the city the automobile dealers should be most active in . . . support [of the Chicago Plan Commission] because of what it means to their business." [33]

Some 135,000 suburban homes in sixty cities were already chiefly dependent on motor vehicle transportation by 1922, and the exodus of the middle class and businesses accelerated as the automobile culture matured in the 1920s. Massive conversion of the central city to accommodate the motorcar was thus paradoxically undertaken as its cost and problems were avoided by the escape to suburbia that automobility encouraged. *Motor* enthused that, in making possible the proliferation of suburban country clubs, the motorcar had "added a new phase of growing social importance to the social life of this country." [34] But a more significant development in American social life was that the central city increasingly came to be an isolated ghetto of the deprived of American society as the middle class retreated to a modified version of the Jeffersonian vision of a nation of yeoman farmers. The implications of this progressive bifurcation of American society into urban ghettos and middle-class residential suburbs would not become apparent to the middle class, unfortunately, until the deterioration of living conditions in the central city manifested itself in widespread riots during the mid-1960s.

Automotive safety, on the other hand, was already recognized as a major problem by the mid-1920s. Although improved roads and better control of motor vehicle traffic progressively reduced the number of fatalities per miles of automobile travel in the 1920s, more automobiles traveling at higher speeds meant a mounting toll of fatalities, injuries, and property damage in absolute figures. In 1924, automobile accidents accounted for 23,600 deaths (including the deaths of 10,000 children), over 700,000 injuries, and over a billion dollars in property damage—"regarded as one of the big economic problems of the day" by *Motor Age*.

The automobile industry consistently turned out cars with more horsepower that were capable of higher speeds than could be driven legally, much less safely, on the highways of the day. The industry also put styling ahead of safety in automotive design. Newspaper accounts of accidents frequently mentioned the failure of steering mechanisms, brakes, tires, and other components. Yet the NACC Traffic and Safety Committee analysis of 280 automobile accident fatalities in 1924 traced only 7 to a defect in the vehicle. According to the NACC committee, physical conditions, such as visibility and conditions of the pavement, accounted for 92 of the fatalities, while 150 were the fault of pedestrians. The remaining 152 were attributed to the motorist, with excessive speed accounting for 48 and violations of "rules of the road" for 40. To reduce accidents the NACC committee recommended depriving "the careless motorist" of his car, giving better instruction on how to drive in wet weather, adjusting headlights properly, guarding children better, appointing traffic administrators, and keeping records of the causes of fatalities.[35]

The automobile industry dominated the National Safety Council, and about all that came out of the council's 1925 and 1926 meetings was a warm endorsement of uniform state traffic codes and the pious statement that "more must be done to see that those using the highways come to have a better understanding of what the laws are and additional educational work must be carried on to make the public realize the urgent need of being more careful. Several speakers expressed the opinion that there are thousands holding operators' licenses who are not fit to drive cars. Some expressed the opinion that applicants for operators' licenses should be compelled to undergo at least an optical, hearing, and mental test if not a general physical examination." The industry prided itself, however, that NACC statistics showed that "the traffic accident situation isn't as bad as some make it." [36]

It was evident in the specialized automobile journals that automobility had stopped being a progressive force for change and by the mid-1920s was beginning to petrify into a complacent maturity. The journals had been inaugurated as heralds of a new horseless age. Most tried to cover the entire spectrum of the automobile movement and were addressed to the motoring public. By World War I, however, they had become narrow trade journals catering to the automobile industry, especially to the interests of automobile dealers. *Motor* held out the longest, but in 1924, after twenty-one years of publication for car owners, it, too, became a trade magazine. By then the earlier confident predictions about the utopian benefits of mass automobility in *Motor*'s columns had given way to superficial platitudes. "Motoring is one of the most effective forms of health insurance that modern life has produced, as a palliative to its intensified, speeded-up social and commercial processes," said the health commissioner of New York City in a 1922 *Motor* article. "Do you realize, that without the motorcar golf could never have become the popular game that it is today." "An automobile is as much an asset to a present-day American citizen as a deposit in a bank," said another writer. "There has been a tendency in some quarters to an expression of opinion that the automobile industry has about reached the limit of its development. . . . that the industry has already passed this limit and has persuaded the country to absorb more cars than it was justified in carrying." He argued, however, that "this country has got to maintain its present ratio of motor vehicles, because its life has been gradually formed upon the foundations of speed and mobility that the motor vehicle has brought to it." *Motor* asked Thomas A. Edison in 1924: "If the automobile develops in the next twenty-five years at the same rate as in the past twenty-five, what will be the most startling transformation in everyday life?" The best answer that the dean of American inventors could give was: "Everybody who can will go out camping in the summer." [37]

Automobility was the driving force behind Coolidge prosperity, and the boom of the 1920s was shattered with the saturation of the market for new cars after 1925. It would be simplistic, of course, to say that market saturation in the automobile industry "caused" the Great Depression in the sense that it was a sufficient condition for what occurred. There are too many variables involved that are too complexly interrelated. What I am arguing here is that automobility played a key role in creating the most important necessary conditions underlying the Great Depression and that this role has not been recognized adequately by historians. Undoubtedly, the great affection that Americans have had for automobility has mitigated against perceiving that the automobile revolution contributed much to bringing about the worst socioeconomic crisis in American history.

It would be nice to know precisely when automobile manufacturers and dealers began to get uneasy about conditions. Walter P. Chrysler said that "early in 1929 it had seemed to me that I could feel the winds of disaster blowing." Alfred P. Sloan, Jr., remembered that "on October 4, 1929, shortly before the stock market crash, I addressed a general letter to the [GM] organization noting the end of expansion and promulgating a new policy of economy for the corporation." "As it turned out," he said, "I was not, of course, pessimistic enough; indeed, it would soon be a question whether we were able to cope with the unbelievable course of events." Yet Charles W. Nash, in an address delivered to the annual meeting of the National Automobile Dealers Association (NADA), had said as early as 1925: "I read something the other day in an ad where a fellow was boohooing the idea of the saturation point. I am going to say to you men tonight, regardless of the fact that I will be contradicted in the press and by a lot of shining lights, that the saturation point was reached two years ago; not now but two years ago." Nash thought the industry had reached "the point of the survival of the fittest" and added that "production must be limited to fit the demand." [38]

Beginning in the 1920–1921 recession, numerous articles in the automobile trade journals dealt with the possibility of market saturation, but, unlike Nash, they generally failed to face the problem squarely. The tendency instead was to state with bravado rationalizations intended to maintain business confidence. A 1925 editorial in *Motor Age*, for example, claimed that "the retail organization in the automotive industry knows that saturation in automotive ownership does not exist today. . . . The dealer who is convinced that the saturation point is reached in his market is ready to turn some profitable business over to his competitors." As late as January 1930, *Motor* printed that people "will continue to buy automobiles. They have been doing it for a quarter century with no let-downs of consequence. They won't walk. They don't like old cars—and they aren't broke. Business executives may be a bit pessimistic because *they* 'lost in the market.' It would do most of them good if they would take a day off and talk to the great common people. They would learn that the stock market is *not* America and that the 'home town folks' are ready to make 1930 a good year." [39]

Mounting evidence ran counter to such optimism. NADA studies showed that replacement demand accounted for over 70 percent of the new car market as early as 1924—three years before NACC statistics revealed the same shift. In 1926 a field survey conducted by James B. Dalton, the industrial editor of *Motor*, revealed that "not more than 30 percent of all dealers are making money; 30 percent are making a bare living, and the rest are losing money. Dealer mortality has been so heavy that some companies have found it necessary to ship on consignment. . . . Repossessions by finance companies have further complicated the used car situation and depressed the market." [40]

In July 1929 Dalton reported that "thumbs down is the attitude of bankers on loans for the wholesale buying of new automobiles to all save the most soundly financed dealers. . . . With the Federal Reserve Board constantly stressing the dangers of the credit situation, and with the entire nation jumpy because of its frequent warnings, the automotive industry—more completely dependent than any other upon the use of credit for the merchandising of its products—is feeling a real pinch." The bankers felt "that persons of moderate means who trade in their cars every year or two and are perpetually paying installments on an automobile are carrying things a bit too far." In October, on the eve of the stock market crash, Dalton wrote, "How long this uninterrupted progress can continue without a major reverse is the question which is perplexing economists and business strategists." He added: "The march forward will be checked by a shortage of credit if by nothing else. Americans are a race of gamblers and they will speculate in one way or another when they have as much money as they have now. . . . Ten years have passed [since the post–World War I recession] and just as little attention is being paid to Federal Reserve warnings which then were aimed at speculative excesses of a business nature but now are aimed at stock market recklessness." Dalton concluded that "business is weaker than it was in 1920. Excessive productive capacity and the bitter competition which has resulted have brought profit margins very low whereas the reverse was true at the close of the war. Production costs and selling prices are so delicately balanced that even a moderate recession in demand would convert a profit into a loss." [41]

"There is precisely one thing wrong with the automobile industry today," Clarence E. Eldridge, sales manager of the REO Motor Car Company, told the Minnesota Automobile Dealers Association as the stock market crashed. "That one thing is that there has been built up by this greatest of all industries a capacity for building, and a capacity for selling, approximately twice as many automobiles as the market, either present or potential, can absorb." Eldridge excoriated the industry for not recognizing earlier the realistic limits to the new car market and for its innovations that were intended to obviate the fact of market saturation: "The exploitation of high-cost markets, both foreign and domestic; the imposition upon the dealers of arbitrarily determined quotas, together with a reduction of territory, for the purpose of compelling the dealers to sell more cars; the exhaustion of the possibilities, so far as creating additional buyers, of installment selling; and finally the utterly short-sighted policy of accelerating the obsolescence of comparatively new cars, for the purpose of temporarily stimulating sales of new cars—all of the methods, sound or unsound, which might sell new cars were put into effect." Stripping away still another myth of the automobile market, Eldridge pointed out that "the basic problem is not one of how to sell used cars or to handle the used car problem, but how more intelligently to adjust production to the absorptive capacity of the market. And that responsibility, I say quite frankly, rests in one place and one place only—with the automobile manufacturers. It is they who by their insatiable ambition, their blind worship at the shrine of the godess, 'quantity production,' have created this situation—this situation which, unless speedily corrected, seems to me to threaten the very existence of the entire merchandising structure of the automobile industry." [42]

By the mid-1920s the market for both new and used cars was being maintained primarily by installment sales. As early as 1922, 73 percent of cars were sold on time. "Take Off Your Hat to the Man Who Buys on Time," *Motor* urged automobile dealers in 1925. "Time-buying has caused more intensive work than any scheme of mere money-saving ever devised—meritorious though such plans may be." [43] But by then the automobile finance companies themselves had begun to fear that time sales had been overextended. Dealers facing the onset of market saturation were already trying to extend the customary 12-month maximum for payments to 18 and 24 months, with lower down payments than the usual third. Some were even passing on to the finance companies inflated bills of sale that credited the buyer with a down payment he had never made. Credit losses tended to increase as credit was further extended. In 1926, for example, the credit loss on new car paper was only 0.16 percent for terms of 12 months with one-third down, versus a 4.58 percent credit loss when terms were extended to 19 months or more with 24 percent or less down. So after 1925 the finance companies tightened credit terms. In 1927 the share of new cars sold on time dropped to 58 percent, and there was an estimated sharp decline of $643 million that year in the volume of installment sales of both new and used cars.

The stabilization of the demand for automobiles was bound to have catastrophic reverberations that would end the boom, for the growth of many ancillary industries, as well as the expansion of automobile manufacturing, was threatened. The prospects were particularly glum for the petroleum industry, which by 1927 faced a drop in the price of crude oil below the cost of production and heavy losses in refining attributable to overexpansion to meet the needs of the motorcar. In 1923–1924, skyrocketing prices for gasoline presaged a fuel shortage that touched off investigations of the oil industry by both Senator Robert M. LaFollette, of Wisconsin, and the Federal Trade Commission, as well as several muckraking articles by Ida M. Tarbell, the well-known critic of the Standard Oil Company. By the end of 1926, however, huge new oil fields developed in Oklahoma and Texas had led to overproduction, which promised to be lasting because "the market was no longer expanding as it had before 1925. Not only did the vast flow of crude threaten decreasing prices but also a temporary increase in costs. . . . the new crude, heavy in sulpher, demanded changes in the refining equipment which processed it." Alfred D. Chandler, Jr., points out, for example, that, "as a result, [Standard Oil of New] Jersey's profit record for 1927 was the lowest since 1912. Earnings fell from $117.7 million in 1926 to $40.4 million in 1927. Not only did the refining activities show heavy losses, but domestic production showed a small net loss." [44]

The gravity of the situation was compounded by the onset of technological stagnation in the automobile industry. By the late 1920s no manufacturing innovation was in sight that was of comparable importance to the continuous-strip mill for rolling sheet steel or the continuous-process technique for manufacturing plate glass, much less anything that could have the impact of the moving-belt assembly line a decade before. Moreover, no product innovation in sight could approach in importance the effects of the shift to the closed car in the twenties. Only 10.3 percent of the cars built in 1919 were closed, but 82.8 percent of the cars produced in 1927 were closed. "This change in the demand for automobiles had a marked influence on the demand for fabricating materials; for example, much larger quantities of plate glass were required for closed cars and a different sort of upholstery from that which had commonly been used in open cars," the Hoover Committee on Recent Economic Changes pointed out in 1929. "The increased production of automobiles and the increased number in use does not tell the whole story of the effect of automobiles upon demand, because, with the increased number of closed cars in service and the improvement in roads, all-the-year-round use became far more common. The effect of this more constant use was to increase the demand for gasoline, lubricants, and tires, to provide an almost new market for alcohol, glycerine, and other non-freezing preparations, and, not least, to increase the demand for labor for repair and maintenance service." [45]

The major innovations in automotive technology that distinguish the modern motorcar from the 1908 Model T that had not yet been incorporated by the late 1920s were the all-steel body, infinitely variable automatic transmissions, and "drop frame" construction, which dropped the passenger compartment from its high perch upon the axles in the cars of the 1920s to its now familiar position down between the front and rear wheels, lowering the height and center of gravity of the car. The self-starter, which obviated the onerous and dangerous problem of using a hand crank to start the car, was developed by Charles F. Kettering under the supervision of Henry M. Leland in 1911 and gained rapid acceptance. Kettering and Thomas Midgeley, Jr., of the General Motors Research Corporation, discovered in the early 1920s that the addition of tetraethyl lead to gasoline greatly reduced engine knock. In 1926 Dr. Graham Edgar of the Ethyl Gasoline Corporation, formed by General Motors and Standard Oil of Indiana in 1924 to market the product, conceived a scale to rate the octane (antiknock quality) of fuels. Ethyl gasoline, the octane rating of fuels, and better crankshaft balancing to reduce vibrations were the most important breakthroughs that led to the introduction of the high-compression engine in the mid-1920s. By then, four-wheel brakes, low-pressure "balloon" tires, and "wishbone"-type front-wheel suspension had also appeared. Syncromesh transmission and safety plate glass in all windows were features of the 1928 Cadillac. In contrast with the Model T that came only in black after 1913 because only black enamel would dry fast enough, mass-produced cars of all hues and shades of the rainbow became possible when Duco lacquer made its debut in the "True Blue" of the 1924 Oakland.

Not only had most of the basic innovations that add up to the modern motorcar been made by the late 1920s but the increased emphasis on styling after 1925 was disastrous for the smaller automobile manufacturers. The styling changes in the "annual model," which signified planned obsolescence, were intended, in Sloan's words, "to create demand for the new value and, so to speak, create a certain amount of dissatisfaction with past models as compared with the new one, and yet the current and old models must still be capable of giving satisfaction to the vast used-car market." But bringing out the annual model involved enormous retooling costs that were beyond the capability of the small automobile producer. Increased emphasis on style also meant higher production costs, particularly in stamping processes, where the most significant economies of scale accrued to the benefit of the large-volume producer. In addition, some stylistic changes, such as the closed car of the 1920s and the integral trunk and all-steel top of the 1930s, put various accessory manufacturers out of business. Sloan recalled, for example, that the integral trunk "was another case where styling changes made some people unhappy, for these developments meant an apparent loss of accessory business in trunk racks, tire covers, and the like, at a time when accessories were very profitable items. But such is the price of progress." [46]

Increasingly in the 1930s, capital investment in the automobile industry was being stimulated much more by the demands of planned obsolescence and the dictates of style than by basic innovations in automotive and manufacturing technologies. *Business Week* reported in its issue of November 10, 1934, for example: "With no overwhelming need for wholesale modernization, the industry would like to roll along for a while without any capital outlay. The cars themselves are good, already have everything a purchaser should want in the way of personal transportation. . . . Several manufacturers thought they had done enough to make the prospects dissatisfied with their present cars and planned to bring out new models with noticeable but unimportant changes. But competition, and the increasing necessity of trimming the last penny off every possible operation are forcing last minute shifts. So the new models now being translated from paper to steel will have the traditional radical differences. And the equipment makers . . . will get more business than they expected. And, one may add, the consumer will pay most of the bill." [47]

By the late 1920s an end also seemed imminent to the vast governmental expenditures for road construction and improvement brought about by mass personal automobility. In *The Road and the Car in American Life*, Professor Rae has summarized well the many inadequacies, by today's standards, of the American system of roads up to 1950.[48] In fact, the American system of roads never has and undoubtedly never can be made adequate to the demands of our motor vehicle traffic. One reason is that every attempt to make roads adequate for existing motor vehicle performance and current volume of traffic has inevitably encouraged the automobile industry to build still larger and faster cars and the public to drive more of them farther on more occasions. Whether American roads were adequate by the late 1920s from some abstract set of standards is thus not very meaningful. The important fact is that it seemed obvious that phenomenal progress in road construction and improvement had been made during the 1920s and that an adequate system of roads for the vehicles in use was nearing completion. The President's Committee on Recent Social Trends, for example, concluded: "Should there be no further increase in the volume of motor vehicle traffic, the utility of new construction and improvement projects would naturally diminish as present highway programs approached the period of completion. This in turn would lead to a more careful weighing of the relative advantages of additional highway facilities as against a reduction of highway taxes." [49] There was so little enthusiasm for express highways in the 1930s that the Pennsylvania Turnpike Commission was unable to sell its bonds. The Roosevelt administration spent huge sums on road construction and improvement during the depression not because F.D.R. thought we needed better highways but because it was a convenient and noncontroversial way to provide jobs for the unemployed and stimulate the economy.

Although better roads and the Model T got rural America out of the mud in the 1920s, automobility was also in large part responsible for the depressed condition of agriculture, which involved a ruinous combination of overproduction of staple crops and higher fixed prices for equipment and chemical fertilizers. Along with the farmer's automobile came the widespread displacement of farm horses by the tractor, which necessitated a switch to artificial fertilizers, encouraged the use of other expensive machinery to increase productivity, displaced farm workers, and usually involved a mortgage on the family farm. Ultimately, automobility made the small family farm obsolete. The Hoover Committee on Recent Economic Changes, for example, pointed out that "the most dramatic and probably the most significant single factor which has entered into the productive situation of agriculture within the last few years has come with the increased mechanization of the farm, primarily as a result of the internal combustion engine." The number of tractors in use on American farms increased from 147,600 in 1919 to over 825,900 by 1929. It was obvious that "the introduction of the tractor implies and necessitates a sweeping revision of the whole character of our agricultural industry and of our ideas with reference to farm organization and management, land values and other phases of rural economy. . . . We are coming slowly to perceive that it sets a new pace and rather than fitting itself unobtrusively into our agriculture, creates a demand that agriculture be quite drastically readjusted in accordance with its needs and potentialities." The committee concluded that the tractor "permits enormous economies in the production of staple agricultural products, but its effective utilization demands larger operating units and a more specialized type of economic organization; it permits also of a considerable release of manpower." [50]

For many businesses, too, the automobile boom of the 1920s was either illusory or deleterious. Especially on short-haul passenger traffic, the motor vehicle cut heavily into the business of the railroads. "The steady decline in railway passenger traffic since 1920 is evidence that the competition of motor vehicles is severe," reported the Hoover Committee in 1929. "The automobile is being used more and more on relatively short trips, both for business and pleasure, that formerly were made by rail. The public has recently shown a decided preference for the motor coach over the steam railway coach and the trolley car." The loss of commuters in suburban traffic "has brought about curtailment of train service or abandonment of branch lines, when such action is permitted by the regulatory authorities, and the effect of poorer railway service has been to stimulate the transfer of passengers to the highway." "The possibility of further inroads on railway revenues by highway competition depends in part upon Congressional action," the committee concluded. "To a large extent, motor vehicles, notably motor trucks, are unregulated except in minor particulars. . . . broadly speaking, the trucks have a free hand in the matter of rates and assume no continuing obligation to serve. Under such circumstances, the railways have justification for complaint against unfair competition."[51]

Motor Age reported in early 1924 that "dealer organizations in several sections are preparing to take steps to combat the propaganda against the purchase of automobiles on time which has been instituted by associations of clothing dealers and others who have become alarmed because of the falling off in their own business and are attributing it to enormous sales of motor cars on installments." Articles in the *National Retail Clothier* in the early 1920s showed that "retail clothiers are unanimous in blaming the automobile for the admitted slump in the retail clothing trade," the Lynds found. "In one city, to quote an example cited in the articles, a store 'put on a campaign that usually resulted in a business of 150 suits and overcoats on a Saturday afternoon. This season the campaign netted seventeen sales, while an automobile agency across the street sold twenty-five cars on the weekly payment plan.' " [52]

The unsettling impact of the motor vehicle on retailing and wholesaling was significant. By opening up much larger trading areas, automobility killed off the village general store and lessened deposits in small local banks. The big mail-order houses—Sears, Roebuck and Montgomery Ward—were forced to assume the new business risks involved in opening chains of retail stores. Before the advent of the automobile, the mail-order houses had catered to the isolated rural population. Retailing "had been concentrated into the center of cities and towns into which all avenues of transportation funnelled." But, as Robert E. Wood, the former general merchandise manager at Montgomery Ward who became vice-president of Sears, Roebuck, explained, "When the automobile reached the masses, it changed this condition and made shopping mobile. In the great cities Sears located its stores well outside the main shopping districts, on cheap land, usually on arterial highways, with ample parking space." Downtown merchants in medium-sized cities saw business move to the periphery of town or the metropolis and were forced to specialize in a single line of goods. "And by the end of the decade many downtown merchants were realizing the extent to which the motor vehicle was sapping the vitality of the business district," relates Brownell. "In 1926, Thomas E. Pitts reluctantly closed his well-known cigar store and soft drink bar at Five Points, a major intersection in downtown Atlanta. 'I think the real thing that did it,' he lamented, 'was automobiles, and more automobiles. Traffic got so congested that the only hope was to keep it going. Hundreds used to stop; now thousands pass. Five Points has become a thoroughfare, instead of a center.' " These developments in retailing completely unsettled wholesale trade. Competition became much sharper among wholesalers, and many firms found they could no longer operate economically in the expanded trading areas brought about by automobility. The Hoover Committee reported in 1929 that "relatively few wholesale firms have as yet readjusted their methods for dealing with the new conditions." [53]

Nor did the automobile boom of the 1920s mean prosperity even for most of the automobile industry. By the mid-1920s, as we have seen, most automobile dealers were breaking even or losing money. In the 1920s the franchised dealership system became universal, wiping out the wholesalers who had served as middlemen between the automobile manufacturers and the dealers in the early days of the industry. With the closure of entry into automobile manufacturing in the 1920s and the solidification of the industry into an oligopoly of giant corporations, most small automobile producers, and with them most parts and accessories manufacturers, faced ruin. "Unhappily, there is more of tragedy, courage and dogged determination than of romance in the events which are now unfolding," wrote James Dalton in the October 1924 issue of *Motor*. "Old and honored names are being erased from the roster and it seems inevitable that more of them must go, either by voluntary liquidation while there is still something to save, or by failure. . . . The industry is slowly but steadily contracting, *not in the volume of its products but in the number of companies making them.*" Dalton predicted: "The effects promise to be far-reaching not only for accessories manufacturers but for jobbers and dealers. No vivid imagination is required to visualize the result. It will mean a radical readjustment in methods of distributing a large volume of merchandise which has been highly profitable in the past. . . . it is practically certain that at least 90 percent of the business will always be in the hands of a comparatively few powerful manufacturers." [54]

There was indeed some justice in the outcome that the main benefits of the automobile boom accrued to a relatively small number of capitalists, for the boom was mainly due to vast capital expenditures to reshape the American economy and society to fit the motor vehicle—something largely accomplished by the late 1920s. During the decade the production of capital goods and nonresidential construction rose much more rapidly than the production of commodities designed for direct consumption, including residential construction. This huge, rapid expansion in capital investment undoubtedly encouraged an unrealistic emphasis upon the priority of savings for investment. And it encouraged this at the expense of demands for better income distribution and great increases in personal disposable income.

The paradox confronting Americans by the late 1920s was that, while the automobile boom was the product of capital investment, automobility had caused a concomitant shift to a new consumer-goods-oriented economy and society. The diffusion of mass-production techniques (innovated in the automobile industry) tremendously increased the output of all commodities. Even more important, "the great expansion in the automobile and electrical industries had far reaching effects in diverting the consumers' purchasing power from old to new products and placing in the hands of consumers stocks of durable products which have a slow rate of obsolescence and which, consequently, need to be replaced only after a lapse of considerable intervals of time." During the twenties the production of such durable consumer-goods items increased 72 percent, compared with an increase of less than 15 percent in the production of more staple, perishable commodities.[55]

Personal disposable income did not increase sufficiently and income distribution was inadequate during the 1920s to support the phenomenal increase in the production of durable consumer goods with low replacement demand. The decade was a time of relatively full employment, and the real wages of workers employed in manufacturing rose about 17 percent between 1919 and 1929. However, per capita disposable income rose only about 9 percent during that period, and the rise was fairly well concentrated in the upper-middle- and upper-income brackets. Despite an almost 50 percent gain in manufacturing output, contrary to the optimistic predictions of Henry Ford and other apostles of industrial efficiency, the number of workers employed in manufacturing remained constant—the big gain in new employment being in relatively poorly paying service trades. The collapse of the trade union movement after the 1920–1921 recession was one important reason why workers did not share adequately in the gains of the automobile boom. Wages and prices remained relatively stable from 1922 to 1929, freezing the level of demand for an ever-increasing amount of consumer goods. On the other hand, net corporate profits soared from $3.9 billion in 1922 to $7.2 billion in 1929, and bank deposits, almost wholly from the upper-middle and upper classes, increased from $41.1 billion to $57.9 billion. As we have seen, these excessive savings lacked productive outlets for investment, so they became the main source of the runaway bull market of the late 1920s.

The main problem was that the more equal income distribution and higher per capita disposable income needed to maintain the automobile boom was eschewed in favor of unnecessarily high profits. Thus the mass-production techniques innovated in the automobile industry had by the late 1920s simply led to overproduction, which could not be absorbed through advertising, salesmanship, or the extension of consumer installment credit. And once market saturation in the automobile industry became apparent, there was no incentive for capitalists to invest still more capital in the future of automobility.

The American people could not have done worse in 1932 had they deliberately set out to elect a president who was ignorant of the implications of the automobile revolution. Franklin Delano Roosevelt's public statements about the automobile while he was governor of New York reveal a naïveté and short-sightedness even beyond Warren G. Harding's a decade earlier. In his speeches Roosevelt continually hailed the motorcar for "making it possible for those of us who live in the cities to get out into the country, whole families at a time," and for "helping to correct a lop-sided situation" in the distribution of population by "making farm life more socially interesting as well as more financially profitable." Roosevelt thought that to pay for "new forms of necessary governmental expenditure brought about by changes of modern civilization. . . . a gasoline tax is the best solution of the problem." As late as the summer of 1931 he enthused that "the possibility of diversifying our industrial life by sending a fair proportion of it into the rural districts is one of the definite possibilities of the future. Cheap electric power, good roads, and automobiles make such a rural industrial development possible." "The automobile, the bus, and the truck have become as important in the transportation of finished products and in some cases of materials as in the movement of workers. Huge vans of manufactured goods travel great distances from factory to market on the public roads," said F.D.R., acknowledging the obvious. "We have seen how transportation has reduced distances and made rural living practicable today where it was not a generation or more ago, when the pattern of the factory town of the old style was devised." [56]

Probably the main reason that the New Deal failed to return the nation to prosperity, much less resolve the basic crises of our emergent urban-industrial social order, was that the Roosevelt administration never identified adequately the sources of the depression. Walter Lippmann perhaps hit the nail on the head when he called Roosevelt "a pleasant man who, without any important qualifications for the office, would very much like to be President." Raymond Moley, leader of the so-called Brain Trust, said in 1939 that "to look upon [New Deal] policies as the result of a unified plan was to believe that the accumulation of stuffed snakes, baseball pictures, school flags, old tennis shoes, carpenter's tools, geometry books, and chemistry sets in a boy's bedroom could have been put there by an interior decorator." The diverse and most often contradictory "pragmatic" responses of the Roosevelt administration to the depression had as a unifying principle only that underconsumption was the problem. But William E. Leuchtenburg points out nevertheless that the "Heavenly City" of the supposedly antiutopian New Dealers was "the greenbelt town, clean, green, and white, with children playing in light, airy spacious schools . . . immaculate farmsteads on broad, rectangular streets." [57]

Fundamental reform was impossible in part because the New Deal failed to question the central values intimately associated with automobility—material prosperity and progress through unlimited production and consumption of consumer goods, and the fusing of rural and urban advantages in a suburban Utopia. Even had the New Deal rejected these tenets of the automobile culture, however, it would undoubtedly have been politically inexpedient to have attempted to curb or drastically change the nature of American automobility. For automobility was one of the few aspects of American life that did not come under critical, disillusioned questioning by the man in the street during the 1930s.

Aware that the recovery of the automobile industry was important to restoring the prosperity of the 1920s, however, President Roosevelt took a personal interest in the National Recovery Administration code drafted for the automobile industry. "The subjects to which the code committee gave greatest attention were hours, wages, and management labor relations," writes Sidney Fine in his definitive study. Maximum weekly hours for workers were set at forty-eight, and it was stipulated that working hours averaged on an annual basis should not exceed thirty-five hours a week, a substantial reduction from the average weekly hours worked in the automobile industry in the 1920s. But Fine notes that 95 percent of the auto workers were already making more than the 43 cent minimum hourly wage set by the code before it was approved by the president on August 26, 1933. Under Section 7(a) of the National Industrial Recovery Act, workers ostensibly were given the right to organize and engage in collective bargaining with management. Yet Roosevelt overrode his own Labor Advisory Board and permitted an affirmation of the automobile industry's open shop policy to stand in the code. The automobile code did not encompass the parts and accessories manufacturers, contained no reference to trade practices, and failed to define the relationship between automobile manufacturers and their dealers and suppliers. "The Consumers' Advisory Board pointed out that the code was of little interest to consumers. . . . It noted that the highly competitive character of the industry protected the consumer in so far as price was concerned." The NACC was made the code authority and was entrusted with its administration, while neither organized labor nor the consumer was represented. Henry Ford refused to sign, and the Roosevelt administration did not have sufficient will or the power to make him sign. Thus the code at best reduced average hours, which the depression was doing anyway, and maintained workers' wages—which accounted for only 10 percent of the wholesale price of a car. As Fine says, "the automobile manufacturers, in final analysis, had their way." [58]

On May 27, 1935, a unanimous decision of the Supreme Court in *Schecter Poultry Corporation* v. *the United States* declared the National Industrial Recovery Act unconstitutional. The best summary of the pathetic ineffectiveness of the automobile industry code was probably given by Alfred Reeves, who spoke for the Automobile Manufacturers Association (AMA), the successor of the NACC. Reeves said that "neither the industry nor its employees benefitted from the code while it existed and neither have [*sic*] suffered any loss from its termination." The code certainly did not create jobs for automobile workers or improve the working conditions of those fortunate enough to remain employed. It did nothing to lower the prices of cars for the consumer. It did not even lead to higher profits for the manufacturer. And it did nothing to check the attrition of the small automobile producer and the parts and accessories manufacturers from the automobile industry, which had accelerated in the 1920s and snowballed in the depression. The main impact of the NIRA was that it stimulated labor organization and gave an impetus for management to pay more attention to labor relations.[59]

"Whether native- or foreign-born, white or black, male or female, the workers in the [automobile] industry in the pre–New Deal era had at least one characteristic in common," Fine observes. "They were, in the vast majority, almost entirely innocent of trade unionism in so far as their personal work experience was concerned." Rae describes the halfhearted attempts of the American Federation of Labor (AFL) to unionize the automobile industry in the 1920s and early 1930s as "monumental ineptitude. . . . The leadership of the AFL was obviously more concerned with protecting the jurisdictional rights of existing craft unions than with developing an organizational structure that would meet the needs of the automobile workers." However, no greater success was achieved by the radical International Workers of the World (IWW).[60]

Labor unrest in the automobile industry spread with massive unemployment and the deterioration of working conditions as the depression deepened. On March 7, 1932, the miniscule, communist-dominated Auto Workers Union staged a march of the unemployed on the Ford River Rouge plant that ended in a violent encounter with the Dearborn police. In 1933 the parts and accessories manufacturers were plagued by spontaneous, sporadic strikes. Section 7(a) encouraged the AFL to establish a network of "United Automobile Workers Federal Unions," open to automobile workers whose skills did not fit other AFL unions. The automobile manufacturers tried to neutralize Section 7(a) by setting up espionage systems to rout union sympathizers from their plants and by trying to organize company unions.

The National Labor Relations (Wagner-Connery) Act of July 5, 1935, replaced Section 7(a) after the NIRA was declared unconstitutional. The so-called Wagner Act set up a National Labor Relations Board. It was empowered to conduct elections to determine workers' bargaining agents and units and to restrain employers from "unfair labor practices," including the discharging of workers for union membership and the setting up of employer-dominated company unions. Roosevelt at first opposed the Wagner bill but reversed himself and declared it "must" legislation. "The Wagner Act was one of the most drastic legislative innovations of the decade," observes Leuchtenburg. "It threw the weight of government behind the right of labor to bargain collectively, and compelled employers to accede peacefully to the unionization of their plants. It imposed no reciprocal obligations of any kind on unions. No one, then or later, fully understood why Congress passed so radical a law with so little opposition and by such overwhelming margins." Perhaps the main reason, as Leuchtenburg concludes, was that "the Wagner Act and the movement for industrial unionism were motivated in part by the desire to contain 'unbalanced and radical' labor groups." [61]

Coincident with the passage of the Wagner Act, the AFL issued a charter to the International Union, United Automobile Workers of America (UAW). And within the AFL, in November 1935, a group headed by John L. Lewis, Sidney Hillman, and David Dubinsky set up the Committee for Industrial Organization (CIO) with the objective of abandoning the craft union principle of the AFL and organizing industrial unions in the mass-production industries that had resisted unionization. The CIO separated from the AFL in August 1936, taking along the UAW, headed by Homer Martin and the aggressive young Reuther brothers, Walter and Victor. At this time only about 15 percent of the automobile workers were organized.

By the end of 1936 the UAW had closed most General Motors plants through the newly innovated tactic of the sit-down strike. Workers stopped work but remained in the plants so that strike-breakers could not be brought in. After Governor Frank Murphy of Michigan, wanting to avoid bloodshed, refused to call out the troops to evict the workers, GM capitulated and on February 11, 1937, accepted the UAW as the bargaining agent for its workers. Chrysler capitulated to the UAW sit-down tactics two months later. Because the Roosevelt administration failed to enforce the law, however, the Ford Motor Company remained in violation of the Wagner Act, the constitutionality of which had been upheld by the Supreme Court, until 1941. Members of the Ford Service Department brutally beat Walter Reuther and several other organizers in the notorious "battle of the overpass" at the River Rouge plant on May 26, 1937. A spontaneous walkout of the Ford workers on April 1, 1941, following the discharge of several union members, closed down the River Rouge plant. Negotiations led to an NLRB election that resulted in an overwhelming majority for the UAW. On June 20 Henry Ford finally signed a formal contract with the UAW, ironically agreeing to more generous terms than GM or Chrysler.[62]

Highway construction and improvement were the only areas other than labor relations in which the New Deal affected American automobility. The federal government gave its first support to building a national system of roads with the passage of the Federal Aid Road Act of 1916, which appropriated $75 million to be spent by the secretary of agriculture for the improvement of post roads over a five-year period. The great growth in automobile registrations and the demonstration of the value of long-distance trucking in World War I led to the Federal Highway Act of 1921, which provided federal aid to the states, through fifty-fifty matching grants, for building a connected interstate system of highways. Under the act $75 million were appropriated for 1922 alone. After Roosevelt came to power, federal aid was extended to urban segments of primary roads in 1934 and to secondary "feeder" roads in 1936—in Rae's words, "a major change in national highway policy." In addition, to offset declines in state and local expenditures for streets and roads, and as a "time-honored method of relieving unemployment," the New Deal spent vast sums of federal money on highways. "By 1939 relief and recovery accounted for 80 percent of all federal expenditures for roads and 40 percent of the total outlay on highways from all sources," writes Rae. "Between 1933 and 1942 federal relief agencies spent $4 billion on roads and streets."[63]

The automobile industry began to prosper again with the general upswing in the economy as the Roosevelt administration shifted its emphasis from relief and recovery to national defense in 1939–1940. William S. Knudsen, who had replaced Alfred P. Sloan, Jr., as president of General Motors on May 3, 1937, left GM on May 27, 1940, to accept an appointment at no salary on the Advisory Committee of the Council for National Defense. He was made codirector, with Sidney Hillman, of the Office of Production Management (OPM) on January 7, 1941, to coordinate defense production, purchasing, and priorities in consultation with Secretary of War Henry L. Stimson and Secretary of the Navy Frank Knox. The OPM was under the Supply, Priority, and Allocations Board (SPAB), chaired by Vice-President Henry Wallace. When the SPAB was abolished on January 16, 1942, its functions were taken over by the War Production Board (WPB), chaired by Donald M. Nelson. Knudsen was "demoted" to lieutenant general and director of war production in the War Department. He resigned from the army on June 1, 1945, to become a member of the General Motors board of directors.

Two of the most salient realities of contemporary American life were thus inaugurated in Roosevelt's third term in office: the linking of prosperity since 1940, even in predominantly consumer-goods industries, to huge military expenditures; and the increasing involvement of top executives in the military-industrial complex. Knudsen's changing of hats proved a harbinger of Charles E. Wilson, the GM president from 1941 to 1953, being appointed secretary of defense in the Eisenhower administration, and Robert S. McNamara, president of the Ford Motor Company, being secretary of defense under Presidents Kennedy and Johnson.

The contributions of the automobile industry to the war effort are most fully recounted in the Automobile Manufacturers Association, *Freedom's Arsenal: The Story of the Automotive Council for War Production* (Detroit: Automobile Manufacturers Association, 1950). The AMA sponsored the formation of the Automotive Council for War

Production (ACWP) shortly after the attack on Pearl Harbor. Twelve divisions of the ACWP coordinated the conversion of the industry's resources to the war effort. Alvan Macauley, president of both the AMA and the Packard Motor Company, became chairman of the ACWP. Its chief executive officer was George K. Romney, managing director of the AMA. Romney's capable performance brought him national recognition—not only the start of a brilliant career in the postwar auto industry, as champion of the compact car at American Motors, but the start as well of a career in public life. He was elected governor of Michigan in 1962, 1964, and 1966; was a candidate for the Republican presidential nomination in 1968 (but withdrew his name in February 1968); and was appointed secretary of the Department of Housing and Urban Development in the Nixon administration on January 22, 1969.

World War II brought great curtailment in automobile use in the United States. The manufacture of motor vehicles for the civilian market ceased on February 22, 1942, despite the reluctance of automobile manufacturers faced with an expanding market for the first time since the 1920s. Tires and gasoline were severely rationed for the duration of the war. Motor vehicle miles of travel decreased from 334 billion in 1941 to 213 billion in 1944, highway expenditures fell from their 1938 high of $2.659 million to a 1944 low of $1.369 million, and receipts from special motor vehicle use taxes dropped from $2.186 million in 1941 to a low of $1.649 million in 1944. Cars that had been nursed through the depression long after they were ready to be junked were patched up further to survive through the war. Consequently, the wholesale value of replacement parts for the domestic market, $718 million in 1941, rose to a new high of $778 million in 1944 after hitting a $472 million low in 1942. Although the production of passenger cars was only 102,000 in 1943 and 447,000 in 1944, the production of trucks and buses doubled from 567,800 in 1940 to 1.069 million in 1941 and was over 1.7 million in 1944. Before the war ended, the automobile industry had produced for the military 4.131 million engines, 5.947 million guns, 2.812 million tanks and trucks, and 27,000 completed aircraft. Automobile manufacturers made some seventy-five essential military items, most of them unrelated to the motor vehicle. The military materials produced by the automobile industry during World War II had a total value of $29 billion and constituted one-fifth of the nation's entire war production. "The automobile industry was the country's greatest reservoir of 'know how' and skill in the technique of making, accurately and reliably, the largest possible number of items in the shortest possible time," concludes Rae.[64] American superiority in mass-production techniques developed in the automobile industry was indeed the main reason why the Allies won World War II.

Following the war, pent-up demand for cars and general affluence ensured the automobile industry banner sales, which lasted into the mid-1950s. The automobile industry further solidified into a tight, joint-profit-maximizing oligopoly. Ambitious highway improvement programs at the state level were capped by the Interstate Highway Act of 1956, which committed the federal government to pay 90 percent of the construction costs for 41,000 miles of toll-free express highways.

As the smug, self-satisfied 1950s gave way to the discontentment and disenchantment of the 1960s, however, what had been the automotive dream became the automotive nightmare for an increasing number of Americans. The automobile culture remained an all-encompassing reality. Yet the automobile revolution ironically had sown the seeds of its own destruction. The sentiments that once supported unlimited automobility were rapidly being eroded as the motorcar came to be recognized as a major social problem.

7 THE DISENCHANTMENT

By the late 1950s, many Americans began to have critical second thoughts about the automobile industry and its product. John Keats caught the new mood well in his witty diatribe against the postwar American automobile culture, *The Insolent Chariots*. Said Keats, "The American's marriage to the American automobile is now at an end, and it is only a matter of minutes to the final pistol shot, although who pulls the trigger has yet to be determined." [1]

A handful of social critics such as Lewis Mumford fastened on the broader sociocultural and environmental issues, but the complaints of the 1950s against the automobile culture were in the main consumer-oriented. George K. Romney, while managing director of the Automobile Manufacturers Association (AMA), "felt the industry made a mistake in not preventing dealers from overcharging and forcing motorists to buy unwanted accessories during the postwar car shortage." [2] And when the seller's market for new cars changed to a buyer's market with the settlement of the Korean War in 1953, the sharpened competitive conditions resulted in dealers generally engaging in sales practices that not only were highly unethical but often skirted illegality. The now familiar sales "blitz" was introduced in 1953, and high-pressure tactics came to include grillings by teams

When writing contemporary history, one is tempted by each day's newspaper to revise or add to the text. The line becomes increasingly hazy between writing history and journalistic reporting. Inevitably a point is reached when one must stop collecting data and hope that one's generalizations prove to be adequate, if imperfect, predictions about major trends. My reaching that point roughly coincided with President Richard M. Nixon's resignation from office in August 1974, and developments after his resignation are not covered in my analysis. However, I do not believe that changes in presidential administrations have been very meaningful in the past for the periodization of American history. Nor do I think it probable that the Ford administration will depart from the status quo in its policies.

of salesmen in special rooms equipped with bugging devices. Customers were subjected to the "plain pack" (inflated charges for dealer preparation of the car); the "top pack" (an inflated trade-in allowance added to the price of the new car); the "finance pack" (exorbitant rates of interest on installment sales that most often involved a kickback to the dealer from the finance agency); the "switch" (luring the customer into the salesroom with an advertised bargain, then getting him to accept a worse deal on another car); the "bush" (hiking an initially quoted price during the course of the sale by upping the figures on a conditional sales contract signed by the customer); and the "highball" (reneging on an initially high trade-in offer after the customer committed himself to buying a new car). Few customers could have walked out of a salesroom without feeling that they had been victimized, and many people still shop for a new car with trepidation. Senator A. S. Mike Monroney spoke for most consumers when he said that the retail selling of automobiles by the mid-1950s had come to exhibit "the morality of an Oriental Bazaar." [3]

Despite disclaimers from Detroit, the evidence is unequivocal that the shoddy treatment of customers by dealers emanated from long-standing policies of the automobile manufacturers. The manufacturers forced their franchised dealers to accept too many cars and to maintain large stocks of unwanted parts and accessories. The allocations of popular models were tied to the acceptance of quotas of slower-selling cars. With the annual model change, components were arbitrarily changed in minor ways, forcing dealers to buy expensive new repair tools and needlessly to increase inventories of parts and accessories. Cars came off the assembly line with too many minor flaws that the dealer had to remedy at his expense for the customer. Dealers were forced to contribute to national advertising funds that did little to promote local sales. Books had to be kept in ways that exaggerated the dealers' profits, thereby increasing their taxes. High-volume "stimulator" dealerships were franchised in territories where competition was already ruinous. Phantom freight rates from Detroit were charged on cars assembled at much closer branch assembly plants. Franchises were arbitrarily canceled without adequate compensation for the dealers' investment. These dealers' complaints were investigated as early as 1938 by the Federal Trade Commission.[4] But virtually nothing was done to correct them until, at the request of the National Automobile Dealers Association (NADA), automobile marketing practices were investigated in 1955–1956 by a subcommittee of the United States Senate Committee on Interstate and Foreign Commerce.[5] With passage of the so-called Automobile Dealers Day in Court Act of 1956 (Public Law 1026), the worst abuses were corrected, and there was a general easing up of sales pressures on dealers. However, Detroit still defines dealer-manufacturer relations in ways that encourage the exploitation of customers so that the dealers can maintain average profits about equal to those for all retail businesses.[6]

Increasingly in the 1950s Detroit also faced the mounting criticism of its product. As early as 1938 the automotive engineer Delmar G. Roos, who contributed to the development of the jeep, stated a common-sense sine qua non of rational automotive design: "The object of an automobile is to transport a given number of people with reasonable comfort, with the least consumption of gasoline, oil and rubber, and for the slightest operating cost and prime price." An AMA analysis of extensive statistics on automobile use compiled by the Public Roads Administration revealed that 85 percent of all automobile trips were thirteen miles or less and were for essential purposes. Clearly, it was foolish to use, in the words of the AMA's Christy Borth, "two tons of automobile to transport a 105-pound blond." A survey undertaken by the Federation of Women's Clubs agreed with this criticism of Detroit's product; and the mayors of both New York City and Los Angeles took public stands for smaller cars to reduce smog, traffic congestion, and parking problems. In an article that attracted wide attention, Dr. S. I. Hayakawa, the prominent semanticist, wrote that, "except for some interesting experiments at the fringes of the market by American Motors and Studebaker, the dominating forces in the industry—General Motors, Ford, and Chrysler—are still carrying on (in 1958) their assault on consumer intelligence. The Big Three are producing no cars that are not expensive, hideous and (except for a few sizes) costly to operate and powered far beyond any ordinary needs." During the 1950s George K. Romney, the president of American Motors, was a lone voice in the industry campaigning against what he called the "Dinosaur in the Driveway." He was vindicated when his compact Rambler became "the only success story of the American automobile industry in 1958, a year which saw more cars imported than exported for the first time in the century." Romney reasoned that "consumers are rebelling against the size, large horsepower and the excessive styling changes made each year by many auto manufacturers." [7]

Detroit's reluctance to enter the small-car market was due to a traditional truism in automobile manufacturing—large cars are far more profitable to build than small ones. Fixed investments in plant and machinery, advertising expenses, and labor costs are about the same for a subcompact and a standard-size car, and raw material costs do not vary more than perhaps $500. Yet the standard-size car can be sold for as much as several thousand dollars more than the subcompact. Similarly, dealers' profit margins average 25 percent of the wholesale price for standard-size cars, 21 percent for compacts and intermediates, but only 17 percent for subcompacts. In addition to the consideration that the production of small cars shifts sales away from the far more profitable large cars, the buyers of economy cars are less likely to order them loaded with luxury extras, which typically are marked up much higher than the basic car, earning profits of 50 to 100 percent in some instances.

Led by the low-priced makes (Ford, Chevrolet, and Plymouth), a significant movement toward larger-size automobiles was inaugurated in the mid-1950s. As Lawrence J. White says, "Between 1949 and 1959, low, medium, and high price makes grew in all relevant dimensions. After 1959 the high and medium price makes tended to remain about the same size or shrink slightly, while the low price makes continued to grow." A result was that by 1958 "the current intermediate-sized cars, represented by the Ford Fairlane and Oldsmobile F-85, are larger than was the full-sized Ford of 1949." The so-called horsepower race of the 1950s and 1960s was initiated with the introduction of the "Kettering engine"—a V-8, overhead-valve engine operating at a 7.5:1 compression ratio with high-octane gas that gave the 1949 Cadillac 160 horsepower on 331 cubic inches of displacement. In 1968, White points out, "the low priced three offered V-8's in the 200 horsepower range on their full-sized cars, sixes in the 150 horsepower range, with optional engines offering up to 400 horsepower. The minimum compression ratio in the industry was 8.25:1, with most standard engines falling in the 8.50:1 range; compression ratios as high as 11.00:1 were offered." Along with larger, more powerful cars, automatic transmissions, power steering, power brakes, and air conditioning came to be considered essential equipment, with about 90 percent of the standard-size cars sold having these "options" by the 1974 model year.[8]

The costs of automobile ownership rose accordingly. From 1949, when the Office of Price Administration (OPA) lifted its set prices, to 1971 the average wholesale value of an American-made passenger car increased from $1,229 to $2,481. The basic price of a Ford V-8, four-door sedan, for example, rose from $885 in 1946 to $1,546 in 1949, with the lifting of OPA controls; and suggested retail prices (including dealer preparation) for Ford V-8, four-door sedans ranged from $2,826 for the Maverick to $4,044 for the LTD Brougham in 1972, the last model year for which *Automotive Industries* included price data in its annual statistical edition. Operating costs also skyrocketed because heavier, more powerful cars with more convenience options guzzled gasoline and oil and were harder on tires (generally undersized for the weight of the car, anyway, to enhance a stylish low profile). Even a large Cadillac got 20 miles to a gallon of gasoline in 1949, but by 1973 American passenger cars averaged only 13.5 miles per gallon. The accelerated subordination of utility to style made cars increasingly more prone to extensive damage from even minor accidents, so repair bills and insurance premiums soared. In addition, motorists paid out countless billions in motor vehicle use taxes to revamp our streets and highways to accommodate ever wider, longer, heavier, and faster motorcars. All costs considered, the Department of Transportation estimated in 1974 that the average owner would pay out $15,893 to drive his standard-size car 100,000 miles over a ten-year period.

Cars also became less safe. Not only were increasingly less maneuverable cars traveling at faster speeds on the highway, but these cars were generally overpowered, undertired, and underbraked for their weights. Far more emphasis was placed upon styling than upon sound engineering in design, and several major styling innovations, such as the hardtop and the wraparound windshield, were obvious safety hazards. The emphasis upon comfort rather than upon safety dictated poorly designed seats, springing that was too soft, and an overall loss of "road feel." Accidents caused by mechanical failures resulted from the poor design of basic components and poor quality control. Until the 1968 model year, cars were also poorly designed to prevent occupants from "secondary collisions" when an accident occurred: doors tended to fly open, dashboards had too many needless protrusions, steering columns did not collapse, and cars lacked restraining devices to keep occupants from being thrown through windshields.[9]

The marketing strategy of planned product obsolescence innovated by Alfred P. Sloan, Jr., in the 1920s was implemented with a vengeance as the auto market became saturated in the 1950s and 1960s. Cars were made less durable, incurring a massive waste of scarce resources. Lowell Dodge, director of the Center for Auto

Safety, points out that data presented by Lawrence J. White indicate that "80.70 percent of cars made by the big three (GM, Chrysler, and Ford) which were nine years old on July 1, 1955 were still on the road that day. On July 1, 1967 only 55.23 percent of the nine-year-old cars made by the same companies were still on the road. The decrease occurs with a regularity that makes it look very much as if it were planned that way, or resulted cumulatively from cost-cutting programs. Analysis of further data confirms the trend toward decreased durability." In addition, "the strategy [of planned obsolescence] is implemented by purposeful proliferation of model types, which totaled 370 in 1967, to induce owners to trade up to something a little more glamorous." Dodge also notes that "Ford, Chrysler, American Motors, and GM all market cars delivered to retail buyers with an average number of 24 defects each, some safety related. The costs of completing the assembly of new cars are neatly shifted to owners by means of poorly performed warranty service, refusals of warranty coverage, and ineffectual dealing, with the consequent frustrations and complaints." [10]

These industry-engendered trends toward irrational automotive design culminated in the brief craze for high-performance, so-called muscle cars in the late 1960s, when countertrends in the domestic market for new cars toward economy and utility were becoming increasingly apparent. Mounting inflation, shortages of fuel and materials, and continuing environmental concerns promise to make this reversion to rational automotive design permanent by the late 1970s.

The American automobile industry faced mounting competition from foreign imports. The Volkswagen "Beetle"—basically un-changed in styling since its conception in 1937—overcame early newspaper aspersion as "Hitler's car," reaching a record sale of 569,292 units in the United States in 1968; by 1970, Americans had bought over 4 million VWs. Despite the Big Three's introduction of compact and subcompact models to compete with imports, the share of the U.S. market for new cars accounted for by foreign competitors increased from 5 percent in 1963 to 16 percent in 1971. Since 1968, Japanese producers have been the most aggressive and dynamic force in the American automobile market. By late 1971 the Japanese alone were selling more cars in Southern California, the bellwether of our automobile culture, than either Ford or Chevrolet. In world markets, Detroit slipped even worse vis-à-vis foreign competitors: the U.S. share of the world market for passenger cars plunged from 72 percent in 1955 to only 36 percent in 1970.

In response to the increasingly stiffer Japanese and Common Market competition, the American automobile industry in the early 1970s belatedly and reluctantly shifted its emphasis away from so-called traditional four-door family sedans. It began to concentrate upon producing smaller, more economical, and sportier-looking so-called contemporary models that brought lower unit profits. Changes in the engine specifications of American passenger cars from the 1968 to the 1974 model year illustrate this trend well: average brake horsepower (bhp) decreased from 252.2 to 182.5; average rpm at maximum bhp decreased from 4,547 to 4,062; the average compression ratio decreased from 9.47 to 8.26, while the average displacement increased from 331.5 to 359.8 cubic inches. The two devaluations of the dollar by the Nixon administration, combined with worldwide inflation, also helped Detroit dull the competition from foreign imports: by the first quarter of 1974 the port of entry price of a VW "Super Beetle" without options or accessories had climbed to $2,849, as opposed to a basic price of $2,442 for a Ford Pinto. Consequently, although imports continued to account for about 15 percent of U.S. sales, six out of ten small cars sold in the United States by 1974 were American-made—up significantly from only four out of ten in 1969.

The shift to smaller cars was dramatically accelerated in 1973 as a result of runaway inflation and consumer concern over a rapidly developing fuel shortage. In December 1973, for the first time in the

United States, the sales of cars with wheelbases under 112 inches surpassed those of standard-size cars, and they continued to account for 53 percent of the market during the first quarter of 1974. Automobile manufacturers were unable to supply the demand for small cars, while inventories of larger models piled up to double the normal 60–65 days in storage lots and dealers' showrooms. Wholesale auctions of used big cars showed average prices down $600–$1,000 over the previous year.

Only American Motors, which had continued to emphasize compact and subcompact models, was prepared for this marked shift in demand. The timetables of the Big Three for switching over production to smaller models had not anticipated that this shift would occur before the 1977 model year. Giant GM's plans, as late as December 1973, called for compacts and subcompacts to account for less than 25 percent of its production for the 1974 model year. Chrysler hoped to increase its 1974 profits by concentrating on the more profitable big cars. Ford, on the other hand, hoped by March 1974 to shift 50 percent of its production to five compact and subcompact models. Henry Ford II announced: "I'm a small-car man. I'm a promoter of small cars. . . . The big car as we know it today is on its way out. That's gone forever." He predicted that small cars would soon account for two-thirds of the U.S. market. Whether the smaller car would ultimately mean lower prices to the consumer was conjectural, however, because auto manufacturers planned to make up for declining unit profits on small-car sales by loading them with luxury extras. "Wait until you see all the optional equipment on that Mustang II," Ford President Lee A. Iacocca explained to a *Newsweek* reporter. "We can't start selling stripped cars; no use kidding you on that. . . . The American motorist wants economy— at any price." [11]

Unreasonable insistence upon incredibly high and constant profits is the main reason why American automobile manufacturers lost ground to Common Market and Japanese producers both at home and abroad. The American industry has been reluctant to switch over to the production of smaller cars at smaller unit profits. It has been equally reluctant to reinvest an adequate proportion of its huge profits into improving its product and improving manufacturing techniques to raise the level of its productivity. Contrary to popular belief, the American automobile industry's inability to compete has very little to do with the high hourly wages paid to American automobile workers. As Emma Rothschild concludes, "If it were correct that German, Japanese, and American manufacturers were equally productive, the entire labor cost advantage of VWs sold on the American market would be cancelled out by transportation costs: the advantage of Toyota makers in labor costs would be only $50. International differences in raw material costs are small; in any case American car manufacturers buy Japanese steel, and Japanese steelmakers buy American coke and ore. Foreign manufacturers produce cars cheaply, then, because they have a high level of productivity, and because they accept smaller profits than American corporations. GM makes about three times as great a profit on each vehicle it produces as its foreign competitors: a profit of $239 per vehicle world-wide in 1969, compared to $75 per vehicle for Toyota, $59 per vehicle for VW, and $57 per vehicle for Datsun-Nissan." [12]

The postwar American automobile industry has earned excessive profits not only in comparison with foreign automobile manufacturers but also in comparison with other American industries. In the first scholarly analysis of the economics of the postwar American automobile industry, Lawrence J. White points out that during the 1946–1967 period the industry averaged an 11.51 percent rate of return on total assets and a 16.67 return on net worth, compared with average profits for all manufacturing corporations of 6.64 and 9.02, respectively, on these criteria.[13] White cites Gordon R. Conrad and Irving H. Plotkin, who tried to estimate the relation between rates of return and risk, using a sample of 783 companies grouped into 59 industries.[14] The sample included Detroit's Big Three plus the leading "independents," Studebaker and American Motors. Using the extremely weak criterion that 8.6 percent was the return on a riskless investment in an industry where some monopoly profits were earned, the five automobile companies had an average rate of return of 17.9898 percent and an average variance of 58.127 percent for the 1950–1965 period. When the variance is accounted for in the equation, the expected average rate of return, adjusted for risk for the automobile industry, is 13.4 percent, showing that the actual rates of return included excess profits over and above a generous risk premium. Of the 59 industries examined by Conrad and Plotkin, only the cosmetics industry, notorious for overpricing its products, showed a greater margin between the actual rate of return and the risk-adjusted rate of return. White points out that normal profits would have meant 3.5 percent lower wholesale prices on new cars.

Especially in view of the excessive profits earned, White finds that the performance of the postwar automobile industry leaves much to be desired. He points out that "the automobile industry may be described as a technologically stagnant industry in terms of its product. Cars are not fundamentally different from what they were in 1946; very little new technology has been instigated by the industry. The product has improved over the last twenty years, but these have been small improvements with no fundamental changes. The sources for these improvements have often been the components suppliers, rather than the auto companies themselves; and the auto companies have often been slow to adopt these improvements." He also notes that foreign automobile manufacturers during this same period developed and produced commercially the rotary piston engine, a pneumatic suspension system, a commercially feasible fuel-injection system, and a diesel engine for use in passenger cars. Product improvement to make cars safer and less polluting had to be forced on American automobile manufacturers by the government. In addition, the industry was slow in responding to the compact car boom of the late 1950s and the subcompact boom of the late 1960s. As White says, "Throughout the postwar period, one gets the impression that the Big Three were a tight oligopoly, convinced that they and they alone knew what kinds of cars the American public wanted. Not too surprisingly, those kinds of cars also appeared to be the most profitable for them to produce."

When one turns to manufacturing technology, the record of the automobile industry looks better: "The motor vehicle has out-distanced the rest of manufacturing in its labor productivity gains, particularly on the production worker productivity basis." However, White finds that, "when there have been new fundamental processes developed [in automobile manufacturing] . . . the initial development of these processes has usually taken place outside of the automobile industry. The industry has usually been fairly prompt in adopting and adapting these processes, but, again, as in automotive technology, it appears to have let others take the risks of initial development." In sharp contrast to the auto industry's earlier impact on the technologies of ancillary industries, "in nonautomotive manufacturing areas, like steel and glass, the auto companies do not appear to have made any special contributions to new technology and appear to have been somewhat slow in adopting the major technological developments of these industries." [15]

High average profits for the automobile industry as a whole reflect in large part the performance of General Motors, the industry leader, which averaged 14.67 percent on total assets and 20.67 percent on net worth in the 1946–1967 period. Excluding General Motors, average profits for the automobile industry on these criteria were 7.76 and 11.41 percent, respectively. GM's superior performance since the 1920s has not been due to any significant edge over its competitors in making better cars available to the consumer at lower prices. The main reason for the giant corporation's consistent, huge profits is that GM innovated a corporate structure, management techniques, and financial controls that vastly increased the internal efficiency of the firm and insulated it against the short-range vicissitudes of the market. Another reason is that, as the leader of a tight, joint-profit-maximizing oligopoly in automobile manufacturing, GM has been able to define competitive conditions in the automobile industry in ways that guarantee the firm excessive profits at a minimal risk of capital. George Schwartz, assistant director of the United Automobile Workers' (UAW) research department, points out the ironic result that, "in the auto industry, the lowest risk producer earns the highest return and the highest risk producer the lowest." [16]

Pierre S. du Pont and Alfred P. Sloan, Jr., were probably the first entrepreneurs fully to recognize that giant enterprise in a technologically sophisticated consumer-goods industry necessitated major changes in the structure and operations of the firm. At General Motors in the 1920s they pioneered the decentralized, multidivisional structure of the modern industrial corporation. Entrepreneurial decisions were separated from managerial ones and became group decisions based on objective criteria and expertise. New emphasis was put upon the collection and interpretation of data essential to long-range planning and upon channels of communication within the firm. The concept of the ideal executive changed from the traditional risk-taking entrepreneur to the security-oriented technician who worked well in a group.[17]

Under du Pont and Sloan, GM's vice-president of finance, Donaldson Brown, developed an ingenious system of financial controls. "Under his concept," Sloan explained, "General Motors' economic objective was to produce not necessarily the highest attainable rate of return on the capital employed, but the highest return consistent with attainable volume in the market. The long-term rate of return was to be the highest expectation consistent with a sound growth of the business, or what we called 'the economic return attainable.' " This goal turned out to be about a 20 percent return on capital investment. An equation for computing return on investment worked out by Brown "was used to measure the effectiveness of each division's operation as well as to evaluate broad investment decisions." Then in 1925 Brown conceptualized a pricing policy, "which related a definite, long-term return-on-investment objective to average or 'standard volume' expectations over a number of years." The concept of standard volume permitted GM to determine unit costs (including taxes on profits) on the basis of "the estimated rate of operations at the normal or average annual utilization of capacity." Unit cost estimates were thus based on a conservative assessment of how many cars GM could expect to sell over a period of years at given prices. As a result, GM was able to set unit prices that would guarantee a minimally acceptable long-range profit on its capital investment, with a constant proportion of profits on actual sales being set aside for expansion of the business. With standard volume pricing, therefore, the profit margins acceptable to GM were protected against short-range cyclical or seasonal drops in demand for GM products. And when demand, which was conservatively estimated, increased beyond expectations, GM gained profit windfalls because the unit costs upon which its car prices were based had been estimated at a lower (consequently costlier) volume of production.[18]

These innovations made General Motors by the late 1920s the predominant force in an increasingly tighter, joint-profit-maximizing oligopoly in our major industry. When GM became the archetype, widely copied after World War II, of the rational, depersonalized business organization run by a technostructure, American capitalism was transformed.

The mature automobile industry, most especially General Motors, forms the implicit model of contemporary American capitalism cogently criticized in John Kenneth Galbraith's *The New Industrial State*. Galbraith points to GM as an outstanding example of a corporation that, because of its huge size and the small number of much weaker competitors, is able to set prices for its products and dictate consumer tastes and preferences. The outcome, of course, is that the consumer, enthroned as king in the mythology of American capitalism, is no longer sovereign. As Galbraith says, "The mature corporation has readily at hand the means for controlling the prices at which it sells as well as those at which it buys. Similarly, it has means for managing what the consumer buys at the prices which it controls. This control and management is required by its planning. The planning proceeds from use of technology and capital, the commitment of time that these require and the diminished effectiveness of the market for specialized technical products and skills." [19]

It is obvious that the American automobile industry operates on principles antithetical to the myths of the competitive free enterprise system. "Whether it be styling, engineering, distribution or pricing, the auto industry always seems to end up playing follow the leader," reported *Time* early in 1973. "If giant General Motors announces higher prices on new-model cars, for example, Ford and Chrysler customarily follow suit—even though they may have earlier announced lower prices for their new cars. During triennial rounds of labor negotiations, identical company wage offers usually appear on the three separate bargaining tables within minutes of one another." [20]

The relationship between the UAW and the automobile manufacturers in the postwar period also makes obvious the fallacy of the myth of New Deal reform that strong labor unions would check the abuses of large corporations. By 1970 the militant labor-management confrontations of the 1930s had simmered down to what UAW president Leonard Woodcock called "a civilized relationship." After a bitter strike against GM in the winter of 1945/46, the UAW until 1970 chose as its strike target every three years one of GM's much weaker competitors. The union could gain from them much more generous settlements, to which all auto manufacturers were bound by a 1955 pact. The union's concentration upon the weaker firms in the industry was a major factor in the decline of the marginal independents and the consolidation of GM's monopoly power. Its narrow concentration upon increased wages and costly fringe benefits—easily passed on to the consumer in the form of higher prices by the industry price leader—left GM's huge profit margins and preeminence in the auto industry untouched. When at long last the UAW leadership again selected GM as its strike target in 1970—to preserve credibility with the rank and file—the result was one of the costliest strikes in American history, a strike, however, that merely preserved the status quo.

In his study of the 1970 GM-UAW strike and the "civilized relationship" between the company and the union, labor reporter William Serrin concludes that, despite Walter Reuther's reformist platitudes, "the UAW does not work for change, not meaningful, fundamental change; it works for the perpetuation of its position, for the status quo." Serrin demonstrates that "industrial democracy is as foreign to the UAW as it is to General Motors" and adds that "the [UAW] leadership seemingly has little trust in the rank-and-file; it will not go to the workers and say that a large wage increase is unjustified, or that there are goals of greater importance than winning increased wages—let us change the factory system rather than increase wages or take more time off the job." [21]

The factory system in American automobile manufacturing needs fundamental change. For neither the American economy nor, in the long run, Detroit's profit margins can survive our growing productivity problem and increasing alienation on the assembly line, which threatens the quality of Detroit's product. A generation of assembly-line workers socialized into middle-class values and expectations by the public school system and the mass media can no longer tolerate the monotonous boredom of repetitive labor. Absenteeism in automobile plants has climbed to 13 percent (higher still on Mondays and Fridays) versus only 3 percent a few years ago. Alcoholism, drug use, and industrial sabotage have become commonplace on the assembly line. The problem is that the worker has changed while automobiles continue to be made essentially as they were in the 1920s. As Charles Reich says, "No person with a strongly developed aesthetic sense, a love of nature, a passion for music, a desire for reflection, or a strongly marked independence could possibly be happy in a factory or white collar job." [22] Of all factory jobs, work on an automobile plant assembly line is probably the most dehumanizing, for about 75 percent of the jobs in automobile manufacturing are unskilled versus only 10 percent in the rest of American industry.

Emma Rothschild perspicaciously analyzes Detroit's mounting labor-productivity problem. She blames the "technological inertia" and "managerial intransigence" that have kept the American auto industry wedded to outmoded "Fordist" mass-production methods and equally outmoded "Sloanist" marketing strategies. The basic patterns of assembly-line production and regimentation of factory labor innovated at the Ford Highland Park plant in 1913–1914 continue to be refined and intensified rather than changed. Concomitantly, Detroit persists in implementing the marketing strategies innovated by Alfred P. Sloan, Jr., at GM in the 1920s: constant "upgrading" of product and planned obsolescence, through the annual model change, to make cars each year more expensive, complicated, and nonutilitarian. "Sloanism" is antithetical to rational automotive design, wasteful of limited natural resources, and predicated on the unrealistic assumption that the auto industry should gain an increasing percentage of the consumer's dollar. Most important, automobiles designed to conform with "Sloanist" marketing strategies have become far too complicated and expensive to produce efficiently and competitively with "Fordist" mass-production methods. The American auto industry is thus caught on the horns of a self-created dilemma. Rather than simplifying and stabilizing automotive designs, American automobile manufacturers have clung to "Sloanist" marketing strategies while attempting to cut production costs to the bone through intensified "Fordist" regimentation of the factory. This combination has encouraged demoralization and discontent on the assembly line and lowered the quality of Detroit's product.[23]

As one might expect, given the technological stagnation of the American automobile industry, the most radical departure from the assembly-line method of production is being pioneered abroad at Saab-Scandia and at Volvo. At Saab's new Sodertalje plant in 1972, the production line for assembling engines was replaced with "production teams." Groups of three workers are responsible for assembling the entire engine, with each worker doing the whole series of assembling tasks. Volvo began assembling whole automobiles with twenty-man work teams at two new plants, costing a total of $50 million, completed in 1974. The Saab experiment—closely watched by Detroit—has had mixed results. Saab claims that better-quality engines are produced by the production-team method, and the experiment undoubtedly has had great advertising and public relations value. However, for the same production rate as on an assembly line, capital costs for plant and equipment and for job training are higher, and the job turnover rate at Saab is about the same. Also, it has been impossible so far to do away with repetitive line-production jobs for three-quarters of the 200 workers at Saab's engine plant. Finally, Saab spokesmen have been the first to point out that what is feasible for the Sodertalje plant's annual production of only 110,000 engines probably would not be good for General Motors. To set up a group assembly system to produce, say, a million engines annually would involve far more formidable problems because of both space requirements and the high cost of the additional machine tools that must be installed in every assembly bay.[24]

The American automobile industry is not apt, therefore, to solve its mounting labor-productivity problem by switching to the group assembly system. American automobiles are already overpriced in saturated domestic and world markets; so the additional production costs could not easily be passed on to the consumer, and cutting profit margins remains anathema to Detroit. Nor can American automobile manufacturers hope to achieve with present-day American laborers the paternalistic labor-management relations that are a factor in the high productivity of Japanese assembly-line workers.

Recognizing these facts, Detroit has tried to solve its labor-productivity problems through intensified "Fordism" on domestic assembly lines and through the expansion of overseas manufacturing operations. That the former will not work has been demonstrated at GM's Lordstown, Ohio, Vega plant—the most technologically advanced and costly factory in modern automotive history, where extensive automation permits turning out 101 cars an hour instead of the usual 55 to 60. The Lordstown plant quickly gained notoriety as a hotbed of labor unrest and production problems, while the Vega, in Rothschild's words, came to be "criticized by the American consumer movement with an urgency unknown since the downfall of the Chevrolet Corvair." On the other hand, Detroit may well keep afloat for a while through increased dependence upon captive imports, such as the Dodge Colt and the Mercury Capri, plus an accelerated farming out of the manufacture of components for domestically assembled models to the lowest bidding foreign firm. "Capitalist Darwinism can expect no end in the efficiency of *Homo Sapiens*," explains Rothschild. "Industrial species are fated to boom and die perpetually, as business evolves from one need to the next. . . . Low-technology and labor-intensive industries [such as the auto industry] move to ever less developed countries with low-paid workers." But this corporate imperialism will be at the expense of the further exploitation of Third World people, unemployment for American workers, and the health of our national economy. UAW president Leonard Woodcock has warned that the current proliferation of multinational corporations threatens political-economic domination of the world by fewer than two hundred gargantuan firms within a decade.[25]

Despite the American automobile industry's problems, there were many indications into the early 1970s that Detroit would continue to be prosperous and powerful for the foreseeable future. The American automobile culture continued to flourish throughout the 1960s. Drive-in facilities were extended from motion picture theaters and restaurants to banks, grocery stores, and even churches; the cults of the hot rod and the sports car gained devotees; interest in restoring antique automobiles grew by leaps and bounds; and a newly apparent mass market for recreational vehicles resulted in an avalanche of motor homes, campers, snowmobiles, and trail bikes decimating our national parks and forests. The best indications of the automobile culture's continuing vitality in 1972 were that motor vehicle factory sales exceeded 11.3 million units, registrations surpassed 117.4 million units (plus 1.7 million publicly owned motor vehicles), and 83 percent of American families owned cars, compared with only 59 percent as late as 1950. Production in 1972 lagged behind the demand for new cars, and record-breaking factory sales were made for the fourth straight year in 1973. Most observers agreed that to the average person the automobile remained an important symbol of individualism, personal freedom, and mobility in our increasingly collectivized and bureaucratized society.

Looking beyond these surface manifestations of America's marriage to the motorcar, however, it was evident by the early 1970s that the love affair had ended. Much of the earlier romance of motoring was lost to a generation of Americans, reared in an automobile culture, who accepted the motorcar as a mundane part of the establishment. And for most Americans automobility had lost the quasi-religious connotations criticized by Lewis Mumford in the early 1960s and had become mainly utilitarian. "The novelty and status of car ownership are long gone," reported the *Wall Street Journal* in 1971. "People today look at their cars as appliances to get them economically from place to place and to be replaced when they wear out." [26]

By the early 1970s automobility also was no longer a historically progressive force for change in American civilization. Unlimited mass accommodation to automobility ended as government came to recognize the automobile as a major social problem and to regulate the automobile industry. Although that industry still provided one out of every six jobs in the United States, its hegemony in our society and economy had been progressively eroded over the preceding generation by proliferation of the size, importance, and power of government, which provided one out of every five jobs by 1970. With increased international involvement, the rise of a nuclear warfare state, and the exploration of outer space, new industries more closely associated with the military-industrial complex (especially aerospace) became, together with the federal government, more important forces for change than the mature automobile industry. By 1970 automobility was having far less impact on changing American institutions and values than either television or the computer. And with the progressive saturation of markets for durable consumer goods our economy was tending to become more service-oriented.

By the early 1970s saturation points had been reached in both the domestic and the world market for motorcars. In 1973 the United States had one car for every 2.25 people—more cars than people in the Los Angeles area. The market for cars was also saturated in Japan and in the developed nations of Europe—not in the ratio of cars to population but in the ratio of cars to land and paved roads. The low per capita incomes and the inequitable income distribution in underdeveloped countries posed an impossible barrier to the development of new automobile cultures. The expansion of mass personal automobility anywhere in the world was further prohibited by environmental concerns and growing awareness of dwindling world oil reserves. As Emma Rothschild says, "There is perpetually for the auto companies of the 1970s, a danger that next year or next decade the limits of the car market may collide with the limits of human irrationality." [27]

For all these reasons, projections for a vast increase in the number of motor vehicles on our roads over the next several decades, and arguments that we must, therefore, continue to accommodate to automobility, have lost credibility. John B. Rae makes what will probably be the last as well as the best defense of our automobile culture in *The Road and the Car in American Life.* "Unless there is a radical change in our social and economic structure, people will continue to want and use transportation that will give them maximum freedom to move about and to choose where they live, work, or locate their businesses," Rae concludes. "Putting artificial restraints on highway transportation can yield only economic and social stagnation. The Road and the Car together have an enormous capacity for promoting economic growth, raising standards of living and creating a good society. The challenge before us is to implement this capacity." [28] Many of Rae's arguments in defense of the road and the car seem incontrovertible, especially those focusing on the indispensable motortruck. Nevertheless, his analysis proceeds from value assumptions that have come to be as critically questioned as automobility: virtuous materialism, unlimited economic growth, unbounded faith in technological progress, and the sanctity of consumer needs and consumer democracy. Consequently, he fails to consider the inevitable limits to our reliance on the motorcar for mass transit posed by a deteriorating environment and the energy crisis. My opinion is that his caveat regarding "a radical change in our social and economic structure" seems more likely to occur by the turn into the twenty-first century than that we will (or should) meet the challenges essential to preserving our automobile culture.

Meaningful governmental regulation of the automobile industry and its product began in the mid-1960s, when it became apparent that Detroit was dragging its feet on voluntarily solving two problems of public concern—motor vehicle safety and environmental pollution. Automotive design came to be regulated by the federal government with passage of the Motor Vehicle Air Pollution Act of 1965 and the National Traffic and Motor Safety Act of 1966. Then, in a notable rejection of the tenets of the market economy, prices for new cars, as well as the wages of automobile workers, were made subject to governmental approval with the Nixon administration's 1971–1974 wage and price controls to curb inflation. Continuing concern over the environment and energy promises, by the late 1970s, severe legislation to limit the size and horsepower of passenger cars and to curb their use in urban areas and in our national parks. We can also expect the abuse of monopoly power in the automobile and oil industries to become a major issue, with critics asking for reforms ranging from traditional (and invariably ineffective) trust-busting to the nationalization of automobile manufacturing and oil production. As Senator Barry Goldwater warned in the wake of the 1974 fuel shortage: "The American private enterprise system—especially its basic industry segment—is headed for new and serious trouble in Congress. . . . I predict that Congress will, before long, be considering a barrage of bills to nationalize businesses or to impose greater controls or taxes on the domestic and foreign earnings of American industry." [29]

Reactionary defenders of the mythical free enterprise system ignore the reality that our highway system is already nationalized and that irrational proliferation of the post–World War II automobile culture occurred less because of consumer demand in a competitive market than because of the government's massive indirect subsidization of the automobile and oil industries, especially through the Interstate Highway Act of 1956. That act was the most ambitious public works program undertaken in our history. It committed the federal government to pay from a Highway Trust Fund 90 percent of the construction costs for 41,000 miles of toll-free express highways, to be completed by June 30, 1976. Between 1947 and 1970 the combined highway expenditures of the local, state, and federal governments in the United States totaled $249 billion.

Senator Gaylord Nelson calculated that over the preceding generation only 1 percent of governmental expenditures for transportation was for urban mass transit as opposed to 75 percent for highways. The lion's share of this huge expenditure for highways since 1956 has come from special use taxes on cars, gasoline, tires, lubricants, and parts paid by motorists into the Highway Trust Fund—which could be used only for highway expenditures until August 13, 1973. On that date President Nixon signed a compromise $22.9 billion highway aid bill providing for the first diversion of the fund to urban mass transit and extending the timetable for completion of the Interstate System to June 30, 1979. By the time the sacrosanct Highway Trust Fund was broken, 82 percent of the Interstate System was completed, another 16 percent was under construction, and, with the nation facing an imminent fuel shortage, the president was calling for a national 55-mph speed limit over the system's 80-mph express highways.

In her outspoken, well-researched *Superhighway—Super Hoax*,[30] Helen Leavitt describes how the Interstate System and its nondivertible Highway Trust Fund killed off possibilities for developing a balanced transportation system in the 1960s and benefitted mainly the special group of highway interests she calls collectively "the Road Gang"—including the automobile manufacturers and dealers; the automobile clubs; the oil oligopoly; truckers and the teamsters' union; and state highway administrators. She demonstrates convincingly that the Interstate System has not lived up to the claims made by "the Road Gang" to help sell it to the public. The system was never, as its proponents claimed, vital to national defense, and our superhighways have proved neither economical nor especially safe compared with mass-transit alternatives. The urban expressways built as part of the system have not, as we were led to anticipate, alleviated urban traffic congestion at peak hours. Instead, the building of urban expressways has destroyed cohesive urban neighborhoods and city parks, further alienated racial minorities, and contributed to the declining tax base of the central city. "As Eisenhower [who signed the Interstate Highway Act] himself might appreciate by now, things have changed," points out Ernest B. Furgurson. "The automobile has metamorphosed, from servant to master. The highway has passed the point of merely linking towns and cities, until now it functions mainly to channel congestion and pollution back and forth from cities to suburbs. . . . To continue to ram roads into our cities without making a major effort to develop parallel systems is to assure our strangulation." [31]

Despite the feverish building of improved highways after passage of the Interstate Highway Act, motor vehicle fatalities increased from 38,137 in 1960 to some 55,500 in 1968, the model year in which federal safety standards were imposed on new cars. By the mid-1960s over 4 million Americans a year were injured in automobile accidents. There were 570 fatalities for every 10 billion miles of travel by car—versus only 14 for every 10 billion miles flown, 13 for every 10 billion miles traveled by bus, and 5 for every 10 billion miles traveled by train.

Yet the automobile industry remained reluctant to subordinate styling to safety on the self-fulfilling assumption that "safety doesn't sell." Despite a 1955 pact between the automobile manufacturers that forbade them to support formal automobile racing or to advertise horsepower ratings, automobile advertisements continued to stress performance and portray cars as outlets for antisocial instincts. (The agreement not to support racing was widely violated as well, with the Ford Motor Company alone spending an estimated $20–30 million a year on racing activities in the mid-1960s.) An industry-sponsored Vehicle Equipment Safety Compact authorized by Congress in 1958 had passed only one safety standard (on tires) by 1965 and had no full-time staff members until 1966. In 1965 the Senate Government Operations Committee's Subcommittee on Executive Reorganization began investigating automotive safety under the leadership of its chairman, Senator Abraham A. Ribicoff.

Testimony revealed that General Motors had spent only $1.25 million on safety research in 1964 (GM later claimed $193 million) while making $1.7 billion in profits. And while the industry continued to deemphasize the role of cars in accidents, it was brought out by Ribicoff that since 1960 over 8 million cars (about one out of every five manufactured) had been recalled for defects, many of them safety related. Ralph Nader, then a consultant for the Ribicoff Committee, estimated that styling changes accounted for $700 of a car's retail price and suggested that most of this money should be diverted to making cars safer.[32]

Public consciousness of the safety issue reached new heights with the publication in late 1965 of Nader's *Unsafe at Any Speed: The Designed-in Dangers of the American Automobile.*[33] Nader's emphasis on the oversteering of the 1960–1963 Chevrolet Corvair was perhaps unfortunate. Nevertheless, his main contentions were sound. He pointed out forcefully the dangers of the "secondary collision" and the subordination of safety to styling in automotive design. The same points were made in a better-balanced book that attracted far less attention—Jeffrey O'Connell and Arthur Myers, *Safety Last: An Indictment of the Auto Industry.*[34]

In 1964 Congress set safety standards for motor vehicles purchased by the General Services Administration (GSA) for the federal government. By late 1965 several governmental groups in addition to Ribicoff's Subcommittee on Executive Reorganization were concerned with the issue of automotive safety. The most important were the staff of Senator Gaylord Nelson; the Senate Commerce Committee, chaired by Senator Warren G. Magnuson; and Joseph G. Califano, a special assistant to President Lyndon Johnson in charge of working up a 1966 legislative program that included a traffic safety bill. That an administration-backed bill would become law was guaranteed by the poor performance of executives of the automobile industry before congressional committees and by a scandalous case of personal harassment of Ralph Nader by GM, for which GM president James M. Roche apologized before the Ribicoff Committee and a national television audience. Nader brought a civil suit against GM for invasion of privacy, which the corporation settled out of court for $425,000.

The National Traffic and Motor Vehicle Safety Act of 1966 established an agency under the secretary of commerce (now the National Highway Traffic Safety Administration—NHTSA—in the Department of Transportation) to set safety standards for new cars beginning with the 1968 model year. The agency initially adopted the seventeen standards issued by the GSA for 1967 model cars purchased for the government. These standards included safety belts, padded visors and dashes (with recessed control and instrument knobs), safety door latches and hinges, impact-absorbing steering columns, dual braking systems, standard bumper heights, and glare reduction surfaces. With twenty-eight standards adopted by the 1969 model year, the Department of Transportation claimed a reduction in the rate of increase in highway fatalities from an average of 6.9 percent in the five years before 1966 to only 2.3 percent in the two years following passage of the National Traffic and Motor Vehicle Safety Act. Decreases both in bodily injury claims and in the number of injuries per automobile accident were also reported. Although annual traffic deaths remained fairly stable at about 55,000 in absolute numbers, by 1973 the combination of safer cars and improved highways was credited with decreasing by nearly 20 percent since 1966 the fatalities per hundred million vehicle miles traveled. The record seems especially good when one considers that as late as 1973 almost half our motor vehicle population antedated the incorporation of the 1968 safety standards and only three out of every ten drivers used safety belts. The failure to use safety belts accounted for about 10,000 unnecessary traffic fatalities a year by 1973. By 1974, compliance with federal safety standards had added more than $300 to the price of an average car.

The National Traffic and Motor Vehicle Safety Act also attempted to goad automobile manufacturers into eliminating defects from their cars by requiring public announcements of recalls. But the act seems to have had little success in reducing defects. By mid-1972 Detroit had recalled some 30.6 million motor vehicles since the reporting requirements went into effect, and the pace of recalls seemed to be accelerating. An estimated 5.8 million motor vehicles were recalled in the first half of 1972—an amount nearly equal to production. About three-fourths of the recalls up to that point were accounted for by General Motors.

The shift in emphasis in the safety crusade during the 1960s from the driver to defects in the car was long overdue and beneficial. However, the automobile industry tended to become a convenient scapegoat while other essential reforms were neglected. State governments lagged in instituting stringent periodic safety inspections of all cars registered because of expense and unpopularity with voters until the National Highway Traffic and Safety Administration in 1973 set standards giving states the choice of periodically inspecting brakes, steering, suspension, and tires or losing 10 percent of their federal highway funding. It acted after determining that wear of these components caused 6 percent and contributed to an additional 11 percent of all motor vehicle accidents.

State governments also consistently raised rather than lowered speed limits until, in response to the fuel shortage, a national 55-mph speed limit was put into effect on January 1, 1974. In the last two months of 1973 the sixteen states that had already reduced speed limits to conserve fuel experienced an 18.6 percent drop in highway fatalities, compared with only a 2 percent drop in the rest of the nation. With the imposition of the 55-mph speed limit nationally, the highway death toll for the first four months of 1974 showed a 23–26 percent reduction over the fatalities reported for the same months in 1973. It is estimated that from November 1973 through April 1974 some 4,700 lives were saved by the lower speed limits.

Although driving is in theory a privilege granted by the state, the necessity of being able to drive in our automobile culture has in practice made driving another inalienable American right. The training and certification of drivers remain hopelessly inadequate, with the result that operators' licenses are commonly handed out to people who are barely competent to drive a car, much less able to cope with emergency situations. Homicide and suicide by automobile are commonplace, but we have done virtually nothing to keep the psychologically disturbed off our highways. Despite data revealing that the abusive use of alcohol is involved in about half our highway fatalities, the drunks continue to drive. Our poor system of law enforcement furthermore assures that only 2 percent of the 2 million drivers who lose their licenses each year are actually taken off the road.

By the mid-1960s the rising carnage on the highway was only one indication of the deleterious impact of mass automobility on the quality of American life. What was once considered a healthy decentralization of business and residential patterns became the problem of "urban sprawl," and urbanologists began in many ways to question the wisdom of continuing to accommodate the city to the motorcar. The automobile suburb decentralized even more an already overly decentralized structure for political decision making, and the duplication of essential governmental services led to an inordinate rise in the costs of municipal government. Most important, the proliferation of the automobile culture contributed to the historical oppression of the dispossessed and racial minorities. "This combination—the equipping of all but the very poor with private automobiles, the enormous burst of highway construction, and the surburban housing of the white middle and upper class—not only consumed the resources of the country to the exclusion of alternative uses; they also led to further changes in economic patterns," points out Dan Lacy. "Industries were no longer confined to central urban locations that employees could reach by mass transportation. . . . Suburban locations were especially attractive to electronic and service industries . . . the most rapidly growing industries providing the most attractive job opportunities. The very ease of private automobile transportation led to a decay and abandonment of public transportation even where it existed, and there was little incentive for the establishment of new transit or bus lines to serve the new areas. Blacks who could not afford to own and maintain cars in the city were hopelessly blocked from employment in precisely those types of plants in which opportunities were largest and most promising." [35]

That this shift away from mass transit was not altogether due to consumer choice expressed in a competitive market was indicated by testimony in February 1974 at a hearing of Senator Philip A. Hart's antitrust subcommittee investigating the restructuring of the auto-mobile and ground transportation industries. Bradford C. Snell, the subcommittee's assistant counsel, charged that General Motors played a dominant role in destroying 100 electric surface rail systems in forty-five cities between 1932 and 1956. National City Lines—a holding company formed in 1936 by GM, Standard Oil of Califor-nia, and the Firestone Tire and Rubber Co.—had spent $9 million by 1950 to obtain control of street railway companies in sixteen states and convert them to less efficient GM buses. The companies were then sold to operators who signed contracts specifying that they would buy GM equipment. "Nowhere was the ruin from GM's motorization program more apparent than in Southern California," said Snell. National City Lines in 1940 began buying up and scrapping parts of Pacific Electric, the world's largest interurban electric rail system, which by 1945 served 110 million passengers in fifty-six smog-free Southern California communities. Eleven hundred miles of Pacific Electric's track were torn up, and the system went out of service in 1961, as Southern California commuters came to rely narrowly on freeways. By 1974 Los Angeles was struggling to reestablish the viable mass-transit system it had lost. Mayor Tom Bradley complained before the Hart subcommittee that GM had restricted competition and thwarted technological advances in bus manufacture. He anticipated that the Southern California Rapid Transit District alone needed 1,400 new buses, while nationwide production was only 3,700 in 1973. San Francisco Mayor Joseph Alioto, an antitrust lawyer, charged that a once fine electric rail system in the Bay Area also had been destroyed by "the terrifying power of the auto monopoly." He alleged that "the basic monopolistic practice in the auto industry is the interlacing and interlocking control of competing modes of transportation." [36]

As once smog-free cities and national parks deteriorated with the irrational proliferation of the automobile culture during the 1960s, environmentalists gained a broad base of popular support. People began to be concerned about the adverse impact of indiscriminate freeway building and urban sprawl upon the scenic beauty of the American countryside and about the preservation of our few remaining free-flowing streams and wilderness areas. "True outdoor fulfillment has become a six-wheel bus with a boat on top, trail bikes on carriers fore and aft, and, frequently, a dune buggy or compact runabout towed behind," lamented a former enthusiast of motorized camping in 1973. "Everywhere there is physical damage caused by the conflict between forest or meadow and the alien machine." In a long-overdue attempt to reduce congestion and air pollution in Yosemite National Park, restrictions were placed on access by automobile in 1972. The master plans for several other national parks contemplate banning the automobile entirely in the foreseeable future. Similarly, by early 1973, Southern California's freeway program—the most ambitious in the nation—was near collapse. "Clearly, the freewheeling, freeway-building days of the early 1960s, when every mile of freshly paved freeway was considered a blessing, are gone," reported the *Los Angeles Times*. "The changing mood about Southern California's freeway program has cast serious doubts on the future of all routes not yet built." A survey conducted by the paper indicated that more than half of Californians wanted restraints on freeway building on environmental grounds, and the completion of most freeways still on the drawing boards was being held up while state highway engineers completed environmental impact reports. Larry E. Moss, the Sierra Club's Southern California representative, voiced an increasingly widely shared opinion of the original planners of the state's freeway system: "Time has shown their vision was inadequate. They have put us into a horrible kind of box, committing us to a transportation system that was fundamentally evil." [37]

The paramount ecological issue persisting into the 1970s, of course, is the atmospheric pollution induced by automobility. Although its precise social and economic costs probably never can be accurately or adequately assessed, we know that exhaust fumes from the ever-present motorcar constitute a major cause of heart and respiratory diseases and that the continuation of air pollution at the present level constitutes a grave threat to the future of life itself on earth. In 1966, of an estimated 146 million tons of pollutants discharged into the atmosphere in the United States, 86 million tons were attributed to motor vehicle traffic. Since then, from 60 to 80 percent of atmospheric pollution has generally been attributed to the motorcar, with a figure of 97.5 percent being reported for Orange County, California, in 1973. For every 10,000 miles traveled a decade earlier, the average car without pollution controls discharged into the atmosphere 1,700 pounds of carbon monoxide, 520 pounds of hydrocarbons, and 90 pounds of nitrogen oxides. Motor vehicles were the major source of these pollutants and of lead compounds. The situation has improved greatly, but the battle for clean air is still far from won.

The recognition of the motor vehicle as a major source of air pollution came in the 1950s in smog-ridden Southern California. As with automotive safety, the automobile manufacturers did little to solve the problem until forced to by government. Although a joint committee to study motor-vehicle-caused atmospheric pollution was formed by the AMA in 1953 and a cross-licensing agreement covering pollution control devices was signed in 1954, automobile manufacturers were reluctant to add devices to clean up car emissions that would raise costs without adding sales appeal. "The compiled correspondence between Kenneth Hahn, Los Angeles County Supervisor, and the auto companies from 1953–1967 on the subject of automotive air pollution seems to be an accurate reflection of the companies' attitudes," concludes Lawrence J. White. "While assuring Hahn of their sincerest interest in the subject, they tended to take refuge behind the AMA committee and behind the issuance of technical papers; more information was needed they said, more research required. And, besides, better maintenance of vehicles would probably solve most of the problems." [38]

California framed the first legislation to reduce car emissions. Positive crankcase ventilation systems to reduce hydrocarbon discharge were required on all cars sold in California beginning with the 1963 model year. Exhaust control devices to reduce emissions of carbon monoxide, oxide of nitrogen, and lead compounds became mandatory in California beginning with the 1966 model year. The automobile manufacturers balked at installing nationally the devices required by law in California. But public pressure to do so became insurmountable with recognition that California's experience demonstrated that the basic technological problems had been solved. The Motor Vehicle Air Pollution and Control Act of 1965 resulted in national standards comparable to California's for the 1968 model year. These standards allowed an average of no more than 275 parts per million hydrocarbon emissions and 1.5 percent carbon monoxide emissions. By the 1970 model year the standards were raised to permit no more than 180 parts per million of hydrocarbon and 1.0 percent carbon monoxide emissions. Controls to eliminate gasoline evaporation were also required nationwide by 1971.

The passage in 1970 of Senator Edmund S. Muskie's amendments to the Federal Clean Air Act called for further reductions of about 90 percent in emissions, in grams per vehicle mile, to 0.41 carbon monoxide and 3.4 hydrocarbons by 1975, and to only 0.40 nitrogen oxide by 1976 (versus actual 1970 emissions, in grams per vehicle mile, of 46 carbon monoxide, 4.7 hydrocarbons, and 6.0 nitrogen oxide). In 1973 the Environmental Protection Agency (EPA), charged with enforcing the Clean Air Act, bowed to industry pressure that the 1975–1976 standards could not be met and granted the automobile manufacturers a two-year extension. Critics noted that, although the American automobile industry appeared to have reached a technological stalemate in pollution control, the 1975–1976 standards had already been met by three foreign imports—the rotary-engine Mazda, the stratified-charge-engine Honda, and the diesel-powered Mercedes-Benz.

Rather than risk large amounts of capital in innovating fundamental technological breakthroughs in engine design, Detroit pursued the conservative path of proliferating the desmogging devices on an already overly complicated basic power source. Consequently, the 1972 conventional engines were probably the last ones capable of acceptable performance that Detroit can produce. Current desmogged conventional engines get 10 to 15 percent less gas mileage than earlier uncontrolled engines; they are more difficult and expensive to maintain; and they have unsafe tendencies to surge from idle, stall, and "diesel" (keep running after the ignition key has been turned off). Despite their far poorer performance, EPA tests in early 1973 demonstrated that the vast majority of cars built between 1968 and 1971 failed to meet existing antipollution standards.

The main hope of meeting antipollution standards with conventional engines lies in perfecting the dual catalytic converter used with nonleaded fuels. Catalytic converters, required on all 1975 cars sold in California, were installed in GM's 1975 models. The National Academy of Sciences, however, has called the catalytic converter the least promising way of controlling exhaust pollution, and EPA scientists are concerned that significant quantities of platinum and sulfuric acid mist—more poisonous than the emissions controlled—will be released into the atmosphere. The manufacture of the catalytic converter will require huge amounts of scarce and expensive platinum and palladium, the main deposits of which are found in Africa and the USSR. The catalytic converter will add about $150 to the price of a car. Current estimates of the additional cost to equip a conventionally powered car with the total emissions system required by 1977 range from about $200 a car at GM to over $400 at Chrysler.

It thus seems inevitable that Detroit will be forced to adopt an alternative to the conventional internal-combustion engine. In addition to growing expenditures by the automobile industry, the federal government spent some $23 million from 1969 to 1973 to subsidize the development of alternative engines. Senator John Tunney proposed in early 1973 that $900 million be diverted from the Highway Trust Fund for a crash program to develop an alternative to the conventional internal-combustion engine by the late 1970s. William Lear's lack of success in building an operable steam-powered bus and the persistent stalemate in developing satisfactory storage batteries indicate that the alternative will be neither the steamer nor the electric car in the near future. And plans to run conventional engines on hydrogen or manure are still in the dream stage of development. Cleaner-burning propane is already being utilized with excellent results by a number of municipal and commercial motor vehicle fleets, but it is in too short supply for use on a mass scale. The Wankel rotary-piston engine with a thermal reactor is more difficult and expensive to manufacture than a conventional piston engine and consumes about 7 percent more gasoline. The new Honda stratified-charge engine looks more promising, but, like the Wankel, the Honda engine in its present state of development is not capable of powering standard-size American cars. Other recently innovated internal- and external-combustion engines—the Brayton cycle, the Stirling cycle, the Karol split-cycle rotary, and the Rancine cycle—are possible revolutionary technological breakthroughs but are still hardly off the drawing boards. With conventional internal-combustion engine technology at an impasse, Detroit at long last appears to be taking a serious look at these alternatives.[39]

The end of a two-decade trend toward cars that guzzled more and more gasoline was dramatically underlined when sales of small cars skyrocketed to 39 percent of automobile sales (as high as 60 percent in the Los Angeles area) for the first four months of 1973. (As we have noted, by December they had surpassed standard-size cars in sales for the first time in history.) Consumers were responding to the combination of runaway inflation and an imminent fuel shortage that was being investigated by the Nixon administration's Office of Emergency Preparedness (OEP), the Federal Trade Commission (FTC), and the powerful Senate Committee on Internal Affairs chaired by Senator Henry Jackson. In early February 1973, Senator Jackson called for legislation that would impose penalty taxes on large, gas-eating engines, and he predicted gasoline rationing by spring. Although rationing did not occur, filling stations cut out gimmicks such as trading stamps and prizes intended to stimulate purchases; major oil companies began canceling dealerships, especially in the Middle West; gasoline prices rose to an average 5 cents above the fall 1972 price by the Memorial Day weekend, with a doubling of prices anticipated in some areas by mid-summer; and some stations either closed temporarily or limited gasoline sales to five or ten gallons a customer. Denied supply by the major oil companies, the independent dealers—long a welcome dumping ground for surplus gasoline—were the hardest hit, with 1,500 independent stations closed temporarily and 400 closed for good by June. By the year's end 1,600 independent stations would be out of business and 1,750 more closed temporarily. Of a national total of about 218,000 service stations, some 10,000 went out of business in 1973. Also hard hit were municipal governments facing greatly reduced quotas of gasoline at sharply increased prices for huge fleets of motorcars and trucks. Secretary of the Treasury George Schultz disclosed that the administration might ask Congress to raise the federal gasoline tax by 4 or 5 cents a gallon both to cut demand for scarce fuel and to help cool off the economy. Mobil Oil Corporation launched a six-week national advertising campaign to educate drivers on "how to get along on less gasoline." It suggested cutting down on car use, driving at slower speeds, and turning off air conditioners. The Nixon administration made similar suggestions—an ironic outcome given that the administration had consistently tied economic growth to the health of the automobile industry. The president also issued a long-overdue executive order ending a fourteen-year-old quota system limiting oil imports, announced plans to triple the amount of federal lands open for oil exploration on the continental shelf, proposed new tax deductions for the oil oligopoly, and suggested easing clean-air standards to permit the burning of more high-sulfur coal.

Critics both within and outside government charged that the fuel shortage was a hoax—a ploy by the major oil companies to justify raising gasoline prices to boost sagging profit margins; to squeeze out competition from the independents; and to gain public support for an expansion of offshore drilling (blocked by the environmentalists) and for completion of the trans-Alaska pipeline (tied up in environmental litigation in the courts). An FTC investigation to determine whether the shortage was contrived resulted on July 17, 1973, in a massive antitrust complaint against eight major oil companies: Atlantic Richfield, Exxon, Gulf Oil, Mobil Oil, Shell Oil, Standard Oil of California, Standard Oil of Indiana, and Texaco. The companies were charged with attempting to monopolize the oil market by limiting the supply of crude oil to independent refiners and by limiting the sales of refined products to independent wholesalers and retailers. Senator Jackson, who called for the FTC investigation, reported to the press that "there is a growing and increasingly widespread conviction that the fuel shortage is a deliberate, conscious contrivance of the major integrated petroleum companies to destroy the independent marketers, to increase gasoline prices, and to obtain the repeal of environmental legislation." [40]

By September, rapidly rising prices for gasoline were recognized as one of the biggest contributors to the country's inflationary spiral, and the Cost of Living Council (CLC) had won the right to enforce Phase IV guidelines requiring gasoline price cuts effective September 8. The Antitrust Division of the Justice Department was also beginning a grand jury investigation to determine whether there had been a conspiracy to fix gasoline prices. But attention was diverted from this developing wrangle over price-fixing when, after months of threats and public support from their oil oligopoly partners, the Organization of Arab Petroleum Exporting Countries (OAPEC) implemented oil diplomacy in response to the October war with Israel. The OAPEC announced minimal production cuts of 5 percent a month until Israel withdrew from occupied territories and the "legitimate rights" of the Palestinians were restored. The cuts were to be borne by the "enemies" of the Arab cause, which turned out to mean that only the United States and the Netherlands were under a "total embargo" by December. The OAPEC also announced that oil prices henceforth would be determined unilaterally by the producing nations rather than through negotiations with the major oil companies. Posted oil prices for the Persian Gulf nations had risen 130 percent over the October price of $5.11 to $11.65 per barrel by January 1974, as opposed to $2.59 per barrel a year earlier. Other oil-producing nations inevitably followed suit: Nigerian and Venezuelan oil doubled to $14 per barrel, Indonesian oil jumped from $6.00 to $10.80 per barrel, and new export taxes increased the price of Canadian oil from $6.20 to $10.40 per barrel.

CLC rules permitted the increased costs of imported crude oil to be passed on to the consumer. The CLC in addition had quickly reneged on its September 1973 plan to roll back gasoline prices. On

October 31, 1973, the council handed down new guidelines that permitted all segments of the petroleum industry to raise prices once a month commensurate with higher costs. Then, on December 19, 1973, the CLC authorized a $1 per barrel increase in the price of "old" domestic crude oil—enough alone to raise the retail price of gasoline 2.3 cents a gallon and net the oil oligopoly $4.75 billion more in annual profits. So-called new domestic crude oil (oil produced in excess of the quantity produced in 1972) was generously pegged at $10 per barrel. By April 1974 the average price of regular gasoline at the pump had climbed to 54 cents, as opposed to 38 cents a year earlier. It was estimated that during the first quarter of 1974 some $8 to $10 billion of pure inflation were injected into the economy by the rising prices for fuel.

As hard-pressed filling station owners faced ruin from the decline in the volume of sales, the oil oligopoly's profits became, in Senator Jackson's words, "obscene." Gains for the first quarter of 1974 over the first quarter of 1973 were: Shell Oil, 52 percent; Mobil Oil, 66 percent; Gulf Oil, 76 percent; Standard Oil of Indiana, 81 percent; Standard Oil of California, 92 percent; Texaco, 123 percent; and Occidental Petroleum, an incredible 718 percent. Conversely, many independent oil companies—with about 20 percent of the nation's refining capacity and 25 percent of the retail gasoline sales—were having a difficult time staying in business because of the higher prices for crude oil and the decimation of their retail outlets.

An even more significant casualty of the fuel shortage was the automobile industry. Massive layoffs of automobile workers occurred as assembly lines were shifted to smaller models. In the first quarter of 1974, sales slipped 27 percent below the first quarter of 1973. First-quarter 1974 profits were down 85 percent at GM, 66 percent at Ford, and 98 percent at Chrysler. These figures followed fourth-quarter 1973 declines of 22 percent at GM, 76 percent at Ford, and 12 percent at Chrysler. With 90 percent of its production in small cars, American Motors upped its share of the market from

3.7 in 1972 to 5.8 percent in 1973. It was the only American automobile manufacturer to increase sales in the first quarter of 1974. AMC announced its first dividend in eight years in January 1974, only to end up with first-quarter 1974 profits down 58 percent because of parts shortages and suppliers' strikes. Sales of recreational vehicles, which the industry hoped would escalate in the 1970s, proved especially vulnerable. Their production was down 90 percent by February 1974 at the Forest City, Iowa, plant of Winnebago Industries, the country's largest producer of motor homes. Winnebago stock dropped from a 1972 high of $48\frac{1}{4}$ to a low of $3\frac{1}{8}$ in 1974. The National Automobile Dealers Association reported in May that over 100 new car dealerships had been forced out of business in 1974 and anticipated that as many as 1,000 more might fold by the year's end.

The "total embargo" threatened by the OAPEC turned out to be a paper tiger. About 700,000 barrels of Arab oil a day were somehow being "leaked" into the United States by December 1973, and storage tanks were reported to be full. It also became increasingly difficult for the motorist waiting two hours in line for a ten-gallon gasoline dole to understand how the federal government projected our 11 percent dependence on Arab oil into a 17 percent shortage that failed to materialize—supposedly because of an 8 percent saving in fuel consumption due to the 55-mph speed limit, a ban on Sunday gasoline sales, and other conservation measures.

Nevertheless, the embargo had accomplished its objectives when lifted on March 13, 1974. The Arab oil-producing nations had gained vastly increased revenues and the upper hand on their oil oligopoly partners. The Nixon administration abandoned our traditional pro-Israel policy and reached a new détente, including the sharing of nuclear energy, with the Arab nations in June. Libya's nationalization of three American oil companies and Saudi Arabia's gaining of a 60 percent control of gigantic ARAMCO by June were offset by the oil oligopoly reaping windfall profits, tightening its control over the domestic market, and obtaining the federal government's approval for increased offshore drilling and construction of the trans-Alaska pipeline.

Indeed, among the Nixon administration's first responses to the Arab oil embargo were ending the ban against drilling in the Santa Barbara channel on November 13 and signing the Alaska pipeline bill on November 17, 1973. The president also advocated the relaxation of clean air standards. After taking these steps toward national "self-sufficiency," the president read an energy message to the nation on November 25, 1973, announcing an "energy policy" that amounted to no more than a list of cutbacks on fuel consumption by consumers. Nor did an "energy policy" become apparent after the creation in early December of the Federal Energy Administration (FEA), headed by William E. Simon, to coordinate fuel pricing, allocation, and conservation. With the ending of the embargo, the "crisis" was declared a "problem" by the president, and Simon told Congress that an omnibus energy bill was no longer necessary. (The administration had vetoed an earlier energy bill that would have rolled back domestic crude-oil prices).

Despite the evidence indicating that the fuel shortage was a short-term hoax, there is a very real long-range energy crisis that demands a national energy policy. The oil oligopoly, with the aid of the federal government, merely capitalized on mounting legitimate concern over our declining petroleum reserves. Domestic oil reserves were reported in mid-1973 to be 52 billion barrels—about a ten-year supply. In 1972 we imported about 27 percent of our crude petroleum, and projections were that we would import over 50 percent by 1980. Barring major new discoveries, only Saudi Arabia and Iran can count on increased oil production after 1980. And if the number of motor vehicles keeps increasing at the present rate, projections are that all known world reserves of petroleum will be exhausted within fifty to seventy years. As Senator Jackson has said, "We have consumed it as if all sources of energy were going out of style."[41]

With only 6 percent of the world's population, the United States has over half the world's motor vehicles. And the automobile is a most inefficient user of energy: about 80 percent of a car's energy intake is wasted through the exhaust pipe. It is therefore doubtful that a world needing oil for petrochemicals, plastics, and tractors will long permit us to engage in the insanity of relying primarily on the road and the car for mass transit. The potential, positive benefits of the fuel shortage from this long-range perspective are well phrased by John Kenneth Galbraith: "If the energy crisis forces us to diminish automobile use in the cities, stops us from building highways and covering the country with concrete and asphalt, forces us to rehabilitate the railroads, causes us to invest in mass transportation and limits the waste of electrical energy, one can only assume that the Arab nations and the big oil companies have united to save the American Republic." [42]

A nationwide poll by the Highway Users Federation in 1973 showed that 57 percent of the respondents favored restrictions on automobile use in cities. In mid-1973, bold EPA plans were announced to control air-quality standards through severe cutbacks in automotive transportation, necessitating the building of alternative mass-transit systems by the 1980s. The plan for Southern California, for example, called for a 50 percent curtailment of freeway traffic, a ban on new parking facilities, and gasoline rationing by 1977. An important point was the linking of local land-use planning with air-quality standards. Delays in the timetable were accepted by the EPA after the California Air Resources Board (CARB) pointed out that the 1977 deadline for some air standards for the South Coast Basin could not be met "without almost complete depopulation of that region." On March 23, 1974, the Nixon administration proposed amendments to the Clean Air Act that would delay until 1987 the requirements meeting air-quality standards through transportation controls.

With the development of the energy crisis and an impending major depression, environmentalists have rapidly lost ground in

Washington and in state legislatures. Yet these are the death knells of the automobile culture. Even the automobile manufacturers hope to diversify into "total transportation" companies by the turn into the twenty-first century. They anticipate that their main business by then will be selling modular transportation systems to the government. The automobile culture and the values that sustained it are no longer tenable. In the words of Russel E. Train, "Our energy and our environmental ills both stem from essentially the same source: the patterns of growth and development that waste our energy resources just as surely and as shamefully as they lay waste to our natural environment." The point made in a *Los Angeles Times*' editorial has become a truism: "It is no longer simply a question of environment or aesthetics or convenience—of helping reduce air pollution and street congestion and commuting time by having adequate alternatives to private autos. It has also become a question of personal and national economic interest." [43]

The ending of the age of automobility undoubtedly marks a significant turning point in American historical development. For automobility has had a more profound impact on Americans in the twentieth century than even Frederick Jackson Turner's frontier had on our nineteenth-century forebears. The question for the future is whether the new era of American history that is dawning will continue to develop as the age of the superstate serving the supercorporation, with self-interest, greed, and waste being its cardinal, and ultimately self-destructive, values. An alternative future characterized by true community and expanded democracy, free from the privatism, materialism, escapism, and exploitation that the automobile culture encouraged, is also within our grasp. Achieving it requires only our will, intelligence, and collective effort.

NOTES

INTRODUCTION

1 George Rogers Taylor, ed., *The Turner Thesis*, rev. ed. (Lexington, Mass.: D. C. Heath and Company, 1956), pp. v, 1.

2 The most cogent and comprehensive criticism of the Turner thesis remains George W. Pierson, "The Frontier and American Institutions," *New England Quarterly*, 15:244–255 (June 1942). For revisions of the Turner thesis as a special case of more general theories of abundance, migration, and institution building, see especially David M. Potter, *People of Plenty: Economic Abundance and the American Character* (Chicago: University of Chicago Press, 1954); Everett S. Lee, "The Turner Thesis Reexamined," *American Quarterly*, 13:77–83 (Spring 1961); George W. Pierson, "The M-Factor in American History," ibid., 14:275–289 (Summer 1962); and Stanley M. Elkins and Erick McKitrick, "A Meaning for Turner's Frontier: Democracy in the Old Northwest," *Political Science Quarterly*, 69:321–353 (September 1954).

3 *Recent Social Trends in the United States*, Report of the President's Research Committee on Social Trends, 2 vols. (New York and London: McGraw-Hill, 1933), p. 172.

4 Raymond L. Bruckberger, *The Image of America* (New York: Viking Press, 1959), pp. 196–197.

5 *American Historical Review*, 53:748–759 (July 1948).

6 Ralph C. Epstein, *The Automobile Industry* (Chicago and New York: A. W. Shaw Co., 1928), and Lawrence H. Seltzer, *A Financial History of the American Automobile Industry* (Boston and New York: Houghton Mifflin, 1929).

7 Allan Nevins, in collaboration with Frank E. Hill, *Ford: The Times, the Man, the Company, 1865–1915; Ford: Expansion and Challenge, 1915–1933;* and *Ford: Decline and Rebirth, 1933–1962* (New York: Charles Scribner's Sons, 1954, 1957, 1963).

8 John B. Rae, *The American Automobile: A Brief History* (Chicago: University of Chicago Press, 1965).

9 James J. Flink, *America Adopts the Automobile, 1895–1910* (Cambridge, Mass.: M.I.T. Press, 1970), is the first of a two-volume study of the origins of the American automobile revolution. It discusses the significant relationships between the development of the industry as a whole and the changing sociocultural milieu within which this development occurred. John B. Rae, *The Road and the Car in American Life* (Cambridge, Mass.: M.I.T. Press, 1971), deals with the impact of the road and the car, considered as an integral unit, on American life from the introduction of the motor vehicle to the present and assesses the future potential of American automobility. Lawrence J. White, *The Automobile Industry since 1945* (Cambridge, Mass.: Harvard University Press, 1971), the first scholarly study of the economics of the post–World War II industry, goes beyond the normal praise and apologetics to be

critical and offer suggestions for sweeping changes in public policy. Reynold M. Wik, *Henry Ford and Grass-roots America* (Ann Arbor: University of Michigan Press, 1972), is a study of the impact of the Model T on rural life.

10 Glenn A. Niemeyer was chairman of the AHA session, "The Impact of the Automobile on American Historical Development." Papers were read by John B. Rae and the present author. The commentators were David L. Lewis and John L. Hancock.

11 *American Quarterly*, 24:451–473 (October 1972).

CHAPTER 1: PROLOGUE: THE AUTOMOTIVE IDEA, ANTIQUITY TO 1900

1 John B. Rae, *The American Automobile: A Brief History* (Chicago: University of Chicago Press, 1965), p. 1.

2 L. Scott Bailey, "The Other Revolution: The Birth and Development of the American Automobile," in *The American Car since 1775*, by the editors of *Automobile Quarterly* (New York: E. P. Dutton & Co., 1971), p. 10.

3 See especially John B. Rae, *The Road and the Car in American Life* (Cambridge, Mass.: M.I.T. Press, 1971), pp. 23–31.

4 Ibid., pp. 31–33.

5 For the early history of automotive technology in the United States the best source is Bailey, "The Other Revolution." The best book on George Selden and the Selden patent suit is William Greenleaf, *Monopoly on Wheels: Henry Ford and the Selden Automobile Patent Suit* (Detroit: Wayne State University Press, 1961).

6 "Salutatory," *Horseless Age*, 1:1 (November 1895).

7 Ibid.

8 Bailey, "The Other Revolution," pp. 52–58.

9 Ibid., pp. 68–93, and James J. Flink, *America Adopts the Automobile, 1895–1910* (Cambridge, Mass.: M.I.T. Press, 1970), pp. 21–22.

10 Flink, *America Adopts the Automobile*, pp. 25–31.

11 "Manufacture in New England," *Motor Age*, 1:4 (September 12, 1899).

CHAPTER 2: EARLY IMPLEMENTATION IN AMERICA

1 The points made in this chapter are elaborated and more fully documented in James J. Flink, *America Adopts the Automobile, 1895–1910* (Cambridge, Mass.: M.I.T. Press, 1970).

2 "Fairly Howling," *Motor World*, 1:17 (October 11, 1900).

3 W. W. Townsend, "Future of the Industry Assessed," *Motor Age*, 3:999 (February 6, 1901).

4 The letter is quoted in full in the *Detroit News*, January 14, 1927.

5 "Our Correspondence Column," *Automobile*, 2:137 (August 1900).

6 William J. Lampton, "The Meaning of the Automobile," *Outing Magazine*, 40:696 (September 1902).

7 "Motorphobia," *Horseless Age*, 12:348–349 (September 30, 1903).

8 "Unfavorable Newspaper Influence and How to Counteract It," *Automobile*, 13:44 (November 9, 1905).

9 James R. Doolittle et al., *The Romance of the Automobile Industry* (New York: Klebold Press, 1916), pp. 322–323.

10 George O. Draper, "A View of the Tour from One Participating," *Horseless Age*, 16:153 (July 26, 1905).

11 Quoted in Chester S. Ricker, "Sixth Annual A.A.A. Reliability Tour," ibid., 24:49 (July 14, 1909).

12 Victor Lougheed, "The Horse and the Automobile," *Automobile*, 18:246 (February 20, 1908).

13 John B. Rae, *American Automobile Manufacturers: The First Forty Years* (Philadelphia: Chilton, 1959), p. 103.

14 "Object to the Abuse of Automobiling," *Motor World*, 4:662 (September 4, 1902).

15 "Automobiles in the Campaign," *Horseless Age*, 14:412 (October 26, 1904).

16 Quoted in "Farmer's Wise Words," *Motor Age*, 8:33 (November 23, 1905).

17 Quoted in William B. Meloney, "The Marvelous Growth of the Automobile Industry in America," *Munsey's Magazine*, 42:21 (October 1909).

18 Ralph C. Epstein, *The Automobile Industry* (Chicago and New York: A. W. Shaw Co., 1928), pp. 94–97.

19 "One Car for Many," *Motor World*, 5:865 (March 5, 1903).

20 Robert S. Lynd and Helen M. Lynd, *Middletown* (New York: Harcourt, Brace, 1929), pp. 251–253.

21 "A Notable Automobile Show," *Outlook*, 85:241 (February 2, 1907).

22 "Installment Sales," *Motor World*, 9:461 (December 15, 1904).

23 "The Automobile Club of America," *Motor Age*, 2:553 (June 28, 1900).

24 "Informal Local Situations," *Automobile*, 8:576 (May 30, 1903).

25 "A.C.A. Is Out of A.A.A.," *Motor Age*, 13:11 (March 19, 1908).

26 "Blood and Boodle," *Motor World*, 1:246 (January 10, 1901).

27 The importance of these factors for the rapid, widespread diffusion of the automobile in the United States was first pointed out in Lawrence H. Seltzer, *A Financial History of the American Automobile Industry* (Boston and New York: Houghton Mifflin, 1928). The best analysis of their pervasive impact upon American civilization remains David M. Potter, *People of Plenty: Economic Abundance and the American Character* (Chicago: University of Chicago Press, 1954).

28 John B. Rae, *The American Automobile: A Brief History* (Chicago: University of Chicago Press, 1965), p. 109.

29 "Government Recognition of Motor Cars," *Motor Age*, 15:6 (March 25, 1909).

30 Joel A. Tarr, "Urban Pollution—Many Long Years Ago," *American Heritage*, 22:65–69, 106 (October 1971). The same points are made, using different examples, in Flink, *America Adopts the Automobile*.

31 "The Motor Car in England," *Scientific American*, 75:423 (December 12, 1896).

32 "The Status of the Horse at the End of the Century," *Harper's Weekly*, 43:1172 (November 18, 1899).

33 "One More Revolution," *Independent*, 55:1163 (May 14, 1903).

34 "Unfair Public Demands," *Motor Age*, 3:4 (June 18, 1903).

35 Some scholars have in fact come to view geographic mobility as the most significant force shaping American civilization. For two such revisionist arguments that make the Turner thesis a special case of a more general theory of migration, see Everett S. Lee, "The Turner Thesis Reexamined," *American Quarterly*, 13:77–83 (Spring 1961), and George W. Pierson, "The M-Factor in American History," *American Quarterly*, 14:275–289 (Summer 1962).

36 Thomas Conyngton, "Motor Carriages and Street Paving," *Scientific American Supplement*, 48:19660 (July 1, 1899).

37 Richard Hofstadter, *The Age of Reform: From Bryan to FDR* (New York: Alfred A. Knopf, 1956), pp. 23–59. For the importance of the agrarian myth in the automobile movement, see also Park Dixon Goist, "Where Town and Country Meet: The Fusing of Urban and Rural Images in Early Automobile Advertising," paper presented to the First National Meeting of the Popular Culture Association, East Lansing, Michigan, April 9, 1971.

38 Quoted in Mitchell Gordon, *Sick Cities: Psychology and Pathology of American Urban Life* (Baltimore: Penguin Books, 1965), p. 13.

39 William F. Dix, "The Automobile as a Vacation Agent," *Independent*, 56:1259–1260 (June 2, 1904).

40 William J. Lampton, "The Meaning of the Automobile," *Outing Magazine*, 40:699 (September 1902).

41 G. W. Atterbury, "The Commercial Car as a Necessity," *Harper's Weekly*, 51:1925 (December 28, 1907).

CHAPTER 3: THE RISE OF THE GIANTS

1 "Who Are the Enemies of the Automobile Industry?" *Horseless Age*, 9:4–5 (January 1, 1902).

2 "Fools and Their Folly," *Motor World*, 1:5 (October 4, 1900).

3 John B. Rae, *American Automobile Manufacturers: The First Forty Years* (Philadelphia: Chilton, 1959), pp. 8, 203.

4 Lawrence H. Seltzer, *A Financial History of the American Automobile Industry* (Boston and New York: Houghton Mifflin, 1928), pp. 19–21. The Chapin quotation was transcribed by Seltzer from notes taken in an interview in Detroit on December 11, 1924.

5 Walter E. Flanders, "Large Capital Now Needed to Embark in Automobile Business," *Detroit Saturday Night*, January 22, 1910. On closure in the American automobile industry, see Harold G. Vatter, "Closure of Entry in the American Automobile Industry," *Oxford Economic Papers*, n.s. 4:213–234 (October 1952).

6 Cleveland Moffett, "Automobiles for the Average Man," *Review of Reviews*, 21:707 (June 1900).

7 For the early hegemony of New England and the rise of Detroit as the center of

automobile manufacturing, see J. T. Sullivan, "New England a 1900 Leader," *Motor Age*, 19:1–4 (March 2, 1911), and L. V. Spencer, "Detroit: The City Built by the Automobile Industry," *Automobile*, 28:791–797 (April 10, 1913).

8 For the history of the Electric Vehicle Company, see John B. Rae, "The Electric Vehicle Company," *Business History Review*, 29:298–311 (December 1955), and his *American Automobile Manufacturers*, pp. 67–72.

9 "Selden Patent Ownership," *Motor Age*, 3:7 (April 16, 1903). The definitive study of the Selden patent controversy is William Greenleaf, *Monopoly on Wheels: Henry Ford and the Selden Patent Suit* (Detroit: Wayne State University Press, 1961).

10 Greenleaf, *Monopoly on Wheels*, pp. 174–175.

11 Hugh Dolnar, "The Ford 4-Cylinder Runabout," *Cycle and Automobile Trade Journal*, 11:108 (August 1, 1906).

12 *Detroit Journal*, January 5, 1906.

13 "Independent Makers Meet in Detroit," *Automobile*, 12:349 (March 4, 1905). For the Ford Motor Company's initial response to the ALAM, see also James Couzens, "Ford on the Selden Association," *Cycle and Automobile Trade Journal*, 8:17 ff. (October 1, 1903).

14 "American Motor Car Manufacturers Association," *Automobile*, 15:704 (November 29, 1906).

15 Greenleaf, *Monopoly on Wheels*, pp. 187–188.

16 Ibid., pp. 248–250.

17 *The Society of Automotive Engineers Transactions* (1910), pp. 125–126, as cited in George V. Thompson, "Intercompany Technical Standardization in the Early Automobile Industry," *Journal of Economic History*, 14:1–20 (Winter 1954). For intercompany standardization, see also Alexander Johnston, "Standardization Turns the Wheels of Progress," *Motor*, 29:84–85, 150 (November 1917), and J. K. Barnes, "The Men Who Standardized Automobile Parts," *World's Work*, 42:204–208 (June 1921).

18 "Standardizing the Automobile," *Scientific American*, 100:40 (January 16, 1909).

19 Charles E. Sorensen, with Samuel T. Williamson, *My Forty Years with Ford* (New York: Collier Books ed., 1962), p. 31.

20 Quoted in Seltzer, *Financial History of the American Automobile Industry*, p. 157.

21 Benjamin Briscoe, "The Inside Story of General Motors," *Detroit Saturday Night*, January 15, 22, and 29 and February 5, 1921.

CHAPTER 4: FORDIZATION: AN IDOL AND ITS IRONIES

1 Allan Nevins, in collaboration with Frank E. Hill, *Ford: The Times, the Man, the Company, 1865–1915* (New York: Charles Scribner's Sons, 1954), p. 480.

2 Roderick Nash, *The Nervous Generation: American Thought, 1917–1930* (Chicago: Rand McNally, 1970), p. 153.

3 Reynold M. Wik, *Henry Ford and Grass-roots America* (Ann Arbor: University of Michigan Press, 1972), pp. 125, 212.

4 Letter from a Minnesotan quoted in ibid., p. 179.

5 National Automobile Chamber of Commerce, *Facts and Figures of the Automobile Industry* (1927 ed.), p. 44.

6 Quoted in Allan Nevins and Frank E. Hill, *Ford: Decline and Rebirth, 1933–1962* (New York: Charles Scribner's Sons, 1963), p. 95.

7 Maurice Hindus, "Ford Conquers Russia," *Outlook*, 146:280–283 (June 29, 1927).

8 Wik, *Henry Ford and Grass-roots America*, p. 4.

9 Interview with Wheeler, *Chicago Tribune*, May 25, 1916.

10 Roger Butterfield, "Henry Ford, the Wayside Inn, and the Problem of 'History Is Bunk,'" *Proceedings of the Massachusetts Historical Society*, 77:55–66 (1965).

11 Walter P. Chrysler, in collaboration with Boyden Sparkes, *Life of an American Workman* (New York: Dodd, Mead, 1937), pp. 134–136.

12 Charles E. Sorensen, in collaboration with Samuel T. Williamson, *My Forty Years with Ford* (New York: Collier Books ed., 1962), pp. 113–114.

13 Ibid., p. 116.

14 Henry Ford, in collaboration with Samuel Crowther, *My Life and Work* (Garden City, N.Y.: Doubleday, Page, 1922), p. 83.

15 Horace L. Arnold and Fay L. Faurote, *Ford Methods and the Ford Shops* (New York: Engineering Magazine Co., 1915).

16 Wik, *Henry Ford and Grass-roots America*, p. 238; Sorensen and Williamson, *My Forty Years with Ford*, p. 124; and Nevins and Hill, *Ford: The Times, the Man, the Company*, p. 474.

17 Sorensen and Williamson, *My Forty Years with Ford*, p. 42, and John Kenneth Galbraith, *The Liberal Hour* (Boston: Houghton Mifflin, 1960), pp. 155, 164–165.

18 Ford and Crowther, *My Life and Work*; idem, *Today and Tomorrow* (Garden City, N.Y.: Doubleday, Page, 1922, 1926); and Henry Ford, *My Philosophy of Industry*, authorized interviews with Fay L. Faurote (New York: Coward-McCann, 1929). Unless otherwise noted, the quotations in this section are from these sources, passim.

19 Allan Nevins, in collaboration with Frank E. Hill, *Ford: Expansion and Challenge, 1915–1933* (New York: Charles Scribner's Sons, 1957), p. 508, and Arnold and Faurote, *Ford Methods and the Ford Shops*, p. 43.

20 John R. Commons et al., "Henry Ford, Miracle Maker," *Independent*, 102:189 (May 1, 1920).

21 Raymond L. Bruckberger, *The Image of America* (New York: Viking Press, 1959), pp. 186–187.

22 Arnold and Faurote, *Ford Methods and the Ford Shops*, pp. 41–42.

23 Ford and Crowther, *My Life and Work*, p. 95.

24 Nevins and Hill, *Ford: The Times*, p. 553.

25 Arnold and Faurote, *Ford Methods and the Ford Shops*, p. 46.

26 Nevins and Hill, *Ford: Expansion and Challenge*, p. 534.

27 Robert S. Lynd and Helen M. Lynd, *Middletown: A Study in Modern American Culture* (New York: Harcourt, Brace, 1929), pp. 31–32.

28 Ford and Crowther, *My Life and Work*, pp. 80, 105, 115.

29 Ibid., pp. 111–112.

30 Nevins and Hill, *Ford: The Times*, pp. 560–561.

31 Samuel S. Marquis, *Henry Ford: An Interpretation* (Boston: Little, Brown, 1923), pp. 34, 149.

32 Ford and Crowther, *My Life and Work*, pp. 129, 146, and Arnold and Faurote, *Ford Methods and the Ford Shops*, p. 61.

33 Nevins and Hill, *Ford: The Times*, pp. 534–535.

34 Marquis, *Henry Ford: An Interpretation*, p. 155.

35 Harry W. Perry, "Our Industry's Part in the War," *Motor*, 31:52 (January 1919).

36 Mrs. Wilfred C. Leland, in collaboration with Minnie Dubbs Millbrook, *Master of Precision: Henry M. Leland* (Detroit: Wayne State University Press, 1966), p. 174.

37 *Detroit Times*, April 16, 1916.

38 Quoted in Nevins and Hill, *Ford: Expansion and Challenge*, pp. 55–56.

39 Ibid., p. 111.

40 Ford and Crowther, *My Life and Work*, pp. 91–92.

41 Keith Sward, *The Legend of Henry Ford* (New York: Holt, Rinehart, and Winston, 1948), pp. 311–312.

42 Jonathan N. Leonard, *The Tragedy of Henry Ford* (New York: G. P. Putnam's Sons, 1932), pp. 15, 230, 235–236.

43 Ibid., pp. 16, 241–242.

44 Wik, *Henry Ford and Grass-roots America*, p. 195.

45 Sorensen and Williamson, *My Forty Years with Ford*, p. 255.

CHAPTER 5: BILLY DURANT AND THE BULL MARKET

1 Walter P. Chrysler, in collaboration with Boyden Sparkes, *Life of an American Workman* (New York: Dodd, Mead, 1937), p. 143; Alfred P. Sloan, Jr., in collaboration with Boyden Sparkes, *Adventures of a White-Collar Man* (New York: Doubleday, Doran, 1941), pp. 106, 110, 112–113; and Henry Greenleaf Pearson, *Son of New England: James Jackson Storrow, 1846–1926* (Boston: Thomas Todd, 1932), p. 139.

2 Earl Sparling, *Mystery Men of Wall Street* (New York: Greenberg, 1930); Mrs. Wilfred C. Leland, in collaboration with Minnie Dubbs Millbrook, *Master of Precision: Henry M. Leland* (Detroit: Wayne State University Press, 1966), pp. 103–104; and Margery Durant, *My Father* (New York: Knickerbocker Press [G. P. Putnam's Sons], 1929).

3 *Detroit Free Press*, March 19, 1947; Pearson, *Son of New England*, p. 138; Eugene W. Lewis, *Motor Memories* (Detroit: Alved, 1947), p. 66; and Dana L. Thomas, *The Plungers and the Peacocks: 150 Years of Wall Street* (New York: Berkley Medallion ed., 1970), p. 116.

4 Carl B. Glasscock, *The Gasoline Age* (Indianapolis: Bobbs-Merrill, 1937), pp. 127–128, and Theodore F. MacManus and Norman Beasley, *Men, Money, and Motors: The Drama of the Automobile* (New York: Harper & Brothers, 1929), p. 100.

5 Alfred P. Sloan, Jr., *My Years with General Motors* (Garden City, N.Y.: Doubleday, 1963), p. 4.

6 Ibid., p. 60.

7 Chrysler and Sparkes, *Life of an American Workman*, pp. 156–157.

8 Sloan and Sparkes, *Adventures of a White-Collar Man*, pp. 111–112, 115–116, 119, and Sloan, *My Years with General Motors*, p. 26.

9 *Detroit News*, February 9, 1956.

10 Chrysler and Sparkes, *Life of an American Workman*, pp. 148, 161.

11 Ibid., p. 202.

12 Sloan and Sparkes, *Adventures of a White-Collar Man*, pp. 104, 107, 112, 120.

13 Sloan, *My Years with General Motors*, p. 38.

14 The best account of the GM crisis of 1920 from the du Pont and Morgan point of view is Alfred D. Chandler, Jr., and Stephen Salsbury, *Pierre S. du Pont and the Making of the Modern Corporation* (New York: Harper & Row, 1971), pp. 475–491. Durant gave his side of the story in most detail in W. A. P. John, "That Man Durant," *Automobile*, 39:70–71 ff. (January 1923).

15 Sloan and Sparkes, *Adventures of a White-Collar Man*, p. 125, and MacManus and Beasley, *Men, Money, and Motors*, p. 231.

16 Thomas, *The Plungers and the Peacocks*, pp. 114–176, is the best account of Durant's stock market activities in the 1920s. But Thomas's contention that John J. Raskob was a member of the Durant group is almost certainly wrong. Mrs. Catherine L. Durant said in a personal interview on December 28, 1971, that Durant and Raskob had no personal or business associations after the GM crisis of 1920.

17 Memorandum on telephone talk with M. W. Willebrandt, February 7, 1929, "Appointments and Misc.," Pre-Presidential papers, and "Appointments Calendar," April 3, 1929, Presidential papers, Herbert Hoover Presidential Library, West Branch, Iowa. There is also a letter of April 4, 1929, from Ms. Willebrandt, the Assistant Attorney General, to Lawrence Ritchie, in the secretary's file, asking, "Won't you please bring to the President's attention the suggestion of seeing W. C. Durant for a few minutes' conference before he goes abroad on April 17th? He will be gone considerable time." Thomas T. Thalken, director of the Herbert Hoover Presidential Library, gave invaluable aid in our effort to substantiate Durant's night visit to the White House, which for years has been an undocumented rumor.

18 *New York Times*, June 5, 1929.

19 "Durant's Dishes," *Time*, 28:61–62 (September 28, 1936).

20 "Durant: Trying Again," *Newsweek*, 13:46–47 (March 27, 1939).

21 Durant to W. H. Washer, November 16, 1943, and *Flint Journal*, n.d., 1946, Fauth Collection, Flint, Michigan.

22 *Detroit Free Press*, March 19, 1947; *Detroit News*, September 7, 1967; and *Flint Journal*, March 19, 1972.

23 "The Fact," *Newsweek*, 50:112 (November 18, 1957), and *Flint Journal*, March 19, 1972.

24 Eulogy in the *Detroit Free Press*, March 19, 1947.

CHAPTER 6: THE AUTOMOBILE CULTURE:
PROSPECTS AND PROBLEMS

1 Robert S. Lynd and Helen M. Lynd, *Middletown: A Study in Modern American Culture* (New York: Harcourt, Brace, 1929), p. 251.

2 Thomas C. Cochran, *The American Business System: A Historical Perspective, 1900–1955* (Cambridge, Mass.: Harvard University Press, 1957), p. 44.

3 "10,449,785 Cars and Trucks Registered in 1921," *Motor Age*, 41:96–97 (February 2, 1922), and "United States Registrations," *Automotive Industries*, 62:277–279 (February 22, 1930). For early regional differences in adoption of the automobile, see especially James J. Flink, *America Adopts the Automobile, 1895–1910* (Cambridge, Mass.: M.I.T. Press, 1970), pp. 74–86.

4 National Automobile Chamber of Commerce (NACC), *Facts and Figures of the Automobile Industry*, 1924 ed., p. 92; ibid., 1927 ed., p. 38; and "2,700,000 Families in Two-or-More Car Class," *Motor Age*, 51:30 (April 4, 1927).

5 John Kane Mills, "Speaking of Incomes," *Motor*, 35:21–22, 64 (February 1921), and NACC, *Facts and Figures of the Automobile Industry* (1924 annual ed.), p. 10.

6 "Depreciation of Used Cars," *Motor World*, 14:21 (October 4, 1906); "What the Industry Thinks of the Used Car Problem," *Motor Age*, 41:18–20 (April 27, 1922); "The Rising Tide of Used Car Trades," ibid., 47:10–11, 22 (May 21, 1925); "Ford's Used Car Sales Policy," ibid., 47:20 (April 9, 1925); and "General Motors Attacks the Used Car Problem," *Motor*, 49:46–47 ff. (June 1928).

7 "Income and Motor Car Ownership," *Motor*, 23:44–45, 118 (March 1915); "Social Ambitions as a Factor in the Automobile Market," *Horseless Age*, 20:105 (July 24, 1907); and Lynd and Lynd, *Middletown*, pp. 254–256.

8 *Recent Economic Changes in the United States*, Report of the Committee on Recent Economic Changes of the President's Conference on Unemployment, 2 vols. (New York: McGraw-Hill, 1929), pp. 416–417.

9 "Forces That Buy," *Automobile*, 30:382 (February 5, 1914), and Park Dixon Goist, " 'Where Town and Country Meet': The Fusing of Urban and Rural Images in Early Automobile Advertising," paper presented to the First National Meeting of the Popular Culture Association, East Lansing, Michigan, April 9, 1971.

10 "Who Made the Banks Dictators?" *Motor Age*, 18:6 (July 28, 1910), and "Bond Houses Now in Open Enmity," *Motor World*, 24:26 (July 7, 1910).

11 "Nothing to the Mortgage-on-the-Farm-to-Buy-a-Car Scare," *Horseless Age*, 26:324–325 (September 7, 1910).

12 "Studebaker Adopts Credit Plan," *Motor World*, 29:723 (December 7, 1911). In several papers done in my seminars at the University of Pennsylvania, Dr. Ronald Clifton contributed to my understanding of the rise of installment selling of automobiles in the 1920s.

13 "Banker Explains Reluctance to Finance Passenger Car Sales," *Motor Age*, 41:32 (March 23, 1922); " 'Get Cash, Pay Cash'—Ford," *Automobile*, 33:178 (July 22, 1915); and "R. E. Olds Warns against Too Liberal Time Payment Plans," *Motor Age*, 44:31 (December 27, 1923).

14 *Recent Economic Changes*, p. 52; "Time Sales Statistics for California Given," *Motor Age*, 49:39 (June 24, 1926); and Walter Engard, "The Blessing of Time Sales," *Motor*, 49:112 (April 1928).

15 John C. Burnham, "The Gasoline Tax and the Automobile Revolution," *Mississippi Valley Historical Review*, 48:435–459 (December 1961).

16 *Recent Social Trends in the United States*, Report of the President's Research Committee on Social Trends, 2 vols. (New York and London: McGraw-Hill, 1933), pp. 1357–1358.

17 Thomas L. White, "The Motor Car and the Cost of Living," *Motor*, 13:65 (March 1910).

18 *Recent Social Trends*, p. 177, and Blaine A. Brownell, "A Symbol of Modernity: Attitudes toward the Automobile in Southern Cities in the 1920s," *American Quarterly*, 24:42–43 (March 1972).

19 Blaine A. Brownell, "Automobiles and the City: The Impact of the Motorcar on Southern Urban Areas in the 1920s," paper read at the annual meeting of the Southern Historical Association, Houston, Texas, November 19, 1971, pp. 3–4, and Thomas D. Clark, *The Emerging South* (New York: Oxford University Press, 1961), pp. 126–127, 130.

20 Brownell, "A Symbol of Modernity," pp. 23–24, 33, 43.

21 Lynd and Lynd, *Middletown*, p. 253, and idem, *Middletown in Transition: A Study in Cultural Conflicts* (New York: Harcourt, Brace, 1937), pp. 265–266.

22 Lynd and Lynd, *Middletown in Transition*, pp. 26, 245.

23 James H. Collins, "The Motor Car Has Created the Spirit of Modern America," *Motor*, 39:186 (January 1923), and Cornelius Vanderbilt, Jr., "The Democracy of the Motor Car," ibid., 37:21 (December 1921).

24 Arthur Raper, *Preface to Peasantry: A Tale of Two Black Belt Counties* (Chapel Hill: University of North Carolina Press, 1936), pp. 174–175.

25 Lynd and Lynd, *Middletown*, pp. 64–65, 95, 257.

26 "The Family Car," *Motor*, 35:19 (February 1921).

27 Lynd and Lynd, *Middletown*, pp. 114, 256–258.

28 John B. Rae, *The American Automobile: A Brief History* (Chicago: University of Chicago Press, 1965), p. 95, and Lynd and Lynd, *Middletown*, p. 137.

29 Lynd and Lynd, *Middletown in Transition*, pp. 266–267, and Automobile Manufacturers Association, *Automobiles of America* (Detroit: Wayne State University Press, 1962), p. 103.

30 NACC, *Facts and Figures*, 1921 ed., pp. 14–15, and Collins, "The Motor Car Has Created the Spirit of Modern America," p. 63.

31 John Steinbeck, *The Grapes of Wrath* (New York: Modern Library ed., 1939), p. 158.

32 "The Motor Truck and the Traffic Problem," *Horseless Age*, 32:698 (October 22, 1913); "The Parking Problem," *Automobile*, 35:1044 (December 21, 1916); "Traffic Problem Becoming Increasingly Important," *Motor Age*, 37:26 (June 10, 1920); Edward Hungerford, "Stop! You Are Congesting the Streets," *Motor*, 39:23–24 ff. (February 1923); and Harold Cary, "Will Passenger Cars Be Barred from City Streets?" *Motor*, 39:34–35 ff. (March 1923).

33 Brownell, "Automobiles and the City," pp. 14, 17, and "Road Space for Cars Is City's Saturation Problem," *Motor Age*, 44:36 (December 13, 1923).

34 John Chapman Hilder, "The Country Club and the Motor Car," *Motor*, 33:74 (January 1920).

35 "Statistics Compiled by Committee of NACC Disclose Fundamental Causes of Motor Fatalities," *Motor Age*, 45:31–32 (April 3, 1924).

36 Lewis Dibble, "Safety Organization Backs State Traffic Uniform Code," ibid., 50:14–15, 32 (November 11, 1926).

37 Royal S. Copeland, "Motoring as Medicine," *Motor*, 38:21 (July 1922); Clarence A. Earl, "Transportation—the Basic Industry," ibid., 37:53, 270, 274 (January 1922); and D. E. Wheeler, "Thomas A. Edison Tells What the Motor Car Has Done for You," ibid., 41:23 (February 1924).

38 Walter P. Chrysler, in collaboration with Boyden Sparkes, *Life of an American Workman* (New York: Dodd, Mead, 1937), p. 197; Alfred P. Sloan, Jr., *My Years with General Motors* (Garden City, N.Y.: Doubleday, 1963), pp. 171–174; and Charles W. Nash, "The Automobile Dealer Has Rights," *Motor*, 43:30–31 (March 1925).

39 "What Is Saturation?" *Motor Age*, 47:31 (February 5, 1921), and Ray W. Sherman, "1930 Should Be a Good Year," *Motor*, 53:67 (January 1930).

40 "NADA Finds Most Sales of Today Are Replacements," *Motor Age*, 48:34 (August 27, 1925), and James Dalton, "Only 30% of Dealers Are Making Money," *Motor*, 46:28–29 ff. (July 1926).

41 James Dalton, "The Bankers Are Getting a Bit Cool," *Motor*, 52:28–29 ff. (July 1929), and "Credit Warnings Not Mere Bogey," ibid., 52:34–35 ff. (October 1929).

42 Clarence E. Eldridge, "One Million Too Many Cars," ibid., 30–33 ff. (November 1929).

43 Ray W. Sherman, "Take Your Hat Off to the Man Who Buys on Time," ibid., 44:27 (October 1925).

44 Alfred D. Chandler, Jr., *Strategy and Structure: Chapters in the History of the American Industrial Enterprise* (Cambridge, Mass.: M.I.T. Press, paperback ed., 1962), p. 208.

45 *Recent Economic Changes*, p. 323.

46 Sloan, *My Years with General Motors*, pp. 265, 276.

47 Quoted in Lynd and Lynd, *Middletown in Transition*, p. 268n.

48 John B. Rae, *The Road and the Car in American Life* (Cambridge, Mass.: M.I.T. Press, 1971), pp. 60–83.

49 *Recent Social Trends*, p. 1360.

50 *Recent Economic Changes*, pp. 556–560, 600.

51 Ibid., pp. 272–274.

52 "Dealers Prepare to Combat Anti-Time Sales Propaganda," *Motor Age*, 45:43 (February 7, 1924), and Lynd and Lynd, *Middletown*, p. 255n.

53 Chandler, *Strategy and Structure*, p. 236; Brownell, "Automobiles and the City," p. 8; and *Recent Economic Changes*, pp. 336–342.

54 James Dalton, "Is the Parts Maker at the End of the Alley?" *Motor*, 42:30–32 (October 1924).

55 *Recent Social Trends*, pp. 232–234.

56 Campaign address, Queens, New York City, October 29, 1928; message to the New

York Legislature on rural tax relief, February 25, 1929; address at the State College of Agriculture, Cornell University, Ithaca, New York, February 14, 1930; address before the Conference of Governors on Land Utilization and State Planning, French Lick, Indiana, June 2, 1931; and address before the American Country Life Conference on the Better Distribution of Population away from Cities, Ithaca, New York, August 19, 1931. I am indebted to Dr. Nancy Pries, one of my former graduate students, for bringing to my attention these and other statements about the automobile made by Roosevelt.

57 *New York Herald-Tribune*, April 28, 1932; Raymond Moley, *After Seven Years* (New York: Harper & Brothers, 1939), pp. 369–370; and William E. Leuchtenburg, *Franklin D. Roosevelt and the New Deal, 1932–1940* (New York: Harper & Row, 1963), p. 345.

58 Sidney Fine, *The Automobile under the Blue Eagle* (Ann Arbor: University of Michigan Press, 1963), pp. 44–74.

59 Ibid., pp. 413, 429.

60 Ibid., p. 13, and Rae, *The American Automobile*, pp. 128–129.

61 Leuchtenburg, *Franklin D. Roosevelt and the New Deal*, pp. 151–336.

62 See especially Sidney Fine, *Sit Down: The General Motors Strike of 1936–1937* (Ann Arbor: University of Michigan Press, 1969), and see Allan Nevins, in collaboration with Frank E. Hill, *Ford: Decline and Rebirth, 1933–1962* (New York: Charles Scribner's Sons, 1963), pp. 133–167.

63 Rae, *The Road and the Car in American Life*, pp. 36–39, 74.

64 Rae, *The American Automobile*, pp. 152–159.

CHAPTER 7: THE DISENCHANTMENT

1 John Keats, *The Insolent Chariots* (Philadelphia: Lippincott, 1958), p. 13.

2 Tom Mahoney, *The Story of George Romney* (New York: Harper, 1960), p. 122.

3 Keats, *The Insolent Chariots*, pp. 131–136.

4 Federal Trade Commission, *Report on the Motor Vehicle Industry* (Washington, D.C.: Government Printing Office, 1939).

5 U.S., Congress, Senate, Committee on Interstate and Foreign Commerce, *Automobile Marketing Practices, Hearings*, 84th Congress, 2nd session, 1956.

6 Lawrence J. White, *The Automobile Industry since 1945* (Cambridge, Mass.: Harvard University Press, 1971), pp. 136–170.

7 Mahoney, *The Story of George Romney*, pp. 19–27, 196–208.

8 White, *The Automobile Industry since 1945*, pp. 216–220.

9 For a comprehensive history of the relationship between automotive safety and styling, see Joel W. Eastman, "Styling vs. Safety: The American Automobile Industry and the Development of Automotive Safety, 1900–1966" (Ph.D. dissertation, University of Florida, 1974).

10 Lowell Dodge, H. L. Duncombe, Jr., and George Schwartz, "*The Automobile Industry since 1945* by Lawrence J. White: A Discussion," *Political Science Quarterly*, 87:422, 425 (September 1972), and White, *The Automobile Industry since 1945*, p. 194.

11 "Detroit Thinks Small," *Newsweek*, 83:54 (April 1, 1974), and "Auto's: Thinking Small," ibid., 82:66 (August 6, 1973).

12 Emma Rothschild, "GM in Trouble—1: The Vega," *New York Review of Books*, 16:14–20 (February 25, 1971).

13 White, *The Automobile Industry since 1945*, p. 248.

14 Gordon R. Conrad and Irving H. Plotkin, "Risk/Return: U.S. Industry Pattern," *Harvard Business Review*, 46:90–99 (March–April 1968).

15 White, *The Automobile Industry since 1945*, pp. 222, 258–259.

16 Dodge, Duncombe, and Schwartz, "*The Automobile Industry since 1945:* A Discussion," p. 437.

17 See especially Alfred P. Sloan, Jr., *My Years with General Motors* (Garden City, N.Y.: Doubleday, 1964); Alfred D. Chandler, Jr., *Strategy and Structure: Chapters in the History of the American Industrial Enterprise* (Cambridge, Mass.: M.I.T. Press, 1962); and Alfred D. Chandler, Jr., and Stephen Salsbury, *Pierre S. du Pont and the Making of the Modern Corporation* (New York: Harper & Row, 1971).

18 Sloan, *My Years with General Motors*, pp. 143–148.

19 John Kenneth Galbraith, *The New Industrial State* (Boston: Houghton Mifflin, 1967), pp. 29–30, 212.

20 "Autos: Follow the Leader," *Time*, 101:59 (January 29, 1973).

21 William Serrin, *The Company and the Union* (New York: Alfred A. Knopf, 1973), p. 304.

22 Charles A. Reich, *The Greening of America* (New York: Random House, 1970), p. 135. For working conditions in the automobile industry, see especially Charles R. Walker and Robert H. Guest, *The Man on the Assembly Line* (Cambridge, Mass.: Harvard University Press, 1952); Eli Chinoy, *Automobile Workers and the American Dream* (Garden City, N.Y.: Doubleday, 1955); and Serrin, *The Company and the Union.*

23 Emma Rothschild, *Paradise Lost: The Decline of the Auto-Industrial Age* (New York: Random House, 1973).

24 Don Cook, "Team Pattern of Car Making: Results Mixed," *Los Angeles Times*, May 14, 1973.

25 Rothschild, *Paradise Lost*, pp. 54, 191, and "Auto Union Leader Warns on Growth of Multinational Firms," *Los Angeles Times*, June 3, 1974.

26 Lewis Mumford, *The City in History: Its Origins, Its Transformations, and Its Prospects* (New York: Harcourt, Brace and World, 1961), pp. 509–511, and Lawrence O'Donnel and Walter Mossberg, "End of the Affair," *Wall Street Journal*, March 30, 1971.

27 Rothschild, *Paradise Lost*, p. 47.

28 John B. Rae, *The Road and the Car in American Life* (Cambridge, Mass.: M.I.T. Press, 1971), pp. 372–373.

29 Barry Goldwater, "A Warning from Goldwater to Businessmen: 'Prepare for the Fight of Your Life,'" *Los Angeles Times*, June 10, 1974.

30 Helen Leavitt, *Superhighway—Super Hoax* (Garden City, N.Y.: Doubleday, 1970);

see also Mark H. Rose, "Express Highway Politics, 1939–1956" (Ph.D. dissertation, Ohio State University, 1973).

31 Ernest B. Furgurson, "America's Great Highway System: The Long, Agonizing Road to Chaosville," *Los Angeles Times*, March 22, 1973.

32 See especially Elizabeth Brenner Drew, "The Politics of Auto Safety," *Atlantic*, 218:95–102 (October 1966).

33 Ralph Nader, *Unsafe at Any Speed: The Designed-in Dangers of the American Automobile* (New York: Grossman, 1965).

34 Jeffrey O'Connell and Arthur Myers, *Safety Last: An Indictment of the Auto Industry* (New York: Random House, 1965).

35 Dan Lacy, *The White Use of Blacks in America* (New York: McGraw-Hill, 1972), p. 216.

36 Morton Mintz, "GM Accused of Helping Destroy Electric Rail Transit in 45 Cities," *Los Angeles Times*, February 25, 1974; "Breakup of GM's Bus 'Monopoly' Urged by Bradley," ibid., February 27, 1974; and "Killing Off the Competition?" *Newsweek*, 83:69 (March 11, 1974).

37 Frances Greiff, "A Motorized Assault on California's Environment," *Los Angeles Times*, March 4, 1973; Ray Herbert, "Southland's Freeway Program Slowly Dying"; Ted Thackrey, Jr., "Californians Still Like Freeways—With Restraints"; and Al Martinez, "Freeways: The 'Dream' That Came True," ibid., March 11, 1973.

38 White, *The Automobile Industry since 1945*, p. 231.

39 See especially Douglass G. Harvey and Robert Menchen, *The Automobile: A Technology Assessment of Advanced Automotive Propulsion Systems* (Columbia, Md.: Hittman Associates, 1974).

40 "Independent Oil Firms' Existence Periled by Production Cutbacks," *Los Angeles Times*, June 17, 1973.

41 "Sen. Jackson Asks Tax on Big Auto Engines," ibid., February 8, 1973.

42 "The Coldest Winter?" *Newsweek*, 82:9 (December 31, 1973).

43 "Losses—and Gains—for the Environment," *Time*, 103:38 (February 4, 1974), and "Will the Highway Lobby Get Its Way?" *Los Angeles Times*, April 3, 1973. For alternatives to the automobile for mass transit, see especially Tabor R. Stone, *Beyond the Automobile: Reshaping the Transportation Environment* (Englewood Cliffs, N.J.: Spectrum, 1971).

INDEX